Harriet Tubman

Recent Titles in Black History Lives

W.E.B. Du Bois: A Life in American History
Charisse Burden-Stelly and Gerald Horne

Thurgood Marshall: A Life in American History
Spencer R. Crew

Barack Obama: A Life in American History
F. Erik Brooks and MaCherie M. Placide

Harriet Tubman

A LIFE IN AMERICAN HISTORY

Kerry Walters

Black History Lives

An Imprint of ABC-CLIO, LLC
Santa Barbara, California • Denver, Colorado

Library of Congress Cataloging-in-Publication Data

Names: Walters, Kerry S., author.
Title: Harriet Tubman : a life in American history / Kerry Walters.
Description: Santa Barbara : ABC-CLIO, 2020. | Series: Black history lives
  | Includes bibliographical references and index.
Identifiers: LCCN 2019033074 (print) | LCCN 2019033075 (ebook) | ISBN
  9781440855689 (hard copy : alk. paper) | ISBN 9781440855696 (ebook)
Subjects: LCSH: Tubman, Harriet, 1822–1913. | Slaves—United
  States—Biography. | African American women abolitionists—Biography. |
  Underground Railroad. | Antislavery movements—United States. | Fugitive
  slaves—United States. | Abolitionists—Biography.
Classification: LCC E444.T82 W35 2020 (print) | LCC E444.T82 (ebook) |
  DDC 326/.8092 [B]—dc23
LC record available at https://lccn.loc.gov/2019033074
LC ebook record available at https://lccn.loc.gov/2019033075

ISBN: 978-1-4408-5568-9 (print)
      978-1-4408-5569-6 (ebook)

24 23 22 21 20   1 2 3 4 5

This book is also available as an eBook.

ABC-CLIO
An Imprint of ABC-CLIO, LLC

ABC-CLIO, LLC
147 Castilian Drive
Santa Barbara, California 93117
www.abc-clio.com

This book is printed on acid-free paper ∞

Manufactured in the United States of America

Contents

Series Foreword vii

Preface ix

CHAPTER 1
A Peculiar Institution *1*

CHAPTER 2
Neglected Weed *19*

CHAPTER 3
From Bondage to Freedom *37*

CHAPTER 4
The Underground Railroad *53*

CHAPTER 5
Return to the Jaws *71*

CHAPTER 6
Small-Scale Guerrilla Warfare *87*

CHAPTER 7
The Struggle Widens *105*

CHAPTER 8
"This Black Heroine" *127*

CHAPTER 9
Impoverished Legend *147*

CHAPTER 10
Mother Tubman *165*

Why Harriet Tubman Matters *183*

Timeline 195

Primary Documents 199

Bibliography 217

Index 223

Series Foreword

The Black History Lives biography series explores and examines the lives of the most iconic figures in African American history, with supplementary material that highlights the subject's significance in our contemporary world. Volumes in this series offer far more than a simple retelling of a subject's life by providing readers with a greater understanding of the outside events and influences that shaped each subject's world, from familial relationships to political and cultural developments.

Each volume includes chronological chapters that detail events of the subject's life. The final chapter explores the cultural and historical significance of the individual and places their actions and beliefs within an overall historical context. Books in the series highlight important information about the individual through sidebars that connect readers to the larger context of social, political, intellectual, and pop culture in American history; a timeline listing significant events; key primary source excerpts; and a comprehensive bibliography for further research.

Preface

Her name (we say it advisedly and without exaggeration) deserves to be handed down to posterity side by side with the names of Joan of Arc, Grace Darling, and Florence Nightingale; for not one of these women has shown more courage and power of endurance in facing danger and death to relieve human suffering, than has this woman in her heroic and successful endeavors to reach and save all whom she might of her oppressed and suffering race, and to pilot them from the land of Bondage to the promised land of Liberty.

—Sarah Bradford (1869, 1)

I was the conductor on the Underground Railroad for eight years, and I can say what most conductors can't say—I never ran my train off the track and I never lost a passenger.

—Harriet Tubman (Bradford 1901, 142)

In her *Harriet Tubman: The Road to Freedom*, biographer Catherine Clinton rather startlingly points out that black women and men who have played significant roles in U.S. history are always at risk of being "disremembered" (Clinton 2004, xi). What she has in mind is the marginalization or invisibility, to use novelist Ralph Ellison's word, to which persons of color have often been consigned by a predominantly white culture.

In Tubman's case, she disappeared for years from public memory after her death in 1913—the first disremembrance—only to be further hidden from view, when she finally resurfaced as a heroine in children's books, by fanciful stories and charming legends that often have little grounding in fact—a second disremembrance. This is unfortunate, because her life and accomplishments are truly remarkable. In many ways, she is the prototypical U.S. hero, who raises herself up from humble origins, over-comes seemingly insurmountable obstacles by dint of sheer determina-tion, dedicates herself to helping others achieve what she did, and makes the world a better place than the one into which she was born.

Fortunately, the amnesia that surrounded her for so long is in remis-sion. In addition to Clinton's work, several biographical treatments of Tub-man have appeared in recent years (I discuss them in this volume's essay "Why Harriet Tubman Matters"), which have helped us better separate the mythological from the historical Tubman. Much about her life remains unknown, and much undoubtedly always will, but we now have a far better understanding of who she was and what she did than ever before. In the process, we've discovered that her actual story—her Underground Rail-road rescues of slaves, her service in the Civil War, and her unflagging devotion to promoting the rights of blacks and women—is every bit as exciting as the legendary one.

More to the point, we've remembered just how important she was in the struggle against the horrible institution of slavery into which she was born, a "peculiar institution," as one of its most famous advocates at the time called it, which held four million men, women, and children in bond-age at the outbreak of the Civil War.

This book offers a portrait of Tubman that makes no claim to original scholarship but, instead, relies heavily on her own recollections and those of her contemporaries as well as the recent spate of scholarly investiga-tions about her. Its purpose is to introduce the reader to Tubman's life and times by situating her within the contexts of antebellum slavery, the aboli-tionist movement and Underground Railroad, the Civil War, the postwar condition of ex-slaves, and the suffrage movement. In addition, the bio-graphical and historical narrative is supplemented by a timeline as well as a number of contemporaneous documents—recollections, letters, and newspaper accounts—which provide a sample of the rich texture of Tub-man's life. A generous bibliography is also provided for those who wish to explore this incredible woman's story further and deeper.

Several of Tubman's nineteenth-century admirers tried to capture her speech by rendering it in "negro dialect." However well-intentioned such practices may have been, they resulted in portraits that the twenty-first century reader finds, at best, condescending and, at worst, demeaning. Consequently, in my biographical narrative, I've nearly always translated the dialect into standard English, although I've left it as it was written in the appended documents.

1

A Peculiar Institution

The peculiar institution of the South that, on the maintenance of which, the very existence of the slaveholding States depends.

—John Calhoun (1994, 175)

FROM KING SUGAR TO KING COTTON

It started with sugar, a sweetness that few people, then or now, can resist. As early as the mid-fourteenth century, European demand for sugar led to the enslavement of both whites and blacks to work vast plantations on islands off the southwestern coast of Africa. By the early sixteenth century, following the discovery of the New World, sugar plantations were established on Caribbean islands and in Brazil. The first New World sugar mill was built in 1515 on Hispaniola (Haiti), and the first African slaves arrived there some three years later.

England in particular had a sweet tooth. By the beginning of the eighteenth century, its people were consuming over thirty thousand hogsheads of sugar a year. A generation later, the annual consumption rate mushroomed to one hundred thousand. In just 150 years, between 1650 and 1800, sugar consumption in the English-speaking world grew by an astonishing 2,500 percent.

To satisfy the escalating demand, a steady supply of slave labor was needed to plant, tend, harvest, and process sugarcane, and English,

Spanish, Dutch, and Portuguese entrepreneurs happily raided African coastlands to meet the need. The island of Barbados in particular became a leading importer of African slaves, whose working life spans in the killing heat were notoriously short and brutal and who, thus, had to be regularly replaced.

African slavery came to North America some time during the first quarter of the seventeenth century; by that time, there were twenty-five thousand slaves working on sugar plantations on Cuba, Hispaniola, and Brazil. The most commonly cited arrival date is August 1619, when twenty Africans were delivered to Virginia aboard a Dutch vessel (horribly misnamed the *Jesus of Lubeck*), but Africans may have reached North America as early as 1608.

There's also some uncertainty about the exact status of these first Africans. They may have been more like indentured servants than actual slaves. In these early days, race wasn't the marker of bondage or freedom that it would shortly become in the North American colonies.

Initially, blacks, whether indentured or enslaved, were put to work as domestic servants in the North; field hands in the South; and, occasionally, as skilled artisans in both regions. For the most part, field hands planted and harvested crops like tobacco, wheat, and corn, especially in the upper southern colonies (and later states). Further south, they were put to work in cotton or rice fields, and even further south, on sugar plantations. Tobacco tended to deplete the soil in the Upper South, thereby gradually reducing the need for slave labor. By the early nineteenth century, Virginia and Maryland had sizeable enough populations of free blacks to cause alarm to white authorities: thirty-four thousand in Maryland, thirty thousand in Virginia, and ninety-four thousand in all the Upper South states. There was a period just before the Revolutionary War, when the number of free blacks actually threatened to match the number of slaves in the Upper South, and Virginia and Maryland enacted strong restrictions on when and under what conditions slaves might be manumitted. In the Deep South, cotton plantations tended to be small because of the tedious and slow work of cleaning harvested cotton.

But Eli Whitney's invention of the cotton gin in the final decade of the eighteenth century ushered in an economic and cultural sea change. The swift pace of cotton-cleaning allowed by the machine meant cotton became a lucrative cash crop almost overnight. Sensing fortunes to be made, southern planters invested in thousands of acres on which to grow cotton and, accordingly, needed a proportionately large number of workers to tend the crop. Between 1770 and 1810, as cotton exports increased from around 10 percent to a full third of the southern economy, the slave population in the southern states doubled to around eight hundred thousand. By the beginning of the Civil War, it had grown to four million, with over half of the nation's slaves working in the cotton fields. King Sugar was supplanted by King Cotton, allowing South Carolina congressman James Henry Hammond to defiantly boast to opponents of slavery from the floor of the House of Representatives: "You dare not make war on cotton—no power on earth dares make war upon it. Cotton is king" (Hammond 1866, 316). His fellow South Carolinian John C. Calhoun spoke for the entire slaveholding class when he insisted that slavery—the South's "peculiar institution," as he called it, with "peculiar" meaning "special"—was a necessary condition for cotton to remain king and that any effort to interfere with it would be met with strenuous resistance, including, if push came to shove, secession. But Calhoun was also convinced that slavery was a boon to the North as well as the South because cotton was so crucial to both their economies.

Only about one-third of southerners actually owned slaves, and only a handful of the wealthiest aristocratic families possessed large numbers of

---

ELI WHITNEY'S COTTON GIN

Massachusetts inventor Eli Whitney's clever machine, which he designed and built in just over a week, revolutionized the cotton industry and made enormous fortunes for both planters and cloth manufacturers, but he saw little profit from it himself. Although his cotton gin ("gin" was short for "engine") was patented in 1794, Whitney wasn't able to have the patent ratified for well over a decade. In the intervening years, hundreds of models were pirated off his original one.

Cotton fibers, which grow in pods, are intermingled with seeds when the pods burst and the cotton is ready for harvest. Before 1794, the process of separating them by hand was laborious. It generally took a single person an entire day to card a single pound's worth of fiber. This made large-scale planting and harvesting of cotton uneconomical.

Whitney's device changed all that, enabling a worker to card as many as fifty-five pounds of cotton lint a day. The machine consisted of a wooden drum with teeth and a mesh screen. Raw cotton was fed into a chamber, the teeth of the hand-rotated drum separated the lint from the seed, and the screen trapped the seeds. Southern planters immediately saw the gin's utility, and, almost overnight, their need for more slaves to plant, harvest, and card cotton expanded.

When his patent on the cotton gin was finally validated, South Carolina, North Carolina, and Tennessee legislators awarded Whitney one-time grants of money for the fortunes they'd made through pirated versions of his invention. By then, he'd moved on to manufacturing government muskets. When he died in 1825, he was a much less wealthy man than he would have been had he been properly remunerated for the gin.

them. But their presence was so vital to the southern labor system that most southerners couldn't imagine life without them. Thomas Drew, pro-slavery advocate and president of the College of William and Mary, voiced this conviction: "It is in truth the slave labor in Virginia which gives value to her soil and habitations. Take away this and you pull down the Atlas that upholds the entire system" (Faust 1981, 30). Although Drew was refer-ring specifically to his home state, his clear implication was that the "entire system" would be unthinkable without slavery incorporated throughout all the slaveholding states.

While both whites and blacks were indentured servants (and possibly even slaves) in North America in the early seventeenth century, it wasn't long before slavery was reserved exclusively for persons of African descent, a practice that encouraged a growing belief that blacks were morally and intellectually inferior to whites. The Virginia House of Burgess voted in 1662 that all children born of African mothers were automatically slaves themselves. New York followed suit in 1665, and Maryland six years later. By the beginning of the eighteenth century, lifelong slavery for Africans and their descendants had become the legal norm. By 1858, the same year that Hammond delivered his King Cotton speech, most southerners agreed with Thomas R. Cobb, a Georgia-born judge who would perish at the Bat-tle of Fredericksburg in 1862, when he wrote that the "presumption of free-dom" rests upon the whiteness of one's skin, while "the black color of the race raises the presumption of slavery" (Cobb 1858, 67). Even opponents of slavery, including many abolitionists, believed that dark skin suggested inferiority.

LAW OF THE LAND

The Articles of Confederation, approved by the Second Continental Congress in 1777 and ratified in 1781, was the initial constitution of the United States. Its authors remained silent on the topic of slavery, content to leave the matter to individual states.

The Constitution of 1787, reflecting a hot debate among delegates about slavery, tried to steer a course that would satisfy both opponents and advo-cates of the peculiar institution. Like the Articles, it left slavery's definition and regulation up to states and required the return of slaves who escaped from one state to another. But it also implicitly acknowledged slavery as an indisputable part of the national landscape in what came to be known as the Three-Fifths Compromise, which mandated that, for tax and census purposes, every African slave counted as only three-fifths of a legal per-son. This relieved southern slave owners of a considerable tax burden while also formalizing the cultural assumption that blacks, being less than fully human, were inferior to whites.

In an attempt to appease slavery's opponents, the Constitution also declared that slaves could no longer be imported from abroad after 1808, and Congress enacted the Northwest Ordinance, which prohibited slavery in territory north of the Ohio River and east of the Mississippi River (including the modern states of Illinois, Indiana, Michigan, Ohio, and Wisconsin), land ceded to the United States as part of the postwar settlement with England.

The autonomy constitutionally granted to states when it came to slavery led to so-called slave laws within each of them that strictly regulated the behavior of Africans held in bondage. For the most part, either implicitly or explicitly, these laws denied any rights whatsoever to slaves. They forbade slaves to travel without consent or hire themselves out to others; practice professions; serve as witnesses in court proceedings against whites; marry without the consent of their masters; bequeath or inherit possessions (the obvious reason being that everything they used, including their own bodies, legally belonged to their owners); travel without a pass; practice medicine; own firearms; or gather in assemblies without the presence of at least one white person. Some laws forbade literacy among slaves and even outlawed Christian preaching.

Moreover, punishments of slave offenses were generally brutal and much harsher than punishments for similar offenses handed down to white malefactors. The Louisiana Slave Code, enacted in 1739 and continuing until the end of the Civil War, served as a punitive model for most other state slave laws. It mandated death "without the benefit of clergy" for slaves who "maliciously" destroyed produce; kilns; barrels of pitch; "or any other goods or commodities of the growth, produce or manufacture of this Province, stealing, and poisoning" (Walters 2015, 174–175). Ironically, short of murder or an exceptionally violent outburst of mayhem, most slave owners in Louisiana and other states with similar draconian slave laws were reluctant to turn their human property over to legal authorities, lest they suffer financially because of the punishments inflicted on the slaves. So slave laws frequently included provisions requiring slaveholders, under threat of penalty, to report slave crimes to the courts.

A landmark judicial ruling in the 1829 case *North Carolina v. Mann* both expressed and reinforced the notion that slaves possessed no legal rights. That year, John Mann rented a slave named Lydia. The relationship between the two was so fraught that Lydia tried to escape, and a furious Mann tracked her down and shot her. He was charged with assault and battery and found guilty by a lower court. The case was appealed to the State Supreme Court, where Judge Thomas Ruffin ruled for the defendant.

Stating that the dominion of masters over slaves must be absolute in order to "render the submission of the slave perfect," Ruffin argued that the absence of such absolute authority would undermine the entire peculiar institution. "We cannot allow the right of the master to be brought into discussion in the courts of justice," he wrote. "The slave, to remain a slave, must be made sensible that there is no appeal from his master; that his [the master's] power is in no instance usurped" (Oakes 1990, 160–161).

Thomas Cobb, in the same book in which he insisted that dark skin carried the presumption of servitude, applauded Ruffin's decision. Any "rights" afforded to slaves, he argued, were legal fictions whose only function was to simplify and streamline judicial procedures.

Even so, slave codes across the South continued to allow for the possibility that masters couldn't do anything they wished with their human property. It's not clear whether the motives for these provisions were based on humanitarian or pecuniary concerns, the latter because slaves represented considerable financial investments, which should not be squandered. But regardless of the reasons, states began to mandate at least some standards, minimal though they were, that curtailed mistreatment of slaves. Kentucky, for example, decreed that slaves could be removed from masters if they were treated inhumanely. What constituted such treatment, of course, wasn't easily provable except in extreme cases, and the removal of slaves from cruel masters simply meant they would be resold to another white person, who might be just as bad and would, in any case, separate them from their families. Alabama went a bit further, requiring masters to feed and clothe slaves properly, to offer medical attention when it was needed, and to provide for slaves too old to work.

Another indication that some slave states admitted, almost despite themselves, that slave rights were a bit more substantial than Cobbs's legal fictions was the 1834 *North Carolina v. Will* case, adjudicated by the same state Supreme Court whose ruling five years earlier had argued that the master's sovereignty over a slave was absolute.

The case involved the slaying of a white overseer by a slave named Will. Will and another field hand got into a scuffle over a hoe, and the overseer, a man named Baxter, began horsewhipping the two of them to break up the fight. Will fled, and Baxter shot him in the back. When the overseer went to the fallen slave and turned him over, Will pulled a knife and fatally stabbed him. The lower court, unsurprisingly, found Will guilty of murder and condemned him to death.

But Will's owner, James Battle, refused to accept the verdict, likely because Will was a good worker and a valuable piece of property. He took the case all the way to the State Supreme Court, which modified the finding of the lower one without totally overruling it. Writing for the court, Judge William Gaston (who also, by the way, wrote North Carolina's official state song) waffled on Ruffin's earlier claim of absolute sovereignty. "Unconditional submission is the general duty of the slave," he admitted, and "unlimited power is, in general, the legal right of the master." But his inclusion of the phrases "general duty" and "in general" suggested that there were some exceptions. "It is certain that the master has not the right to slay his slave," Gaston concluded, "and I hold it to be equally certain that the slave has a right to defend himself against the unlawful attempt of his master to deprive him of life" (Oakes 1990, 161). Unexpectedly, Ruffin was one of the judges who concurred with Gaston. Accordingly, Will's conviction was reduced from murder to manslaughter, just as it would have been for a white man in similar circumstances.

If there was a single overriding motive for Gaston's decision, it was probably, once again, concern for the financial loss that the execution of slaves brought to their owners rather than any humanitarian consideration. As such, Thomas Cobbs's reduction of slave rights to legal fictions may have actually been truer than he knew. The "right" not to be murdered by their masters and the "right" to self-defense may have been legal rationalizations designed more to safeguard human property than to protect slaves—who, after all, were only three-fifths human.

At any rate, the question of slave rights was decided once and for all at the federal level nearly thirteen years after *North Carolina v. Will*, when the United States Supreme Court handed down its decision in the notorious Dred Scott case.

Dred Scott v. Sandford had been moving through the courts since 1846 and had become a closely watched legal battle by defenders and opponents of slavery alike. The plaintiff, Scott, was a Virginia-born slave seeking his freedom on the grounds that his master, an army officer named Sandford, had relocated with him to several free states. Scott's argument was that residence in states where slavery was outlawed made him a de facto free man. Consequently, Sandford's refusal to recognize his freedom was a violation of his rights.

Writing the majority opinion, Chief Justice Roger Taney utterly rejected Scott's suit with a decision that had wide-reaching repercussions. Scott had no right to freedom, argued Taney, because no black, not even a free one, could ever be a citizen of the United States and claim constitutional protection of fundamental rights. Moreover, enslaved blacks had no legal standing as humans, but only as property and, as such, could be transported by their masters to free states without any change in their legal status. In a single judicial decision, Taney not only stripped humanity and constitutional protection from slaves but also nullified an 1819 ban, known as the Missouri Compromise, on slavery north of the 36-30 parallel.

Reaction to Taney's decision was predictable. Slavery proponents applauded it, while opponents deplored it, in the words of the *New York*

Independent, as the "moral assassination of a race." Abraham Lincoln, a rising star in the newly formed Republican Party, announced publicly that he would refuse to recognize it. Speaking for his political allies, he said, "Somebody has to reverse that decision, since it is made, and we mean to reverse it" (Lincoln 1953, 495). At the time, Lincoln presumed that the reversal would be legislative. Four years later, when, as president-elect, he watched slaveholding state after state secede from the Union, he knew that the legal status of slaves would be resolved in a less peaceful way.

Although Taney's decision outraged opponents of slavery, the racism that undergirded it was widely shared. Even free African Americans were subject to so-called black codes in both the North and the South, whose rigorous restrictions reflected the bias that persons of color needed to be kept firmly in hand. Many of these codes prohibited free blacks from assembling in groups of more than four or five unless gathered for worship. Curfews were frequently imposed in cities. In Washington, D.C., for example, blacks on the streets after eight o'clock at night risked arrest and flogging. As tensions between defenders and opponents of slavery increased in the run-up to the Civil War, free southern blacks who received "subversive" mail were also subject to legal penalty. As we'll see in a chapter 6, one of Harriet Tubman's associates, Reverend Samuel Green, was sentenced to ten years in prison simply for owning a copy of Harriet Beecher Stowe's *Uncle Tom's Cabin*. The Dred Scott decision, then, merely codified what many whites already believed about blacks.

PERPETUAL OUTSIDERS

In his poem "Harlem," Langston Hughes memorably asked, "What happens to a dream deferred?" Does it, he wondered, dry up, fester, rot, sag, or explode? Hughes was referring to the destructive effects of racism on free U.S. blacks. But the question equally applied to antebellum U.S. slaves, those unfortunates chillingly described by historian James Oakes as "perpetual outsiders" (Oakes 1990, 31).

In defining just what it meant to be a perpetual outsider, Oakes obviously included the daily grind of slave life with its never-ending round of hard physical work. But he perceptively argued that there are five underlying characteristics essential to U.S. slavery, both of which accounted for its physical burdensomeness as well as the emotional and spiritual weight of perpetual outsiderhood.

The first characteristic of U.S. slavery, already suggested by the almost utterly subordinate legal status of slaves, was its comprehensive subjugation. U.S. slaves, for the most part, were powerless in relation to their masters and white persons in general. It wasn't simply that slaves were owned by another person. It was also that, as human chattel, they had no identities or destinies of their own. The trajectory of their lives was determined by their masters' whims and fortunes, and their identities by the names and status of their owners. As Oates put it, slaves were "noncitizens stripped of virtually all legal rights . . . totally subject to the authority of masters . . . Socially dead and symbolically dishonored, slaves in America experienced their degradation and powerlessness within a legal system that defined the master's authority as a right of property" (Oakes 1990, 31).

The permanence of the total subjugation was a second characteristic of U.S. slavery. Slaves could be manumitted by their masters—Tubman's father was eventually freed, for example—or they could work odd jobs for years to save enough money to buy their own freedom if their owners were willing. As we've seen, the free slave population in Maryland and Virginia grew so large by the beginning of the nineteenth century that white legislators in both states became alarmed. But short of escape, a slave's chance of freedom was utterly dependent on the master's wish. Indentured servitude held out the hope of eventual freedom because it was based on a mutually agreed-upon contract. Slavery was the unilateral control of one person by another. Moreover, it soon became apparent to free slaves that, even if they managed to escape legal bondage, they still labored under the stigma of their color in a society that increasingly viewed dark skin as a sign of inferiority.

The third defining characteristic of U.S. slavery identified by Oates was the atmosphere of violence that surrounded it. There was a multitude of ways in which the physical, emotional, and spiritual well-being of slaves were violated by their lot in life, and all of them stemmed ultimately from their total subjugation to their masters. Violence was inflicted upon them when they were seized or purchased from their African homelands, transported across the Middle Passage to North America, and sold into slavery. A similar kind of violence erupted when they were separated from their slave families by being sold and resold.

Slaves were always subject to physical abuse, usually by overseers or masters, but not infrequently by mistresses and even white children. As we'll see in the next chapter, Harriet Tubman was viciously used by a woman to whom she was hired out when she was still only a child. At times, slaves were forced to physically assault fellow slaves. Solomon Northup, who escaped from slavery and wrote a memoir entitled *Twelve Years a Slave*, records being required to whip another slave with supervised savagery while his master's entire family, including small children, watched the proceedings with what struck him as sadistic pleasure.

It need hardly be mentioned that both the victims and the perpetrators of such actions could easily become desensitized to violence. Beaten slaves sometimes brutalized their fellows, and white children who observed their elders abusing slaves often fell into similar modes of behavior. Thomas

Jefferson worried intensely about white children becoming brutalized by the violence endemic to U.S. slavery. "The parent storms, the child looks on, catches the lineaments of wrath, puts on the same airs in the circle of smaller slaves, gives a loose to the worst of passions, and thus nursed, educated, and daily exercised in tyranny, cannot but be stamped by it with odious peculiarities" (Jefferson 1944, 257). Northrup records personal experience of such debasement, recalling an "intelligent" white boy of ten or twelve years, who, having learned such brutality from his father, regularly rode into the fields where slaves labored to "appl[y] the rawhide, urging the slaves forward with shouts, and occasional expressions of profanity" (Northup 2014, 261).

An especially odious manifestation of violence against slaves is Oates's fourth characteristic of U.S. slavery: sexual abuse. Female slaves were frequently paired by masters with male slaves simply for the purpose of

---

JEFFERSON AND SLAVERY

Thomas Jefferson's double-minded attitude to slavery, morally condemning it but nonetheless continuing to own slaves until the end of his life, wasn't the norm among slave owners, but it wasn't uncommon either. Many slaveholders suffered from moral qualms about human bondage but were unwilling to risk their lifestyles by freeing their human property.

In the only book he wrote, the 1785 *Notes on the State of Virginia*, Jefferson eloquently voiced his concern that the institution of slavery tended to make masters lazy and self-indulgent and slaves angry and deceptive—even though he also suspected that African slaves were probably incapable of caring for themselves if they were freed, a conscience-salving rationalization held by many whites.

Even more worrisome for him, Jefferson feared that slavery itself was a violation of the liberties that he and his fellow Americans (some of them black) had fought to attain. "Indeed I tremble for my country," he wrote, "when I reflect that God is just: that his justice cannot sleep for ever: that considering numbers, nature and natural means only, a revolution of the wheel of fortune, an exchange of situation is among possible events" (Jefferson 1944, 258).

In *Notes on the State of Virginia*, Jefferson expressed the hope that slavery as an economic institution would gradually wither away. As an old man, he was less sure. "We have the wolf by the ears," he glumly wrote to a correspondent, "and we can neither hold him, nor safely let him go. Justice is in one scale, and self-preservation in the other" (Jefferson 1944, 637).

Jefferson's ambivalence toward slavery was exacerbated by his long-standing relationship with one of his own slaves, Sally Hemmings, from whom he may have sired as many as five children. Rumors of the relationship surfaced as early as 1802, but twentieth-century DNA analysis have confirmed it.

procreating more slaves. One especially distasteful but not exceptional example is the fate of a slave named Caroline. Her Eastern Shore master, Edward Covey, purchased her for the express purpose of breeding. Renting a male slave from another owner, he tied the two together every night until Caroline conceived. When she gave birth to twins, Covey sold them (Horton and Horton 2005, 98–99).

The utter subordination of slaves to their masters' whims made the sexual abuse of female slaves by white men nearly inevitable. The abundance of slave children sired by white masters was a barely concealed scandal throughout the southern states. Harriet Tubman's mother may have had a white father. White wives and mothers in slaveholding households secretly deplored but, for the most part, accepted as an inevitability the sexual straying of husbands and sons. Even though polite society pretended to disapprove of and discourage such relations, slave owners had virtual unrestricted sexual access to their human chattel.

The final characteristic of U.S. slavery suggested by Oates is actually the culmination of the first four. It's what he refers to as the "dishonoring" or dehumanization of slaves, a process ratified by law in the Dred Scott decision. Their legal status as subhumans meant that their kinship relations could be ignored by their masters; that they could be forced to perform the filthiest and most demeaning labor; that they were available for the sexual pleasure of their owners; that, with few legal limits, they could be physically and emotionally abused; that their bondage could easily last from cradle to grave; and that, even if they escaped slavery through either legal or illegal means, they would always be viewed as inferior to whites. All this made them perpetual outsiders.

Slaves who escaped bondage were unified in their detestation of it. They fully recognized that it was an institution that demanded that its victims be "tamed" as if they were recalcitrant beasts of burden. Frederick Douglass angrily recalled that he and his fellow slaves were, like farm animals, mere living property. "They were to be broken; so was I" (Douglass 2003, 118). John Parker, a fugitive who would later be a stationmaster and conductor for the Underground Railroad, expressed with unmatched eloquence the dreadful toll of enslavement.

> How I hated slavery as it fettered me, and beat me, and baffled me in my desires . . . It was not the physical part of slavery that made it cruel and degrading, it was the taking away from a human being the initiative, of thinking, of doing his own ways . . . Slavery's curse was not pain of the body, but the pain of the soul. (Parker 1866, 25, 26)

It was precisely this pain of the soul that ultimately led Harriet Tubman to flee her own bondage and, afterward, risk her hard-won freedom by returning to the South to lead others out of bondage.

SLAVE RESISTANCE

For years, both before and after the Civil War, the majority of white Americans chose to believe that slaves were essentially passive and docile creatures who actually benefited from their bondage. Viewed as unable to care for themselves, they needed benevolent owners who would feed and clothe them, provide them with purpose in life, and care for them when they aged. Historian Ulrich B. Phillips influentially reflected and defended this perspective in his 1918 *American Negro Slavery,* a study that continued to be conventional wisdom for years. His conclusions were based primarily on the diaries and letters of white slave owners, which obviously reflected their conviction that blacks were suitable only for slavery.

We now know that this is more caricature than fact. It's undoubtedly the case that many slaves, worn down by hard work, dehumanization, and physical abuse, or simply born with timid dispositions, did accept their bondage as inevitability. But it's also true that slaves' resistance to the peculiar institution that enchained them was more widespread than once thought. As Frederick Douglass observed, many, and perhaps most, slaves were docile in form but not in fact (Douglass 2003, 140). Had Phillips paid less attention to slave owners' memoirs and more to the testimony of ex-slaves like Douglass and Parker, he would have realized this.

Slave resistance took three forms: everyday sabotage, flight, and revolt. The first was most common. The second, the type of resistance exercised by Harriet Tubman and hundreds of others refugees, was less widespread. But, as we'll see in chapter 4, it was a chronic source of worry and irritation to slave owners, representing as it did not only a disregard of their authority and an undermining of the peculiar institution upon which the South relied, but also a huge loss of capital for individual masters and mistresses. The final option, armed revolt or rebellion, was the South's worst nightmare.

Everyday resistance took a number of forms, but each was designed to both ease the burden upon slaves and undermine their masters' fortunes and control. It ranged from telling masters and mistresses what they wanted to hear or acting the part of a simpleton in order to gain their trust, to work slowdowns and outright goldbricking. Sometimes planting and harvesting tools were purposely broken in order to sabotage fieldwork. Slaves sometimes ran off for a few days of rest in nearby woods or swamps, risking the punishment they would receive when they finally returned home. Theft wasn't uncommon, especially of foodstuffs such as chickens and hogs. Many masters, in fact, turned a blind eye to their slaves' thievery as long as it didn't become too costly or frequent.

Slave owners perpetually in need of cash often hired out their slaves to other whites as field hands, domestic help, or skilled labor. Beginning when she was just a child, Tubman worked for several such employees during her years as a slave. The entire wages were usually paid directly to the master, but sometimes slaves were allowed to keep a tiny percentage of whatever they earned. An unintended occasional consequence of this practice was that hired-out slaves came into close contact with free blacks or white tradesmen who disapproved of human bondage. This encouraged resentment of their own bondage by providing them with visions of freedom they might not otherwise have had, thereby increasing the likelihood of resistance when they returned to their masters.

It mustn't be thought that the everyday resistance of slaves was aimed exclusively at lessening the burdens of poverty, hunger, and overwork, although that was certainly one of its goals. It was also an attempt on the part of slaves to assert and affirm their own human dignity and worth. As such, it can be seen as a response to the status of perpetual outsider imposed on them.

A certain amount of goldbricking and theft on the part of their human property might have been acceptable to slave owners. But flight from servitude, or "self-stealing," as it was often called by slavery's defenders, wasn't. It was one thing to lose the value of a purloined chicken or even a few days' labor by a slave who decided to take a break from the fields by running off to a swamp. It was quite another thing to lose a runaway slave, and owners were willing to pay large bounties for their capture and return. There were at least two reasons for this. One was that slave owners invested considerable amounts of money in their slaves, and the loss of any one of them resulted in a loss of capital. The other was that the entire system of slave labor upon which the economy of the South rested was threatened each time a slave succeeded in making his or her way to northern freedom. The flight of slaves from bondage, as well as the strategies they used and the routes they followed, will be explored in chapter 4's examination of the Underground Railroad.

There was one form of slave resistance that terrified southerners, regardless of whether or not they owned slaves: armed revolt. It was a specter that haunted the colonies and antebellum United States for as long as slavery was legal, and for good cause. There were at least ten major slave revolts or conspiracies to revolt prior to the Civil War. The first recorded one occurred as early as 1687 in Westmoreland County, Virginia. Each time that one erupted or was discovered, regardless of how quickly it was put down or conspirators punished, lurid visions of out-of-control blacks slaughtering entire households and sexually assaulting white women terrified the South.

White anxiety about rampaging slaves was stoked when David Walker, a free black who was a clothier in Boston, published an *Appeal to the Colored Citizens of the World* in 1829. Cleverly modeling his book after the

U.S. Constitution, he called its introduction a "preamble" and its four chapters "articles." Walker insisted that "colored citizens" had the same legal rights, at least in the eyes of God, as white ones. He urged blacks to think of themselves as "MEN, and not brutes, as we have been represented, and by millions treated" (Walker 2006, 32). And he issued a chilling warning to all who defended slavery.

> Remember [white] Americans, that we must and shall be free and enlightened as you are. Will you wait until we shall, under God, obtain our liberty by the crushing arm of power? Will it not be dreadful for you? I speak Americans for your own good. We must and shall be free I say, in spite of you . . . And woe, woe, will be to you if we have to obtain our freedom by fighting. (Walker 2006, 72–73)

Walker's call for sedition and even armed revolt thrilled free blacks in the North, especially those who had escaped from servitude, even as it horrified and enraged southern slave owners. Legislators in slave states, realizing what a heady impact Walker's call to arms could have on their human property, quickly outlawed the book and placed a bounty on its author's head. Copies of it still made their way southward, often conveyed by black sailors on northern ships, who deposited them at ports of call. In all likelihood, most slaves never heard of Walker or his book, but the fact that a black man would dare invite race warfare was noted with alarm by white planters.

One of the most naked expressions of their fear was voiced by Mary Boykin Chestnut, the South Carolina blue blood whose published diaries offer an unparalleled portrait of life on a southern plantation. One night, she attended a stage play about the great Indian Rebellion of 1857, in which native soldiers, or sepoys, had revolted in bloodthirsty fury against their British colonial masters. Returning home, Chestnut wrote in her diary that "a thrill of terror ran through me as those yellow and black brutes came jumping over the parapets! Their faces were like so many of the same sort at home"—meaning, of course, southern slaves. "How long," she wondered, "could they resist the seductive and irresistible call, 'only rise, kill, and be free?'" (Horton and Horton 2005, 121).

The most traumatic of all the slave revolts in North America erupted in 1831, only two years after Walker published his *Appeal*. Harriet Tubman was probably around ten years old at the time. It was captained by a religious visionary named Nat Turner, who led a band of fifty slaves on a rampage in Southampton County, Virginia, that led to the violent death of some sixty white men, women, and children. The revolt was put down in quick order by Virginia militia and country officials, and Turner was eventually captured and hanged. But news of the massacre, exacerbated by the wide circulation of a hair-raising pamphlet entitled *The Confessions of Nat*

AFTERMATH OF NAT TURNER'S REVOLT

Nat Turner's bloody rampage truly horrified Virginians. One woman wrote that the entire state felt "like a smothered volcano. We know not when, or where, the flame will burst forth" again (Tragle 1973, 276).

In response to climate of fear, Virginia governor John Floyd recommended that new laws be passed to confine slaves to their masters' estates, to prohibit them from preaching, and to force all freed slaves out of the state. His reasoning would have been obvious to everyone: Nat Turner had traveled to other estates to recruit his rebels, he had been a fiery and persuasive preacher whose words fomented revolt, and the living example of free blacks tempted slaves to discontent.

Just weeks after Turner's execution, one of Thomas Jefferson's grandsons, Thomas Jefferson Randolph, addressed this third possibility by proposing a referendum to end slavery by gradual steps in Virginia. Floyd was sympathetic. Both men apparently thought it better in the long run to rid the state of blacks, slaves as well as free, than to risk another violent uprising. The proposal was extraordinary, given that Virginia's economy rested on slave labor, and indicates just how rattled Randolph and Floyd were by Nat Turner's revolt.

A proposal that might have been laughed out of the legislature months earlier was actually seriously debated for eight full weeks, prompting a Richmond newspaper editor who supported the referendum to write, "Nat Turner, and the blood of his innocent victims, have conquered the silence [on the moral propriety of slavery] of fifty years" (Foner 1972, 8). In the end, the proposal was voted down. Instead, stricter slave laws were passed.

Turner, which described the rebellious slaves as "remorseless murderers" and "savages," whose "flinty bosoms" were impervious to the cries of their victims, spread across the nation, striking fear in the hearts of white southerners and northerners alike (Greenberg 1996, 46).

Throughout her many trips back to the South to rescue fellow slaves, Tubman wasn't opposed to the use of violence. As we'll see, she often carried a pistol, which she was fully prepared to use against white pursuers, as well as any faint-hearted refugee whose timidity put the rescue operation at risk. She also approved of John Brown's 1859 armed raid on the arsenal at Harpers Ferry, which he intended as a prelude to a general slave insurrection, and she came close to accompanying him and his men on the ill-fated mission. She also gladly served as a scout on military expeditions in South Carolina and possibly Florida during the Civil War. Unlike some northern abolitionists who believed that moral persuasion and public pressure rather than violence were the most effective responses to slavery, Tubman's own years of bondage convinced her that slave owners would never voluntarily relinquish their human chattel. In his final note, written shortly before he was hanged, John Brown affirmed his conviction that the sin of slavery would never be "purged" from "this guilty land" except by the shedding of blood. Tubman agreed.

SLAVERY AND DISSONANCE

If those who were enslaved were transformed into perpetual outsiders, those who enslaved them suffered from a curious dissonance that contributed to both white anxiety and the increasingly oppressive treatment of slaves.

Most slaveholders were convinced that the majority of their slaves, especially the ones serving domestically rather than in the fields, were grateful and loyal to them. This patronizing attitude was born partly from the racist assumption that black slaves were childlike in intelligence and, hence, helplessly dependent upon the largesse of white masters, partly from a sentimentally romantic view of plantation life, and partly as a psychological defense against the fears stoked by slave revolts. An antebellum lithograph that hung in more than one plantation home perfectly expresses this idealization of the master-slave relationship. A master and his family are entertained by dancing, jolly field hands, as an aged slave, bent from years of labor, obsequiously says, "God Bless you massa! You feed and clothe us. When we are sick you nurse us, and when too old to work, you provide for us!" (Horton and Horton 2005, 121).

The conviction that their own slaves were contentedly grateful was so deeply engrained that slaveholders were often startled and grieved when circumstances suggested a quite different picture. Mississippi planter John Quitman, convinced as he was of his servant's absolute loyalty, was shaken when his slave John ran. As Quitman's son wrote in bewilderment, "I myself have heard [John] say, that if it were in the power of these abolitionists to give him a thousand freedoms, he would not desert us" (Horton and Horton 2005, 121). A similar sense of betrayal was expressed by Sarah Logue of Tennessee when she discovered the address of one of her runaway slaves. "You know that we reared you as we reared our own children," she wrote him. "That you were never abused, and that shortly before you ran away, when your master asked you if you would like to be sold, you said you would not leave him to go with anybody" (Rodriguez 2007, 677–678). It apparently didn't occur to Quitman or Logue that their slaves, wishing to assert some degree of control over their lives, while at the same time undermining their masters' authority, readily told them what they wanted to hear rather than the truth.

So on the one hand, masters generally considered their own slaves to be loyal and harmless. But on the other hand, they were frightened of black people in general, and especially those who were owned by others. Part of this was the belief, again a self-serving rationalization, that slave discontent and open revolt was the result of some masters not properly controlling their slaves, either by abusing or coddling them. This rationalization, in turn, was founded upon the deep-seated fear that there was something wild and untamable about Africans that made them either a constant, although hopefully low-burning, threat—Mary Chestnut's fear—or utterly unreliable unless kept firmly in hand. Georgia planter John Jacobus Flournoy was convinced, for example, that slaves had "a natural disposition to endless riot [and] for the work of carnage and insurrection" (Blassingame 1979, 231). Roswell King, overseer of a huge Georgia plantation, complained to his employer that the "Ethiopian race" couldn't be trusted and that, given half a chance, they would ungratefully make off for freedom (Franklin and Schweninger 1999, 29). As more slaves ran for freedom, and especially as slave insurrections occurred or conspiracies to revolt were uncovered, these twin convictions became the driving force for ever harsher slave codes and plantation practices that aimed to stifle slave unrest.

This was the complex and harsh culture into which the girl who would become known as Harriet Tubman was born.

2

Neglected Weed

I grew up like a neglected weed—ignorant of liberty, having no experience of it.

—Harriet Tubman (Drew 2008, 52)

CLASHING MEMORIES

Harriet Tubman's earliest memory stretched back to when she was about one-and-a-half years old.

> The first thing I remember, was lying in the cradle. You seen these trees that are hollow. Take a big tree, cut it down, put a bode in each end, make a cradle of it and call it a 'gum. I remember lying in there, when the young ladies in the big house where my mother worked, come catch me up in the air before I could walk. (Telford in Larson 2003, 19)

Like the first memories of many people, Tubman's was nostalgically pleasant, even joyful. She recalls the cradle in which she lay, most likely with vivid remembrances of the wood's texture and aroma. We can easily imagine her guffawing as youngsters do when affectionate hands scoop them up from their beds and playfully toss them in the air. It's a memory that anyone would cherish.

But Tubman was born a slave, as her mention of "the young ladies in the big house" reminds us. To be in bondage in the nineteenth-century United

States, even in a border state like her native Maryland, where slaves were generally treated less harshly than in the Deep South, was to have the pleasant memories of childhood crisscrossed with horrible ones. An especially dreadful memory from when she was about three years old remained with Tubman her entire life.

That's when one of her sisters, a girl aged somewhere between fourteen and sixteen, was sold down south by Edward Brodess, the man who owned Tubman, her mother, and all her siblings. An incompetent farmer and inept manager of money, Brodess, perpetually strapped for cash, put two of his slaves, a fifteen-year-old boy named James and the girl, identified on the deed of sale as Rhody, on the market in 1825. They were sold to Dempsey Kane, a Mississippi slave trader, who slapped down $610 for both of them. Brodess sold cheaply, an indication of just how badly he needed ready cash.

Rhody was almost certainly Tubman's sister Mariah, the second child of their parents, Rit and Ben. It's not clear why she was misnamed on the bill of sale. What's absolutely certain is that her parents and siblings were distraught at having Mariah so abruptly ripped away from them. Being sold to the owners of cotton, rice, or sugarcane plantations in the Deep South was the fear of every slave in the border states of Maryland, Virginia, and Kentucky, because they all knew that the working conditions there were horrible and life expectancy short. Mariah was apparently a fragile child, which may be why Kane was given such a good bargain when he bought her. It's unlikely she could have survived long if she was put to work as a field hand in Mississippi.

The pain of Mariah's sale undoubtedly competed with Tubman's memory of being tossed in the air by friendly hands, helping to fuel her conviction that slavery was "the next thing to hell" (Drew 2008, 52).

DORCHESTER COUNTY

Tubman was born on Maryland's Eastern Shore, a club-shaped peninsula claimed by Delaware and Virginia as well, a state of affairs that gives it the unofficial name of Delmarva. Its primary county is Dorchester, four hundred thousand acres that were landscaped in the early nineteenth century with dense forests, marshes and swamps, port towns, small farms, and a handful of larger plantations. Dorchester is situated between the Choptank and Nanticoke rivers, both of which were convenient navigable routes on which farmers floated their harvests of tobacco, corn, wheat, and flax down to the Chesapeake Bay and on to cosmopolitan ports of sale like Baltimore and the District of Columbia. During the first half of Tubman's life, the county's swampy southern sections were neither farmable nor navigable.

The earliest white settlers on the Eastern Shore made a living from trapping beavers and selling their belts or from mining the rich oyster beds that circled the peninsula. As the beaver population declined, farmers replaced trappers throughout the region. The peninsula's mild and humid climate was ideal for raising crops, especially tobacco.

Originally, most of the peninsula's farms were small holdings. Even though the colony of Maryland began importing slaves in 1642, Eastern Shore farmers primarily made use of white indentured servants to plant, tend, and harvest their crops. By the eighteenth century, however, as some of the original settlers grew rich and expanded their farms to cultivate more tobacco, that began to change. Slaves were purchased not only to work the fields but also to clear forests and drain marshes. Arable land was constantly in demand because tobacco quickly impoverishes the soil. Eventually, in fact, most Dorchester planters switched to other cash crops that were less hard on the land, and an increasing number of them began to exploit the county's hundreds of acres of timber, finding lucrative markets among shipbuilders in Baltimore and New England.

Demand for cheap labor grew so rapidly on the Eastern Shore that, by the beginning of the nineteenth century, more than thirty-eight thousand slaves lived and worked there, accounting for an astounding 36 percent of the total population. As was common throughout the entire slaveholding South, only a handful of Eastern Shore planters owned more than fifteen slaves, and most slave owners possessed far fewer than that. But slavery as a social and economic institution was firmly ensconced as a cultural and economic fact.

There was also pushback, especially after the American Revolution popularized notions of liberty. Maryland Quakers (Religious Society of Friends) led the drive for abolition of slavery, founding a Society for Promoting the Abolition of Slavery, which urged colonial, and then state officials, to outlaw the peculiar institution. The Baltimore Yearly Meeting threw down the gauntlet (if such a martial image is appropriate when speaking of Quakers) in 1787 by condemning slavery on moral and religious grounds and threatening to excommunicate Quakers who continued to own or sell slaves.

As a consequence of this early abolitionist agitation, some Maryland slave owners, Quaker or otherwise, decided that their consciences could no longer allow them to hold fellow human beings in bondage. This was true to a certain extent on the Eastern Shore as well. The real motive that led many Dorchester planters to manumit or free their slaves was economic rather than moral or religious. By the first decades of the nineteenth

---

QUAKERS AND SLAVERY

Quakers, members of the Society of Friends, were the first persons in the U.S. colonies to publicly express serious moral reservations about slavery. The initial statement came in 1688, when several Quakers from Germantown, Pennsylvania, issued a condemnation of the buying and selling of "men-bodies." But their recommendation that Quakers distance themselves from slavery was tabled, and, for the next ninety years, the Society of Friends wrestled on and off again with the issue of whether or not Quakers should own or trade in slaves. Moral sensibility clashed with the spirit of acquisitiveness.

Fifty years after the Germantown declaration, an eccentric Quaker named Benjamin Lay proved to be such an ardent critic of slaveholding Quakers that he was actually expelled from the society. A passionate and dramatic preacher, Lay once kidnapped a Quaker's child to rouse sympathy for the grief felt by Africans whose sons and daughters were stolen by slavers.

Less eccentric and more effective in his efforts to wean Quakers away from slavery was John Woolman, whose eloquent 1753 *Considerations on the Keeping of Negroes* became the most widely circulated antislavery pamphlet of its time. Woolman argued that all races were equal in the eyes of God and that slavery expressed contempt for that truth. Woolman's fellow Quaker Anthony Benezet published scathing denunciations of the international slave trade, which denied any moral distinction between the pirates who stole Africans and the "respectable" U.S. Quakers who purchased them.

By the early 1770s, Quakers throughout the northern colonies had decided against slavery. Philadelphia led the way in denouncing ownership and disowning slaveholders, and the 1773 New England Yearly Meeting did likewise. By 1787, no Quaker north of Virginia owned slaves, and many Quakers in southern states followed suit.

---

century, keeping large numbers of slaves became, for all but the very wealthiest planters, more of a financial drain than an asset.

The reason for this was a decline in the fortunes of the Eastern Shore. Tobacco, which requires extensive care and thus encouraged the purchase of human cultivators, was no longer a staple cash crop. Emphasis had shifted to grains and timber, which required less physical labor and, hence, fewer slaves. An economic peak had been reached during the War of 1812, when British goods ceased to come to the United States. Following the war's end, with embargos lifted against imports, Dorchester County farmers and merchants found that the market for their wares significantly dropped. Consequently, there was even less need for slave labor.

Feeding and housing unproductive slaves was a costly business, so many Eastern Shore slave owners decided to cut their losses and manumit some or all of their slaves. The predictable inclination was to manumit slaves who were unable to work because of age or infirmity. Consequently, the Eastern Shore soon saw an increase in not only the freed able-bodied slaves but also the ones who were unable to care for themselves. By the turn of the nineteenth century, there were over twenty-three hundred freedmen in Dorchester County and forty-five hundred slaves. Only a decade earlier, the freedman population had been just 528 (Larson 2003, 13). At the same time, the white population remained steady at ten thousand because of the drain of white youth to other states.

This fourfold increase in the numbers of manumitted slaves created several problems for the Eastern Shore. The first was the jittery anxiety inevitably felt by southern whites when large numbers of free slaves dwelt in their communities. As we saw in chapter 1, fear of violent black revolt haunted the southern slaveholding states. A second problem was that freed blacks were willing to hire out more cheaply than white laborers and craftsmen, thereby stoking resentment among yeoman farmers and tradesmen alike. A third difficulty was the question of what to do with manumitted slaves who were too old or sickly to care for themselves and who had been manumitted precisely because their upkeep was an expense their owners had no wish to shoulder.

In an effort to do something about the third problem, authorities began to crack down on manumission laws already on the books. Back in 1752, when Maryland was still a crown colony, the courts decreed that only slaves capable of labor and under fifty years of age could be liberated by their masters. The law was revised in 1796 to mandate that the possibility of manumission was reserved for slaves under the age of forty-five. Rigorous enforcement of these existing laws at the beginning of the nineteenth century led to a decrease in manumissions by the end of the first decade.

The problem of too many able-bodied free blacks remained. One response was to enact so-called Black Laws that severely curtailed their legal rights and privileges. Coupled with this disenfranchisement was the rise in Maryland of support for the American Colonization Society's scheme to exile freedmen to the colony of Liberia in Africa. Members of the society, which was established in 1817 with the backing of stalwarts such as Thomas Jefferson, James Madison, James Monroe, and Henry Clay, didn't necessarily have moral objections to slavery. Many of them simply wanted to rid the nation of what they perceived as a potential threat to white sovereignty.

The border state of Maryland, which had one of the largest free black populations in the nation, enthusiastically embraced the idea of colonization, and Dorchester slaveholders especially welcomed the prospect of thinning the county's black population by means of it. But free blacks on the Eastern Shore, just like most free blacks throughout the entire nation, generally resisted the somewhat hare-brained scheme. Many of them had

AMERICAN COLONIZATION SOCIETY

The American Society for Colonizing the Free People of Color of the United States was a contentious affair from the very start. It was founded, in part, to encourage the gradual and compensated emancipation of slaves, but the motives were anything but humanitarian. The society's founders believed that slavery as an institution was flooding the nation with persons of African descent, whom they considered to be inherently inferior to whites. Large numbers of them, free or enslaved, were seen as a menace to the nation's stability. So the society's answer was to export them to overseas colonies, especially one located in Liberia.

Some erstwhile supporters of the society, the most prominent of which was abolitionist William Lloyd Garrison, eventually broke with it because of its racist assumption of black inferiority. Many free blacks living in northern states also objected to its mission, insisting that they were U.S.-born citizens who would find migration to Africa every bit as discombobulating as white Americans would. Shortly after the society's founding, some three thousand black opponents gathered in Philadelphia's Bethel American Methodist Episcopal Church to denounce it.

But some free blacks embraced the idea of migrating to Africa (or other sites such as Haiti). Their reasoning was that neither the white population nor the government would accept them as equals, and that, consequently, it would be better to leave and begin anew. One of the most prominent of them to make this case was the Quaker Paul Cuffee who, a year before the society was founded, bankrolled a small party of blacks who intended to start a colony, Freetown, in British Sierra Leone. Unlike most of his fellow churchmen, Daniel Coker, cofounder and bishop of the American Methodist Episcopal (AME) Church, was also a defender of colonization. Aided by the society, he and nearly one hundred other blacks migrated to Freetown in 1820.

Still, most blacks resisted the society's plan of migration. By the start of the Civil War, less than three thousand of them had actually settled in Liberia. Following the war, the increasingly irrelevant society tottered on until officially disbanding in 1964.

been born in the United States and were understandably reluctant to leave the only home they'd ever known to relocate to an utterly foreign land. Because many black families included both enslaved and freed members, colonization also threatened separation from loved ones.

There was, however, another way to slow down the growth of the free black population on the Eastern Shore, even if colonization didn't seem to be the solution. As the agricultural need for slaves diminished in Dorchester County, the demand for them by Deep South accelerated, as plantation owners who were planting more and more acres with cotton and rice.

Because the importation of slaves into the United States was constitution-ally prohibited after 1808, planters from South Carolina, Alabama, Missis-sippi, Georgia, and Louisiana began shopping for humans in slaveholding border states. Slave traders, recognizing a bonanza when they saw it, either traveled up from the south to scout out business opportunities or hired local agents to encourage cash-poor planters in Maryland and Virginia, both of which soon became known as "breeder states," to sell their slaves. It was in one of these transactions that Tubman's sister Mariah was carted off to her unknown fate in Mississippi.

Because members of the same slave family were frequently owned by different planters, Dorchester slaveholders were traditionally reluctant to sell slaves outside the county. As the agricultural downturn continued, the allure of quick cash from the Deep South proved too tempting. Many of these transactions were made on the sly, because the men and women sell-ing their slaves down south were generally embarrassed by, if not outright ashamed of, what they were doing. As a ruse, some of them even claimed that the slaves they'd sold and whose absence would be noticed by others had run away. One enterprising local, a man named Joe Johnson, made himself a living by serving as the intermediary in these surreptitious slave sales. He eventually ran afoul of the law when he began kidnapping free blacks and stealing enslaved ones to sell to Deep South traders. This was too much even for Dorchester whites to stomach.

The move to sell local slaves to southern plantations located far from the Eastern Shore was a continuous source of dread for slave families. Slaves who otherwise might have tolerated their lot began to seek ways to escape bondage. By 1850, Maryland recorded more successful slave escapes than any other slaveholding state. Part of that would be due to the efforts of Harriet Tubman.

A SLAVE FAMILY

The great abolitionist Frederick Douglass opens his autobiographical *Narrative* with an observation that was both instructive and sorrowful. "I do not remember to have ever met a slave who could tell of his birthday," he wrote. "They seldom come nearer to it than planting-time, harvest-time, cherry-time, spring-time or fall-time" (Douglass 2016, 19).

Some slave owners kept meticulous records of the sale or purchase of their slaves. This made sound financial sense. But recording births, and especially deaths, of slaves was more haphazard, and even if births were recorded in the Big House ledger, slave families often had no way to keep track of such significant dates except, as Douglass suggested, by correlat-ing them with agricultural seasons.

It's somewhat surprising, then, that we have a pretty reliable birth date for Harriet Tubman. For many years, a number of possibilities were floated: 1818, 1820, and 1824. As an adult, Tubman herself usually opined that she was born in 1825. Her gravestone in Auburn, New York, says 1820, and her death certificate offers 1815 as yet another possibility.

We now know, however, that her actual date of birth was almost certainly sometime during the first half of March 1822. A ledger entry dated March 15 of that year records that two dollars was paid to a midwife's care of "Negro Rit," who was also listed as having missed forty-three days of work that winter because of pregnancy. Tubman's mother, Harriet Green, was called Rit or Rittia by everyone who knew her. She gave birth to her daughter, whom she named Araminta, near a place in west-central Dorchester County called Tobacco Stick, doubtlessly named after the cash crop that had been so important at one time to the Eastern Shore economy.

Tubman's father, Ben Ross, and her mother were both slaves. Ben was described by contemporaries as a full-blooded black; we know nothing of his ancestry, although, as we'll see in the next chapter, we know much more about his adult life. Rit appears to have had a white father—this despite an early biographer's claim that Tubman had "not a drop of white blood in her veins" (Bradford 1886, 107)—who might have been the man who owned her mother, Modesty Green. About all we know of Modesty is that she was born in West Africa and was probably a member of the Ashanti tribe, a people known for their fierce courage in battle and valued by white slaveholders for their strength and endurance as field hands. Modesty was probably born in the mid-eighteenth century, and her daughter Rit around 1785.

But like all slaves, Tubman's "lineage" included not only her biological family but also the slave owners who laid legal claim to her. In Tubman's case, that lineage was complicated.

To begin with, her parents belonged to different masters. Ben was the property of a man named Anthony Thompson, a well-to-do planter who held the property on which Tubman was born. Rit was owned by Joseph and Mary Brodess. Mary had inherited Rit from her grandfather, Atthow Pattison—the man rumored to be Rit's father—who died in 1797. The two girls were born about the same time and had likely known one another from childhood and perhaps even played together.

The possibility that Atthow Pattison was Rit's father is strengthened by a provision in his will that stipulated that Rit and her offspring were to be manumitted when they reached the age of forty-five. (Because slavery passed down from mothers instead of fathers, all of Rit's children would necessarily be born slaves, even had she been married to a free black man.)

Three years after Atthow's death, Mary, by then fifteen or sixteen years old, married a youth named Joseph Brodess. His family, located in

Dorchester Country's Bucktown, was respectable enough but had fallen on hard times. In fact, Joseph's elder brother Edward was forced to sell off most of the family's property around the time of the wedding just to make ends meet.

Within a year Mary was pregnant, giving birth in early summer 1801 to a son, Edward. Joseph Brodess, whose financial situation didn't improve, evaded the stress and shame of genteel poverty by dying soon afterward. By the terms of his will, his infant son inherited his land and slaves, including Rit and her children, who, under the law, had become Joseph's property when he married Mary.

Left a widow with a child before her twentieth birthday, Mary was in a precarious position. She wasn't exactly indigent, but the death of a husband in the early nineteenth century left a woman with dismal prospects unless she came from wealth. Like many women who found themselves in similar straits, Mary began looking for a new husband. She found one in Anthony Thompson, the owner of Ben Ross. Thompson, a widower more than twenty years older than his new bride, had several children from his first marriage by the time he wed Mary in 1803. She, Edward, and Rit relocated from Bucktown to live in his house.

This merger of the Brodess and Thompson households brought Ben and Rit together. Although no more legally married than most other slave couples—slave owners could break up slave unions at will—they were devoted to one another and to the nine children born to them between 1808 and 1832. Although Ben remained the property of Thompson, and Rit the property of young Edward Brodess, the Ross family was able to remain intact on the Thompson plantation—at least until Tubman was born.

Mary Brodess Thompson died sometime before 1810, leaving her young son Edward the ward of her now twice-widowed husband, who lived for another quarter century. Thompson served conscientiously as the boy's legal guardian, managing the estate left him by Joseph, two hundred acres near Bucktown and a number of slaves, until Edward turned twenty-one in 1822. Once in full possession of his property—which included Rit and her children—Edward left the Thompson plantation to return to Buckland, ten miles away, from where his father's people hailed. The two men parted on acrimonious terms, squabbling over compensation that Thompson claimed was due him from Edward's inheritance. It's not clear if Edward took Rit and her children with him right away or if he sent for them later, but they were on his Buckland property by the time he married a few months later, while Ben remained with Thompson, his owner. The stable family Ben and Rit had created and nurtured was torn asunder.

Like his father before him, Edward Brodess, his wife Eliza Ann, and their eventual eight children lived on the brink of genteel poverty. It wasn't simply Brodess's ineptitude that kept the family's fortunes low. Part of his distress was caused by the general economic downturn in Eastern Shore agriculture that followed the war of 1812. To make ends meet, Brodess took to hiring out his slaves, including Rit's children, to other planters and tradesmen in the area. The general arrangement in such situations was that the slave's employer would provide board for the slave while paying his or her wages directly to the master. This gave slave owners some additional cash income and absolved them of the expense of feeding hired-out slaves—both welcome possibilities in the Brodess household, which was eager to curtail expenses and increase revenue.

Although he was certainly familiar with it, Brodess also refused to honor the stipulation in his great grandfather Atthow Pattison's will that Rit and her children be freed when they reached the age of forty-five. Their services were simply too valuable to him.

Mediocre harvests, bad money management, and a lust to buy ever more land meant that Brodess was always in need of funds, despite hiring out his slaves. Probably surreptitiously, he began selling his slaves to traders who transported them down south. As we've already seen, Tubman's sister Mariah was the first member of the Ross family to suffer this fate. Sometime in the 1830s, when Tubman wasn't yet ten years old, Brodess also sold off her sister Soph. Although his testimony may have been influenced by his dislike of his stepson, Anthony Thompson swore that Edward had sold the sisters to Deep South planters because doing so fetched a higher price than he would have gotten from in-state buyers.

One can only imagine the effect losing two of her children in this way had on Rit. Ben, too, was undoubtedly upset. But unlike Rit, he no longer lived day-to-day with his children, stuck as he was on the Thompson estate, and so, he probably suffered less immediate pain from the separation. The degree to which Rit was both traumatized and infuriated by Brodess's actions is suggested by what happened when Brodess tried to put Moses, the youngest of Rit and Ben's children, on the auction block shortly after the sale of Linah and Soph. According to Henry, one of Tubman's brothers, Rit got wind of the plan and hid the boy away in Greenbriar Swamp, not far from Brodess's property, before the sale could occur.

Brodess was furious and enlisted another slave to squirrel the boy's whereabouts out of Rit. When that didn't work, he sent the same slave and a neighboring white slaveholder to Rit's cabin to search for Moses. But Rit had had enough. According to Henry, "She ripped out an oath, and said; 'You are after my son; but the first man that comes into my house, I will split his head open.' That frightened them, and they would not come in" (Blassingame 1977, 415).

Afterward, seemingly intimidated by the report of Rit's furious threats against anyone trying to steal another of her children, Brodess appeared at her cabin to disingenuously say how happy he was that Moses was safe. Rit knew, as did he, that she'd bested him.

MINTY

From as early as she could remember, the child named Araminta was called Minty. She lived on the Brodess property with her mother, who served as cook and domestic factotum, and her siblings. There's no evidence to suggest she had much of a relationship with her father, from whom she was separated shortly after her birth, during these early years.

Tubman would later say that Brodess and Eliza Ann were "never unnecessarily cruel" to her (Bradford 1869, 9), but her brothers tell a quite different story. One of them remembered that Eliza Ann was "very devilish," and insisted that were he to tell the full story of the Brodess's cruelty, "it would make your flesh creep and your hair stand on end" (Still 2007, 156). The other bitterly said that Edward wasn't fit even to own a dog (Drew 2008, 60–61).

Because Rit worked at the Great House from dawn to dusk, young Minty, not yet five years old, was left in charge of her infant brother Ben, the same brother who later expressed such dislike of Eliza Ann Brodess. Years afterward, Tubman recalled that she waited impatiently for her mother to leave each morning so that she could play a favorite game with Ben. She would pretend he was "a pig in a bag, and hold him up by the bottom of his dress. I had a nice frolic with that baby, swinging him all round, his feet in the dress and his little head and arms touching the floor, because I was too small to hold him higher." Before Rit returned to the slave cabin late at night, Minty was in the habit of roasting a chunk of pork for a hungry Ben to suck on. "One night," she recalls, "he went to sleep with that hanging out, and when my mother come she thought I'd done killed him" (Telford in Humez 2003, 173).

The story is charming, and the final bit about Rit's fright usually evokes a chuckle. But we ought not to let either blind us to the very real pathos of the recollection. A young girl, still nearly a baby herself, is the only caretaker of her infant brother because her slave mother is forced to work such long hours that she's simply unable to care for her own children. The fact that Rit was frightened when she saw Ben with the pork hanging out of his mouth—she undoubtedly mistook it for his tongue and presumed he was choking—indicates the anxiety she must have felt at leaving her youngsters on their own all day long. That was simply something a slave mother had to do.

Another consequence of her motherless and unsupervised days is that Minty, by her own account, became too "mischievous" for the Brodess's taste. At the age of five, partly to get her out of the way but mainly, one supposes, to bring additional income into the cash-poor household, Minty was hired out for the first time.

PUT TO WORK

There's some confusion in Tubman's recollections of the various jobs she was hired out to do while still a small child. This is only to be understood. Memories, especially earliest ones, have a way of bleeding into one another and fusing together. Regardless of the inaccuracies that crept into her recollections, one thing is certain: young Minty was viewed by Brodess as little more than a flesh-and-blood commodity, just another member of his human herd to be worked for profit.

In telling of her early years, Tubman suggests that although she was initially hired out to serve as a child's nurse, she soon discovered that she was expected to be "maid of all work by day, as well as child's nurse by night," a task that soon exhausted her. Her inability to stay alert led to her being miserably ill-treated by the angry mistress of the Great House where she worked (Bradford 1886, 11). In yet another account, this memory appears to morph into her recollection of being hired by James Cook, whose farm was about ten miles from Buckland, when she was six or seven years old. Even if the two events are separate, Tubman may have been confused about which came first.

If Tubman's memory of her time serving as child's nurse and housekeeper is reliable, it was a truly horrible experience. She worked for a young married woman whom she called Miss Susan. Minty was fed and clothed adequately while in her service, but beaten severely and often whenever Miss Susan was dissatisfied with her performance. Once, ordered to sweep the floors and dust the furniture, the inexperienced youngster botched the job. She told the story to one of her early biographers, who refers to Tubman in the third person.

> At once she took the dusting cloth, and wiped off tables, chairs and mantlepiece. The dust, as dust will do, when it has nowhere else to go, at once settled again, and chairs and tables were soon covered with a white coating, telling a terrible tale against Harriet, when her Mistress came in to see how the work progressed. Reproaches, and savage words, fell upon the ears of the frightened child, and she was commanded to do the work all over again. Then the whip was brought into requisition, and it was laid on with no light hand. Five times before breakfast this process was repeated. (Bradford 1886, 11)

The beatings would have continued but for the intervention of Miss Susan's sister who, alarmed by Minty's screams, rushed into the room and halted the latest onslaught. Instead of reproving Minty, she took the time to explain to the child that it was best to sweep first and dust afterward. Tubman's biographer adds, "A few words might have set the matter right before; but in those days many a poor slave suffered for the stupidity and obstinacy of a master or mistress, more stupid than themselves" (Bradford 1886, 12).

In addition to drudging all day long as a housemaid, Minty was also obliged by her new mistress to care for the infant of the house, both between chores during the daytime, and then all night long. In the night hours, Minty was charged with gently rocking the cradle to make sure that the baby didn't awaken and disturb Miss Susan's sleep. Tubman recalled that she was still so young and small herself that she had to sit on the floor in order to hold the infant. If during her night watch she dropped off to sleep, ceasing the cradle-rocking and awakening the baby, Miss Susan grabbed a switch she kept at her bedside and beat Minty across the neck and shoulders, an energetic and noisy exercise not designed to quiet a squalling infant. Toward the end of her life, Tubman sometimes lowered the collar of her dress to show visitors her scars, defiantly telling them that no matter how badly she was hurt during the beatings that caused them, she refused to cry out in pain (Bradford 1869, 13).

On another occasion, Minty, thinking no one was watching, grabbed a lump of sugar from a bowl and popped it in her mouth. Miss Susan, however, saw the theft and went for the whip. Tubman recalls being so terrified that she bolted out the door. "I just flew, and they didn't catch me. I run, and run, and I run, I passed many a house, but I didn't dare to stop, for they all knew my Missus and they would send me back" (Bradford 1901, 135–136).

Finally, coming upon a pigpen at a neighboring farm, Minty hid in it, battling the sow and piglets for what food she could, for five days and nights, only returning to Miss Susan when she grew too ravenous to stay hidden. This time, the master himself beat her.

That wasn't the only time he laid hands on her. Once, after Minty resisted a whipping from Miss Susan, she received a retaliatory beating from the master severe enough to break ribs, injuring her so badly that she was unable to continue her work. Because some of the fractures didn't mend properly, Tubman carried a knot in her side that hurt her for the rest of her life. Disgusted by her defiant spirit as well as her inability to work because of the beating, Miss Susan finally sent her packing back to the Brodess farm. Rit lovingly nursed her back to health, but Edward and Eliza Ann were probably irritated by the loss of Minty's wages.

As soon as she was physically fit to resume work, Minty was hired out to James Cook, a local farmer who planned to teach her how to weave, apparently with the hope of selling the cloth she would make. She was six or seven years old.

Slave Children at Work

It was a bit unusual for a slave child to be hired out to work at the age of five, as Tubman claimed she was, but it wasn't unheard of. In the "Slave Narrative Collection," interviews of former slaves conducted by the Federal Writers' Project of the Works Progress Administration (WPA) between 1936 and 1938, nearly half of the ex-slaves remembered being put to work before they had reached seven years of age (Steckel 1996, 44).

Customs surrounding the labor of young slaves varied from slave owner to slave owner, depending on his or her temperament; context (for example, whether the owner grew rice and cotton or tobacco); and financial situation (the Brodess family, for example, seemed to have hired Tubman out at such an early age because they were perennially strapped for cash). Sometimes slave children played with the sons and daughters of their masters and had little recognition of the fact that there were fundamental differences in their stations in life. No less a person than Frederick Douglass, reflecting on his earliest days, reported that it took him some time to realize he was a slave. But such cases were probably exceptional. Most slave children, even those not put to work at as early an age as Tubman, witnessed adults, including their own parents, beaten or verbally abused by whites and quickly internalized the realization that even if they played with white children, they were a class apart. As one ex-slave recalled, "I was made to feel, in my boyhood's first experience, that I was inferior and degraded" (Blassingame 1979, 185).

Most slave children were probably given only light tasks up to about ten years of age. After that, they were either sent into the fields, taken on as domestic servants, trained in skills such as hostelry or tailoring, or hired out. At this point, they were treated as adults. Exceptions for their tender years were rarely made when it came to labor expectations, and children could expect the same punishment as adults if they fell short. Slave children grew up fast.

Cook arrived for her on horseback (although she also at least once confused this with the memory of a woman coming to fetch her) and recalled feeling anxious about leaving her mother, siblings, and familiar surroundings. Eliza Ann Brodess had made her a dress for the occasion, an indication that little Minty, like other slave children, ran around either naked or clothed in only a makeshift smock, and that whatever she wore must have been so tattered that the Brodesses were embarrassed to send her out in it.

Once at the Cook homestead, Minty was ushered into the Great House to find the family dining. Already uneasy about her new situation, she was made even more anxious when they offered her something to eat. "I never eat in the house where the white people was," she recalled years later, "and I was ashamed to stand up and eat before them." Sensing her discomfort,

Mrs. Cook offered her a glass of milk. This only made Minty more anxious, and she refused it with the excuse that she didn't care for milk. Once told, however, she had to stick with the fib for the two years she worked for the Cooks. "I was as fond of milk as any young shoot. But all the time I was there I stuck to it, that I didn't drink sweet milk" (Telford in Larson 2003, 37–38).

The civil greeting she received from the Cooks on her arrival proved to be deceptive, because the months she spent in their service were regularly punctuated by beatings and verbal abuse. Additionally, she was as homesick as she'd been earlier at Miss Susan's, pining to "get home and get in my mother's bed" (Telford in Larson 2003, 37–38).

Perhaps it was the ill-treatment she'd received at the hands of Miss Susan, but Minty displayed a willfulness at the Cooks that would remain with her for the rest of her life. She disliked weaving and stubbornly refused to learn the art. Eventually the Cooks gave up on that plan and employed her outdoors, which she genuinely preferred to being stuck inside. Muskrats, whose pelts could be sold and meat eaten, were plentiful in the marshes of Dorchester County, and more than one farmer, including James Cook, regularly set out traps for them. Minty was recruited to routinely inspect the traps and bring back quarry.

Although she preferred being outdoors, the work was hard, especially in the winter months, when she had to wade out into frequently chest-high water to check the traps. Eventually her health gave way, especially after being ordered to the marshes even though she had the measles. Once more, she was sent back to the Brodess farm; once again Rit nursed her back to health.

It's not entirely clear where Minty wound up after her recovery. She may have been sent back to the Cooks for a few more months, or she may have been hired out to someone else. The next definite bit of information about her comes from 1833, when she was ten or eleven years old. Along with playing the pig game with her younger brother, it's one of the few pleasant episodes she recalled from her childhood.

Rit had been hired out to work on a neighboring farm, and Minty, missing her mother dreadfully, risked severe punishment by sneaking away at nights to visit her. One of her brothers always accompanied her to stand guard outside the cabin door, on the lookout for patrols prowling for runaway slaves.

One night—which we can actually pinpoint to November 12—the Leonid meteor shower lit up the night sky. Minty's brother called her out to see the stars, which, she remembered, "were all shooting whichway." Minty and her brother, as well as, undoubtedly, many thousands of others who witnessed the display, "all thought that the end of the world had come" (Humez 2003, 180).

By this time in her life, it's likely that Harriet was working primarily in the fields, either for Brodess or neighboring farmers. Despite her bouts of ill health and the beatings she'd endured as a child, she'd grown to be a strong girl who could carry her weight when it came to outdoor manual labor. In addition to being good at it, fieldwork was the kind of labor she preferred.

Sometime between 1834 and 1835, while working for a farmer she described as "the worst man in the neighborhood," something happened to Tubman that would have lifelong consequences (Telford in Humez 2003, 177). She took the single worst physical blow she ever received during her years as a slave. Ironically, it was an unintended one on the part of the man who delivered it.

Over the years, Tubman shared the story of what happened numerous times. As a consequence, some of the details changed from telling to telling, but the different versions are, in the main, consistent.

One fall afternoon, after working in the fields all day, Tubman was sent with another slave to a dry-goods store to fetch supplies. When she arrived, she stopped at the entrance, hesitating to enter. "I had a shoulder shawl of the mistress's over my head," she recalled, "and when I got to the store I was shamed to go in," presumably because she shouldn't have been wearing her mistress's shawl (Telford in Humez 2003, 177). That she was attests to her streak of defiant independence.

Standing in the doorway, she observed an altercation between a white man, variously described in her accounts as either a master or an overseer, and a slave who had left work without permission. When the slave made a break for the doorway Tubman was blocking, disaster fell upon her in one swift motion. As she told the story, she saw

> The overseer raising up his arm to throw an iron weight at [the slave] and that was the last I knew. That weight struck me in the head and broke my skull and cut a piece of that shawl clean off and drove it in my head. They carried me to the house all bleeding and fainting. I had no bed, no place to lie down on at all, and they lay me on the seat of the loom, and I stayed there all that day and next. (Telford in Humez 2003, 177)

There's no little irony in the fact, given her resistance to James Cook's efforts to teach her weaving, that the wounded Tubman was laid upon a loom. For two days, she hovered between consciousness and coma. Cruelly, on the third one, barely able to stand upright, she was sent to the field again "and there I worked with the blood and sweat rolling down my face till I couldn't see" (Telford in Humez 2003, 177). There's no indication that the white man who so grievously injured her expressed remorse, nor that the farmer to whom she had been hired out offered her proper medical treatment or felt any pity or remorse. She was, after all, not his property, and he had no financial stake in keeping her healthy. So when it became clear that she was unable to carry out her fieldwork, he sent her packing back to Brodess, who in turn promptly tried to sell her. Given her condition, there were no takers. "They said they wouldn't give a sixpence for me," Tubman recalled (Bradford 1869, 14).

Tubman carried the scar of her terrible wound for the rest of her life. More than one acquaintance remarked on the v-shaped indentation in her forehead left by the iron weight. She herself thought that the only reason she survived the injury was because of the thickness of her hair. "My hair had never been combed and it stood out like a bushel basket, and when I'd get through eating I'd wipe the grease off my fingers on my hair. And I expect that the hair saved my life" (Telford in Humez 2003, 177).

The injury left more than a visible scar. It also brought on blinding headaches, seizures, and narcoleptic-like fugues, from which she suffered until the end of her days. (As an old woman, she actually underwent perilous surgery to remove chips of skull from her brain in the hope that the severity of her headaches would lessen.) Her narcoleptic episodes often occurred every hour or so and could last up to fifteen minutes. Remarkably, even though her eyes closed and she snored during them, witnesses testified that she was able to immediately pick up the train of conversation when she awoke. Apparently, some part of her conscious awareness remained functioning.

Yet another legacy from the wound was a heightened religious sense. Like most slaves, Tubman was a fervent Christian from an early age, especially fond, like most slaves, of the story of Moses and the exodus out of Egypt found in the Hebrew scriptures. After her accident, people noted a new zeal in her. She often unexpectedly broke into ecstatic and loud praise of God, experienced visions and heard heavenly voices, and reached a new level of hopeful fearlessness about her condition as a slave. After she escaped from slavery, her religious zeal gave her a strong sense of mission, in which she came to believe that God wanted her to lead her people out of bondage, just as Moses led the Hebrews out of pharaoh's Egypt.

It may be that the head injury provoked temporal lobe epilepsy, a neurological disorder characterized by exactly the kind of symptoms—narcolepsy, headaches, visions, and seizures followed by extreme fatigue—that Tubman displayed. Patients suffering from this form of epilepsy often confuse their visions for religious experiences, which, in turn, encourage hyperreligiosity even in people who, before the onset of epilepsy, may not have been particularly devout.

Whatever the explanation, Tubman clearly displayed more of an obsession with God and matters of the spirit after the accident than before. As she told one of her earliest biographers,

Appears like I prayed all the time, about my work, everywhere; I was always talking to the Lord. When I went to the horse-trough to wash my face, and took up the water in my hands, I said, "Oh Lord, wash me, make me clean." When I took up the towel to wipe my face and hands, I cried, "Oh Lord, for Jesus' sake, wipe away all my sins!" When I took up the broom and began to sweep, I groaned, "Oh, Lord, whatsoever sin there be in my heart, sweep it out, Lord, clear and clean." (Bradford 1869, 14)

3

From Bondage to Freedom

Liberty or death; if I could not have one, I would have the other.

—Harriet Tubman (Bradford 1886, 17)

RECOVERY AND LOSS

It took months for twelve-year-old Minty to recovery from her terrible injury. During her convalescence, Brodess tried to sell her on several more occasions, but no potential buyer was interested in what was clearly damaged goods. Brodess owned her, and, at least for the time being, he was stuck with her. Instead of adding to his income through her labor, he was forced to shell some out in medical treatment for her.

Most likely, she was treated by Dr. Anthony C. Thompson, who, with his brother Absalom, was a medical doctor. Their father, also named Anthony, owned Minty's father, Ben Ross.

Dr. Thompson, described as a spare, bald, and bewigged man, was a go-getter. Not content with simply maintaining a medical practice, he also operated a drug store that sold tonics of his own making, as well as luxuries such as candy he picked up on visits to Baltimore. As we'll see shortly, he branched out into the lumber business after his father's death, even though doing so stretched his personal finances to the breaking point. He was also active in local civic affairs, being an advocate for colonization of freed blacks, a teetotaler, and a school commissioner for the Eastern Shore town of Cambridge. All in all, he was a busy and valued member of the community. Minty was working for him when she headed north to freedom some fifteen years later.

When Minty was finally back on her feet, sometime in either 1834 or 1835, Brodess, surrendering for the moment his hope of selling her, hired her out again. It's not clear to whom. It may have been to Dr. Thompson or to another Eastern Shore man, John T. Stewart. Or it could be that Thompson hired her and then subleased her to Stewart. At any rate, the weight of evidence is that she labored directly for Stewart for the next six years or so, even if Thompson was her immediate employer.

John Stewart was the son of Joseph Stewart, a leading Dorchester County citizen who lived in the Tobacco Stick area. He owned a plantation of over 220 acres, on which he planted wheat and cotton. As with many plantations in the antebellum South, his was practically a small village, complete with a store, windmill, blacksmith shop, slave quarters, outbuildings, and the Great House where the Stewarts lived.

In addition to raising crops, Joseph Stewart was also a master shipbuilder. Since some of his property was on Dorchester's coastline, his shipyard built and launched the vessels he sold to mariners in the middle Atlantic and New England states.

Shipbuilding requires a steady supply of good lumber. To ensure that he was never short of it, Joseph built a seven-mile-long canal, known locally as Stewart's Canal, to transport white oak, walnut, and pine from the dense forests of the interior to his shipyard. Finished in the 1830s, the project took twenty years to complete, primarily because Joseph had his slaves work on it outside of planting and harvesting seasons but also because it was a backbreaking task to drain the marshland through which the canal passed. Disease and accident were rampant during its construction.

Despite the risks, many of the Eastern Shore's freedmen were eager to hire on as laborers. At the end of the day's work, slaves working on the canal generally returned to their cabins, but free black laborers tended to bunk down on site. Many of them, either during the canal's construction or afterward, decided to remain in the vicinity and bought or rented bits of land on which to dwell and farm. As a consequence, there were several free black communities in the Tobacco Stick area. Presumably Minty would have been acquainted with some of their members from the time she began working for John Stewart. Observing the way in which they lived, unbeholden to white masters and unbound by the many legal and social limitations of slavery, must have left a deep impression on the young girl who had already exhibited an independent streak.

Minty was put to a variety of tasks during the years she worked for Stewart. Initially, perhaps because she was still too weak from her injury to do heavy work, she was employed as a domestic servant. Although

STEWART'S CANAL

The seven-mile-long canal that both enslaved and freed blacks labored on from 1810 to 1832 is still visible, although it's now generally called Parsons Creek after the natural tributary to which it connects. Joseph Stewart intended it to link the Big Blackwater River and Parsons Creek into a single artery on which to float timber and agricultural goods from the interior of Dorchester County to Tobacco Stick (now Madison) Bay and on to Baltimore.

Stewart certainly used some of his own slaves in the off-season construction of the canal, but he also hired free blacks and slaves owned by local planters and merchants in the area. It may be that John Tubman, Harriet's first husband, was among them.

The area in which the canal was dug is marshland, and the actual work was backbreaking and dangerous, humid, hot, and mosquito-ridden in the summer months, cold, wet, and even icy in the winter ones. The work required being in water, sometimes waist-deep, all day. Given the sliminess of marsh soil, getting a secure foot grip was undoubtedly difficult. Because few slaves knew how to swim, slipping could mean death by drowning. Slave laborers probably slept in more or less dry spots in the marshlands, close to where they'd finished the day's work. Free blacks may have returned to their homes at night, provided they didn't live too far away. Accidents, as well as illnesses, from respiratory infections to ones caused by bug bites, were common. It was awful work (Larson 2003, 58–62).

One unexpected result of the canal building is that many free blacks who signed on for the construction opted to settle down in the area to work alongside hired-out slaves in the timber industry. This is probably how John Tubman met Harriet's father, Ben, and through him, Harriet.

Tubman often worked as a maid and laundress after she achieved her freedom, while still a slave, she always preferred outdoor to inside work, probably because she didn't like being as close to masters and mistresses as domestic labor required. Both her aversion to inside work as well as her mischievous spirit came through in a memory she shared of only pretending to work in Stewart's house. She would "beat up the feather beds, make believe she was working hard, and when she had blown them up she would throw herself in the middle of them" (Larson 2003, 56).

As she grew stronger—and she would eventually become remarkably so, despite her diminutive height of only five feet; Stewart often bragged about her strength to his friends—her work focus shifted to the plantation store, hauling goods to and from the shipyard. Eventually she wound up working in the fields and in the woods alongside male slaves. She apparently was able to cut half-a-cord of lumber in a single day, no mean accomplishment even for a fully grown male slave.

Working for Stewart during these years was satisfying for Minty, or at least as satisfying as bonded servitude can be. One of the reasons was that she was able to get to know her father, Ben, in a way that Brodess's split-up of her family when she was still an infant had prevented. In fact, her earliest biographer, Franklin Sanborn, records that "frequently Harriet worked for her father" (Bradford 1886, 110). Ben, although belonging to Anthony Thompson, was hired out to Stewart and was an indispensable part of his lumber industry, managing as he did the shipping of surplus timber to Baltimore. The relationship between the two men seems to have been an amicable one and may even be why Stewart agreed to take on Minty. It's likely that three of Tubman's brothers, John, Ben, and Henry, likewise worked for Stewart, perhaps during this same period. When the three of them escaped to Philadelphia, they took on a different surname, as many refugees did, in order to evade slave catchers. The one they chose was Stewart.

Anthony Thompson died in 1836, leaving behind over forty slaves and a good deal of land, all of which was divided between his two sons, Anthony C. and Absalom. The death of a master always stirred up anxiety and even terror in their slaves because it could mean the breakup of slave families, through either estate sales or inheritance. In his will, Thompson provided for the staggered liberation of all his slaves when they reached the age of forty-five, the top legal limit for manumission. Ben Ross was closer to fifty-five when Thompson died. Slave owners often lied about their servants' ages in order to keep them longer, and Ben's falsely recorded birth date mandated that he had five more years of bondage to go, although Anthony C. eventually manumitted him one year early in 1840. Perhaps in contrition for the deception about his age, Thompson also left a provision in his will for Ben to be given ten acres of land to use for his entire lifetime, as well as the right to cut timber on Thompson property as a means of livelihood. It was a surprisingly generous bequest.

Anthony C., enterprising as ever, decided that his future lay in supplying wood to Baltimore shipbuilders. So soon after he came into his inheritance, he sold most of the property left him to buy over two thousand timbered acres in the Poplar Neck region, located in adjacent Caroline County. To do so, he found it necessary to take out a loan of $24,000, which meant he was in danger of losing everything if he couldn't meet his payments. He badly needed Ben Ross, who already had considerable timber experience, to help out in the new venture as a foreman. Ben agreed, and his wife Rit probably accompanied him to Poplar Neck. Minty likely continued working for Stewart, although she would work directly for Thompson in just a few more years.

It's likely that the only member of the Ross clan left at the Brodess estate by this time was nineteen-year-old Ben, because, in December 1842, right before Christmas, he and a yoke ox were seized as surety for a debt for which Edward Brodess and his cousin Richard Pattison were in default. The confiscated ox was stabled, and Ben wound up in jail. Both were to be sold off if some other way to pay the debt wasn't found.

As he sat in jail worrying about what was going to happen to him, a young slave woman was placed in the adjacent cell. In an interview years later, Ben remembered, "Her irons were taken off. She was in great grief, crying all the time, 'Oh, my children! My poor children!'" (Lowry 2008, 102). As it turned out, the woman was his oldest sister Linah, born in 1808.

Linah, the mother of at least one and probably two daughters, was evidently considered by Brodess to be more expendable than either the land he'd have to sell to pay off the loan or Ben, who was probably a more profitable worker than Linah. Another of her brothers, Henry, later testified that Linah was sold to a Georgia planter, fetching a higher price than she would have had she been sold locally. There's no record of the transaction, suggesting that it was done in secrecy. As we saw in chapter 2, Dorchester County slave owners were sometimes embarrassed about selling their slaves to a cruel life on the Deep South rice and cotton plantations. After Linah's sale, the debt was paid off, and Brodess's two beasts of labor, one human and the other bovine, were returned to him.

It's impossible to imagine the anguish that Minty and her family must have experienced over this tragic turn of events. Ben and Rit had already lost two daughters, Mariah and Soph, to the Deep South. Then, out of the blue, they were shocked by the prospect of losing a son—and even more horrified when they discovered that his reprieve from that awful fate was at the cost of another daughter. It was just another reminder to them all that slaves—and even free men, like Ben, with enslaved children—were completely subject to the whims of their masters. No wonder Tubman always insisted that slavery was the next thing to hell.

HARRIET

While still working for John Stewart, a new chapter opened in Minty's personal life: in 1844, she married a man named John Tubman and changed her first name to Harriet while taking her new husband's surname. The reason for the switch from Araminta to Harriet isn't known. She might have done it to honor her mother. Another possibility, suggested by one of her modern biographers, is that the name change may have coincided with some undisclosed conversion experience that Tubman believed to be so life-changing that it called for a new identity (Larson 2003, 62). Whatever the reason, she was henceforth Harriet Tubman.

The marriage between John and Harriet was somewhat unusual, suggesting the likelihood that it was a love match. To begin with, Harriet was twenty-two, older than most slave women were when they first married. Moreover, John was a free dark-skinned mulatto; whether he was born free or was released from slavery is unknown. Given his name, in all likelihood, he came from slave stock owned by members of the extremely wealthy Tubman family, Roman Catholic planters whose roots in the Eastern Shore extended back to the seventeenth century.

We know little about how he made a living or where he and Harriet lived after their marriage. What we do know is this: it was risky business for a free black man to marry a slave woman. In the first place, there was no guarantee that they could remain together physically. The wife's location was entirely at the whim of her master, and she could be hired out at some distance from her husband or, worse yet, sold. So if the two wished to stay together, the husband might be required to uproot himself in order to follow his wife. Moreover, any children that resulted from the union were automatically the property of the wife's owner.

That the child's legal status was identical to the mother's rather than the father's was determined by an 1812 Maryland law that was partly motivated by the growing number of mulatto children whose sires were clearly white men. The law made a slave wife's position even more fragile. If she and her free husband had no children, her owner could choose a new husband for her or sell her. Slave women who failed to breed for their masters were, like any other unfruitful stock, undesirable.

What made slave marriages tenuous was, of course, their extralegal status. They were informal agreements between the man and woman unsanctioned by law and dependent upon their masters' approval. There were, of course, black preachers—although they were increasingly frowned upon after the religious visionary Nat Turner's horrific 1831 slave revolt—who might officiate at slave weddings, but their presence was utterly unnecessary. Most often, the couple to be married gathered with family and friends on a Sunday—the slaves' one day off—for the "jumping the broom" ceremony, a folk ritual that signified marital union.

Anthony C. Thompson continued to sublease Tubman out to John Stewart for another three years after her marriage. The agreed-upon payment to Edward Brodess, $50 to $60 a year, was guaranteed by Thompson. After repaying him from the wages she earned, Tubman was free to keep any other money that came to her from her labor. It wasn't long before she'd saved enough cash to buy a team of steers that she hired out to plow fields, haul timber, and do other sorts of heavy work. It's possible that Tubman, who remained childless all her life, was hoping to save enough money to buy her niece Harriet, one of Linah's now motherless daughters, from Brodess.

Sometime in the mid- to late-1840s, Tubman took $5 from her savings to pay a lawyer to dig into country records. All her life she'd heard rumors in her family about how old Atthow Pattison's will had stipulated that Rit (who may have been Atthow's daughter) was to be manumitted when she reached the age of forty-five, as were her children when they reached the same age. Tubman wanted to know if there was any truth to the family lore.

It took some sleuthing, but the lawyer eventually located the will, which was written in 1791 and probated six years later. Sure enough, the rumors were all true, yet none of his heirs had bothered to honor the will's stipulations. On old Atthow's death, his granddaughter, Mary Pattison, inherited Rit, as her son Edward Brodess eventually did. By then, Rit was most likely in her sixties and should have been set free years earlier. It's not certain that Brodess knew that Atthow had directed the manumission of Rit and her children. Whether he did or didn't, his sale of the three Ross children was clearly illegal. It may be that Brodess knew perfectly well he was violating the will's provisions, because two of the three sales left no official paper trail, suggesting that the transactions had been done on the sly.

Tubman was furious when she discovered that her mother had been hoodwinked out of her freedom. There's no record that she confronted Brodess with what she'd found out or that she tried to take him to law. Doing so would have surely enraged Brodess and placed her, as well as her mother, in jeopardy of being sold in retaliation. It's not unreasonable to infer that this injustice only intensified her hatred of slavery and could well have been a major motivation in her decision to flee bondage.

By 1847, Tubman was working directly for Dr. Thompson, although it's not clear if it was in his Caroline Country timberland or at his home in the town of Cambridge. She fell so ill during the winter of 1848 to 1849 that she was unable to continue her duties, which meant, of course, that she wasn't earning. Thompson, stretched by the huge mortgage he'd taken out to purchase land, was unable to keep on a sick slave, and Brodess, who'd long wanted to rid himself of her, was even more reluctant now to take her back. Tubman knew she was in danger of following her three siblings to the Deep South and leaving behind her husband, parents, and everyone else she loved. Even more to the point, she'd heard rumors that Brodess had already expressed his intention to put her and some of her siblings on the auction block.

During her prolonged illness, she recalled that "from Christmas to March I worked as I could, and I *prayed* through all the long nights— I groaned and prayed for ole master: 'Oh Lord, convert master! Oh Lord, change that man's heart!'" (Bradford 1886, 23–24). As the bleak winter months wore on, it became increasingly apparent to Tubman that her prayers for Brodess's conversions were going unheard and that the peril to her was becoming more imminent. Finally, out of sheer desperation, her prayer went in a drastically different direction.

> I prayed all night long for master, till the first of March; and all the time he was bringing people to look at me, and trying to sell me. Then we hear that some of us was going to be sold to go with the chain-gang down to the cotton and rice fields, and they said I was going, and my brothers, and sisters. Then I changed my prayer. First of March I began to pray, "Oh Lord, if you ain't never going to change that man's heart, kill him, Lord, and take him out of the way." (Bradford 1886, 24)

One week after Tubman began praying for Brodess's downfall, she was stunned to learn that he, in fact, *did* die. Her emotions, understandably, were mixed. On the one hand, she felt relieved and vindicated. "Next thing I heard old master was dead," she later said, "and he died just as he lived." This could only mean that Tubman believed Brodess died in the same state of sin in which he had lived, unrepentant to the end about his abuse of her and her family, and that her dislike of him had been vindicated. On the other hand, she was horrified that her petition to God might have led to the death of anyone, even Brodess. "Oh, then, it appeared like I'd give all the world full of gold, if I had it, to bring that poor soul back." But, she concluded, "I couldn't pray for him no longer" (Bradford 1886, 24). What was done was done.

Tubman's wish that she could bring Brodess back to life was based on her uneasy sense of guilt at somehow playing a hand in his death. She soon discovered another reason for regretting his passing.

BOUND FOR THE PROMISED LAND

Brodess, who died at the age of forty-seven, left his widow and eight children in straitened circumstances. His will, written shortly before his death, stipulated that his land and hard property went to Eliza Ann, but his human property to his children. Contrary to a promise he'd made to his slaves to free them at his death, Brodess apparently had no intention of doing so. There was good reason for that. Never a good businessman, his death saddled his widow with a mountain of debt that threatened the small legacy she and her children had received. Slaves were hard capital that might keep the wolves away from the door.

Brodess had held many of his creditor wolves off as long as he could, paying them a little here and a little there. Once he was gone and could put up no more resistance, they swooped in and demanded payment. When it wasn't forthcoming from his impoverished widow, they filed suit to recover what they were owed. Within weeks of Brodess's death, the Dorchester County Court ordered all of his personal property, except the slaves, to be sold off. In order to save her furniture, linens, and dishes, Eliza Ann deter-mined to buy them back herself. Lacking ready cash, she borrowed $1,000 from a neighbor, John Mills, whom Brodess had named coexecutor of his will. She saved the household items, but then had to find means to repay Mills. The only foreseeable way to do that was to put some of the family slaves on the auction block, even though they technically belonged to Brodess's children rather than her. Eliza petitioned the Orphan's Court in Dorchester County to allow her to do so.

Tubman had feared this would happen from the moment she learned of Brodess's death. She began to have nightmarish visions of slave catchers riding down screaming men and women trying to flee bondage and drag-ging them back to their masters. According to an early biographer, "She would start up at night with the cry, 'Oh, they're comin', they're comin', I must go!'" (Bradford 1869, 15).

Unsurprisingly, the court granted Eliza the permission she sought—what other judgment could have been rendered to a poor widow with a household of children to support?—and in the last week of June 1849, less than four months after Brodess's death, two members of Tubman's family were put up for sale. One of them was Harriet, the twenty-year-old daughter of Linah whom Harriet and John Tubman may have been saving money to buy. The other was Harriet's two-year-old daughter, Mary Jane. Presumably, given Mary Jane's tender age, Eliza Ann was offer-ing mother and daughter as a package deal, but there was no guarantee that she wouldn't sell them separately if the opportunity for a better price presented itself.

For some reason, however, the sale never went through. One reason may have been a messy lawsuit filed against the Brodess estate by one of Atthow Pattison's grandsons, who claimed that all the slaves inherited by Brodess through his mother were, by rights, his. After the lawsuit was dismissed on August 6, another member of the Ross family was put on the market in less than a month. John Mills, coexecutor of Brodess's will, notified buyers in the August 29, 1848, *Cambridge Democrat* that, "I will sell at public sale to the highest bidder for cash, at the Court house door in the town of Cam-bridge, on MONDAY the 10th day of September next, a negro woman named Kizziah, aged about 25 years. She will be sold for life, and a good title will be given."

Kizziah, or Kessiah, was Linah's other daughter. Why Mills and Eliza Ann decided to sell her rather than Harriet and Mary Jane is unclear, but this possibility fell through as well. One explanation is that the Pattison grandson had appealed the decision rejecting his lawsuit, thereby freezing, or at least legally complicating, the sale of any Brodess slave. The other may be that because old Atthow Pattison's will stipulated that Rit and her chil-dren would be freed upon reaching the age of forty-five, Eliza Ann's attempt to sell Kessiah for life was deemed by the local magistrate to be illegal. Whatever the cause, Kessiah was spared.

Then the horror that had befallen the Ross family once before was replayed. Just as Ben had been reprieved at the cost of Linah, so Kessiah was saved at the cost of Harriet and Mary Jane. Put once more on the market, they were sold in June 1850. Thankfully, they were spared Linah's fate of being sent to the Deep South. Instead, an Eastern Shore merchant purchased them.

By that time, Tubman was gone. On September 17, 1849, the very day that Eliza Ann Brodess petitioned the court for permission to sell Kessiah, three members of the Ross family decided they'd had enough. Harriet and her brothers Henry and Ben made a run for freedom. Their absence went unnoticed by Eliza Brodess for several days, suggesting that the brothers, like Harriet, had been hired out and consequently weren't under Eliza's direct supervision. Finally, on October 3, she published a notice of their run and the offer of a reward for their return in the *Cambridge Democrat*.

RAN AWAY from the subscriber on Monday the 17th ult., three negroes, named as follows: HARRY, aged about 19 years, has on one side of his neck a wen, just under the ear, he is of a dark chestnut color, about 5 feet 8 or 9 inches hight [sic]; BEN, aged aged [sic] about 25 years, is very quick to speak when spoken to, he is of a chestnut color, about six feet high; MINTY, aged about 27 years, is of a Chestnut color, fine looking, and about 5 feet high. One hundred dollars reward will be given for each of the above named negroes, if taken out of the State, and $50 each if taken in the State.

The three fugitives didn't make it to freedom. In fact, they didn't even leave the Eastern Shore. From the first, their flight seemed doomed to fail. To begin with, they had only a vague idea of how to get out of Dorchester Country and even less what to do or where to go once they had. Like so many other fugitive slaves, their geographical lore extended no further than the immediate areas where they lived and labored. Moreover, Ben had left behind a wife and children, and Harriet a husband who disapproved of her run for freedom. Whereas she seemed at peace with her decision to flee, assuming that John would eventually follow her north, Ben was distraught at the thought of leaving his young family. The two brothers decided to turn around and return home, and Tubman reluctantly went with them.

It was a risky decision. Runaways were always punished and frequently sold down South immediately upon their return or capture. Why Tubman went back with Ben and Henry is something of a mystery. Perhaps when she realized she'd have to make the journey alone, her courage failed her. Perhaps she felt that she had to accompany her brothers in hope that she could somehow ameliorate any punishment that might be awaiting them. Or perhaps she simply found herself pining more deeply and painfully for John Tubman than she had imagined she would.

There's no record of what awaited them upon their arrival back in Buckland, but whatever punishment they received was light. Tubman apparently resumed working for Thompson right away, and we can presume that the two brothers likewise returned to their labor assignments. Still, it's reasonable to suppose that Eliza Ann Brodess and John Mills made a mental note to rid themselves of these troublesome slaves at the first opportunity. In fact, one story has it that Tubman was warned by another slave a couple of days afterward that plans were in the offing to sell her and her brothers as soon as possible.

Regardless of how frightened or disoriented Tubman may have been on her failed flight to freedom, she quickly regained her nerve, probably steeled by the news of her impending sale. Sometime in late October or early November, she decided to make another try. Years afterward, she remembered that her husband tried to dissuade her from leaving, but she was determined. As she later recalled, "I had reasoned this out in my mind; there was one of two things I had a right to, liberty or death; if I could not have one, I would have the other; for no man should take me alive; I should fight for my liberty as long as my strength lasted, and when the time came for me to go, the Lord would let them take me" (Bradford 1886, 29).

Her longing for freedom, as well as her anxiety about the difficulty in attaining it, expressed itself, as she recalled, in recurring "dreams and visions." She "seemed to see a line, and on the other side of that line were green fields, and lovely flowers, and beautiful white ladies, who stretched out their arms to me over the line, but I couldn't reach them nohow. I always fell before I got to the line" (Bradford 1869, 16). In another telling of her vision, Tubman said that she flew "over fields and towns, and rivers and mountains, looking down upon them like a bird, and reaching at last a great fence or sometimes a river," which she tried to cross. In this version, "just as I was sinkin' down, there would be ladies all drest [sic] in white over there, and they would put out their arms and pull me 'cross" (Bradford 1869, 79).

Both of these accounts are interesting for the same reason. In the first, white women fail to rescue her, not through any fault of their own but because Tubman failed to reach them. In the second, women dressed in white succeed in snatching her from bondage, without any indication that Tubman took an active role in her own journey to freedom other than magically flying through the air. Yet if there was ever a slave who liberated herself by her own daring, initiative, and courage, it was Harriet Tubman. That her visions give the credit to whites may well be an indication of the extent to which even a self-sufficient black woman like Tubman absorbed the cultural myth that slaves were helpless to liberate themselves. It's certainly not a perspective that she held when she began leading other slaves to freedom, nor when she served in the Civil War as a scout and spy.

Always devoted to her family as she was, especially her aging parents, it couldn't have been any easier for Tubman to leave the second time than it was the first. To make matters worse, she couldn't tell anyone of her plans, not even the two brothers who had fled with her before. Dr. Thompson was keeping a watchful eye on her, and she couldn't afford word of her imminent flight to reach him. As much as she wanted to at least say good-bye to her mother, Rit, she knew that doing so was too risky. So on the evening of her departure, she did Rit's chores for her, leaving her the only departing gift, her labor, she felt she could safely give. "Here, mother, go 'long," she told Rit. "I'll do the milkin' to-night and bring it in" (Bradford 1869, 17).

There was another reason Tubman relieved Rit of her duties. After tending to the cows, she was supposed to take the milk to Dr. Thompson's residence. One of his domestic slaves, a girl named Mary, was Tubman's friend, and perhaps a cousin as well. She intended to tell Mary of her plans to leave so that she could pass the news on to Rit after Tubman's departure. Given that several of her children had already been sold, Tubman was worried that Rit would be alarmed if she simply disappeared. She wanted to make sure her mother knew what was going on.

After delivering the milk to the kitchen, Tubman invited Mary to come outside with her so that she could tell her the news in private. Just then, Dr. Thompson, who was "regarded with special awe by his slaves; if they were singing or talking together in the field, or on the road, [they] all hushed till he passed" (Bradford 1869, 18)—rode up on his horse. Mary quickly disappeared back indoors, and Tubman, not wanting to hang around and risk provoking Thompson's suspicion, decided that the only way to safely convey the news of her departure was by way of singing a spiritual.

> I'm sorry I'm going to leave you,
> Farewell, oh farewell;
> But I'll meet you in the morning,
> Farewell, oh farewell.
>
> I'll meet you in the morning,
> I'm bound for the promised land,
> On the other side of Jordan,
> Bound for the promised land.
> (Bradford 1869, 18)

It wasn't unusual to hear slaves singing or humming spirituals as they went about their work, and Tubman hoped that Thompson would discern nothing to be concerned about in her doing so, even though the song's lyrics pretty obviously spoke of a departure. Her memory of what happened

CODED SPIRITUALS

The secrecy that necessarily enshrouded strategies for escaping slavery has given rise to many stories that are thrilling but have little evidence to support them. One of the most persistent is that slaves and free blacks sang out coded Negro spirituals when fugitives were in their areas to alert them to danger or to signal safety.

There were other songs that supposedly gave coded directions for potential runaways to follow on their way to freedom. One of these was "Follow the Drinking Gourd," which appeared to offer precise information about river crossings, safe houses, and so on. "Drinking gourd" refers to the Big Dipper, part of which is the North Star, a runaway's single most important compass point. Legend had it that the song was composed by a free black sailor, Peg Leg Joe, who mapped an escape route from Kentucky to the north and detailed its landmarks in the song's lyrics.

There's no good reason to take either of these claims about coded lyrics literally, although there does seem to be a bit of truth when it came to the songs. Tubman says she sang spirituals on several occasions to let slaves she intended to rescue know that she was in their vicinity. But there's no evidence that such songs were widely used or recognized as codes. It's certainly not clear, for example, that the slave girl Mary understood the hidden meaning behind Tubman's farewell song when she heard it. Moreover, there's even less evidence that some songs, spirituals or otherwise, offered detailed flight instructions to potential fugitives. "Follow the Drinking Gourd," the song usually referenced in such claims, seems to have been published only in 1928. There's no earlier record of it or of other map songs.

The safest conclusion, then, is that coded slave spirituals are more Underground Railroad myths than hard fact.

suggests that it was nonetheless a close call. Walking away from Thompson and still singing, she glanced over her shoulder to see him gazing at her "as if there might be more in this than 'met the ear'" (Bradford 1869, 18). She casually waved at him and continued on her way. As soon as she was out of his sight, she took off for freedom.

We may be fairly certain that Tubman didn't leave without taking at least some food and warm clothing with her. Her first flight with her brothers surely would have impressed upon her the need to be as well provisioned as possible. Had they been a bit more prepared, perhaps the three of them would have pushed on to freedom. Now that early winter was upon her, Tubman knew her trek would be even more difficult.

We know of at least one thing she did take: a bed quilt she had made, one she valued highly. This raises a question. Tubman knew that she had to travel light because she needed to travel quickly. Why load herself down with such a cumbersome thing? Could it be that she couldn't bear to part with it because it was a reminder of the bed she once shared with her husband? May she have taken it as protection against the cold nights that lay ahead of her as she made her way north? Or, finally, may she have intended all along to use it, the only item of real value she possessed, as a payment or bribe for any help she might need along the way?

As it turned out, Tubman indeed did give the quilt to someone, but the gesture looks more like an expression of gratitude than a bribe. Before she fled, "she found a friend in a white lady, who knew her story and helped her on her way" (Bradford 1869, 76). According to someone whose parents knew Tubman when she was an elderly woman, this "white lady" was gifted with the quilt. In return, the lady gave Tubman "a paper with two names upon it, and directions how she might get to the first house where she would receive aid" (Humez 2003, 18). It's unclear what the purpose of the paper was. Tubman couldn't read, and surely the white people in the next house on her way to freedom would have already known where to send her.

Equally unclear is the identity of the white woman. She may have been Hannah Leverton, a Quaker widow who lived not far from the Thompson place and whose daughter was actually married to Thompson's son. The Levertons, like so many other Quakers in that part of the Eastern Shore, were committed abolitionists, and it's possible that Tubman might have heard through the slave grapevine that a runaway wouldn't be turned away by them.

When Tubman showed up at the white woman's house, she was told to rake the front yard, an apparent ruse intended to fool casual passersby into thinking that Tubman was just another slave going about her work. When the woman's husband returned home later that day, he put Tubman in a covered wagon and took her to the next "station" on what had by then become known as the "Underground Railroad," a network of northbound escape routes sprinkled with antislavery households willing and even eager to help runaways get to freedom. (If it was the Leverton household that set her on her way, it would have been Hannah's son Arthur, not her husband Jacob, already dead by the time Tubman took flight, who put her in his wagon.) No doubt Harriet took the "North Star for her guide," as she later said (Bradford 1886, 29). But like so many other fugitives, she was also aided by the Underground Railroad network.

Even with the help of sympathetic abolitionists, Tubman's trek northward to the Pennsylvania border, a good hundred-mile journey, took several days. She traveled primarily by night, sleeping during the sunlit hours either in safe houses or, probably more often, in wooded thickets, hayracks, or marshland. If Eliza Ann sent slave catchers after her once her flight was discovered, there's no record of it. Even so, Tubman was constantly at risk of being detained by any suspicious white she ran across, who would have been perfectly within his legal rights to demand to see a pass authorizing her to travel so far from her home base. Perhaps the piece of paper the white lady gave her was a forged one.

Arriving at the Delaware border, Tubman was probably directed to the Wilmington home of Thomas Garrett, a leading Quaker abolitionist with whom she collaborated in coming years when she returned to the Eastern Shore to rescue family members and other slaves from bondage. Garrett would have put her into contact with other abolitionist friends, who helped her through to Pennsylvania.

Once Tubman finally crossed the Pennsylvania border into freedom, the world seemed to her wonderfully transfigured. "I looked at my hands to see if I was the same person," she remembered. "There was such a glory over everything; the sun came like gold through the trees, and over the fields, and I felt like I was in Heaven" (Bradford 1869, 19). She had left behind everything and everyone she'd ever known, and, like all refugees in strange lands, she had some rough months ahead of her. But after being a slave for all her twenty-seven years, Harriet Tubman was now a free woman, the master of her own fate.

4

The Underground Railroad

The only free road, the Underground Railroad, [has] tunneled under the whole breadth of the land.

—Henry David Thoreau (2001, 412)

DRAPETOMANIA

By the time Tubman made her way to Philadelphia and freedom, slave owners were convinced that the South was hemorrhaging runaways. Their fear outstripped the reality, but the numbers were still daunting, especially when translated into economic terms. The average price of a slave was around $300, making the total value of human capital that fled to the North in the years before the Civil War a staggering $40 million. The loss of revenue prompted Missouri senator and slave owner David Rice Atchison to complain, one year after Tubman's flight, that "depredations to the amount of hundreds of thousands of dollars are committed upon the property of the people of the border slave states of this Union annually" (Siebert 2006, 341).

The problem of slave flight became so troublesome by 1851 that Dr. Samuel Cartwright, a physician who billed himself as an authority on "negro diseases," coined a word to describe it: "drapetomania," a compound term built from the Greek for "runaway" and "madness." According to Cartwright, slave flight was a form of insanity because any "normal" slave would find his or her situation perfectly conducive to health and happiness. Consequently, those suffering from drapetomania were constitutionally flawed, broken by ill-treatment on the part of their masters, or confused from being foolishly coddled by the people who owned them. The best way to "prevent and cure them running away," concluded the doctor, was to treat them firmly but compassionately, as one would children. The patronizing implication was that slaves were psychologically and spiritually underdeveloped and, consequently, would flounder and suffer were it not for the benevolent care and protection of their owners (Cartwright 1851, 331, 333).

"THE CAR EMANCIPATION"

What especially bothered slave owners about the prevalence of drapetomania was the existence of a resource that encouraged slaves in their insanity, one from which Tubman had profited. Intrepid, determined, and resourceful as she was, it's unlikely that she could have made her way to freedom entirely on her own without the help of the Leverton family's participation in a vast and complex network of escape routes for slaves that came to be known as the Underground Railroad. Over the twenty or so years leading up to the Civil War, hundreds of slaves followed it. Some of them turned back or were captured along the way, but an impressive percentage of them made it through to freedom.

There are several stories about how the escape network got its name, but the most common one dates from around 1831. It seems that a Kentucky slave named David Tice ran for his freedom, pursued closely by his master and hounds. Reaching the Ohio River, which lay between him and freedom, Tice jumped in, swam across, and then disappeared so quickly when he reached the other side. His puzzled master concluded he must have discovered access to an "underground road."

Trains were just making their appearance in the United States at around the same time. The earliest ones were unpleasant conveyances. Their dust, cinders, and coal smoke coated passengers until, as one traveler put it, they looked "blacker than the Ethiope" (Stauffer 2008, 4). But despite the discomfort, everyone was fascinated by the speed, upward of thirty miles per hour, that the locomotives could reach. The combination of "Ethiopic" blackface and velocity soon turned the "underground road" in the popular imagination to "underground railroad" or "liberty line," a subterranean track that whisked black slaves away from bondage.

For a while, people who heard the expression took it literally, believing it referred to an actual railroad train that chugged along under the earth's surface. By the mid-1840s, most everyone realized that it referred more realistically to overland routes for slave fugitives. A satirical 1844 advertisement in the *Chicago Western Citizen* carried an illustration of a heavily passengered train steaming into an underground tunnel. Captioned "Liberty Line," the ad boasted that "the improved and splendid Locomotives" regularly ran clients between "Patriarchal Dominion and Libertyville, Upper Canada. Gentlemen and Ladies, who may wish to improve their health or circumstances, by a northern tour; are respectfully invited to give us their patronage" (Harris 1904, 16).

Supporters and critics of the Underground Railroad soon began using rail terminology to refer to it. Escape routes became "lines" or "tracks." Fugitives were referred to as "passengers" or sometimes as "packages." Volunteers became "conductors" or "agents," safe houses became "stations" or "depots," and the people who owned them "stationmasters." Citizens who weren't directly involved as either agents or stationmasters but who contributed supplies and funds were known as "stockholders."

The nomenclature that became associated with the Underground Railroad was deliberately cryptic because all the activities along it were necessarily secretive. It also contributed to the aura of mystery that surrounded the enterprise, and from that mystery arose any number of legends that ballooned the Railroad's actual accomplishments. It was soon falsely presumed, for example, that it had meticulously charted routes traversing every village, town, and city in the nation and that agents and stationmasters took special oaths, punishable if broken by a sure and horrid death, should they divulge the Railroad's secrets. In fact, however, there's no evidence of such secret oaths, and the liberty lines only sketchily penetrated the borders of slave states such as Maryland, Virginia, Delaware, and Kentucky in the Upper South, and were virtually absent in the Deep South. They ran primarily in the free states.

What this meant is that slaves fleeing bondage were usually responsible, unless they had an experienced guide like Harriet Tubman, for finding their way to the nearest Underground Railroad station on their own. Some free blacks in the border slave states, especially Maryland and Delaware, were willing to aid runaways as best they could, offering them temporary places to rest and a little food. Word-of-mouth directions on where to find these friendly havens, as well as the safest back roads to take northward, circulated throughout slave communities. For the most part, fugitive slaves, many of whom had never ventured far from their plantations and for whom the "North" was often vaguely imagined as being thousands and thousands of miles distant, had to initiate their own escapes. Masters, in an effort to deter escape attempts, contributed to the confusion by frequently exaggerating the geographical distance to the free states.

Slaves who lit out for freedom generally left on a Saturday night or a holiday like Christmas, knowing that doing so ensured their absence wouldn't be noticed for at least two days. They traveled light, with few provisions that could slow them down. Usually sleeping wherever they could during the day, they made their way north in the nighttime, often using the North Star as a guide. Stories about being guided by "maps" disguised as quilt embroidery or gospel songs that had coded lyrics are more legend than fact, but it's possible that there's a bit of truth to them.

Exposure to the elements, hunger, manhandling by slave catchers, and postcapture punishment, including the dreaded prospect of being sold to the cotton and rice plantations in the sweltering and unhealthy Deep South, unsurprisingly dissuaded most slaves from attempting to escape. By the start of the Civil War, there were approximately four million slaves in the nation, and only an estimated thirty thousand to sixty thousand fugitives in the three decades leading up to it (and the figure may well be inflated). Even many of the slaves who tried to run ultimately decided, like Tubman's brothers, to turn back out of discouragement or disorientation, taking the chance that their punishment would be less severe if they returned on their own than it would be if they were captured.

For many years before and after the Civil War, the belief was that Underground Railroad agents and stationmasters were exclusively white. The barely concealed assumption behind this conclusion was that slaves were too passive or slow-witted to engineer their own escapes or to aid in the escapes of their fellows. As we saw in chapter 2, slaves were anything but passive in their day-to-day resistance to servitude, and they displayed a great deal of ingenuity in both undermining the authority of their owners and asserting some degree of autonomy in their lives. Accordingly, it comes as no surprise to discover that many Underground Railroad workers were also black, often escaped or manumitted slaves themselves. Working closely as they did with white agents, they participated in the first large-scale interracial collaboration in the United States. One of the most famous Underground Railroad stationmasters, for example, was William Still, a free black who not only managed the busy Philadelphia hub of the Railroad, but kept meticulous records of all the fugitive slaves, including Tubman and her brothers, who came to him seeking assistance.

In addition, free blacks in major northern cities, such as New York, Boston, Philadelphia, and Cincinnati, were driving forces behind forming so-called vigilance committees, charged with aiding runaways as well as protecting them from private slave catchers and official authorities. These committees were essential in finding employment and lodgings for exhausted and often bewildered fugitives, dazed by their sudden departure from a typically rural culture and thrown into busy metropolitan centers. Many of them, including Tubman, initially found freedom discombobulating.

Moreover, free blacks regularly contributed, especially through their church communities, funds and clothing to fugitives who chose to make new lives in Canada rather than the northern United States. As we'll see in chapter 6, the passage of an 1850 law that threatened the well-being and liberty of even freeborn northern blacks convinced many ex-slaves that safety could be found only in Canada, where slavery had been de facto outlawed since the end of the eighteenth century. From first to last, blacks were instrumental in resisting the institution of slavery, aiding fugitives along Underground Railroad lines, and helping them settle once they reached free states.

The upshot was that Dr. Cartwright's 1851 worries about an epidemic of drapetomania were only compounded as the decade progressed, and the Underground Railroad conveyed more slaves to freedom. Opponents

---

VIGILANCE COMMITTEES

Beginning in the mid-1830s, freedmen and sympathetic whites in several northern cities organized what came to be known as vigilance or vigilant committees, charged with helping slave fugitives who had made their way to free states. They offered relief services in the forms of food, clothing, and temporary lodging. They also made sure refugees had safe passage to other communities in the country or in Canada and helped them find local employment. As Tubman and most other runaways discovered, arrival in a strange new city that held neither family nor friends could be a dispiriting experience. Vigilance committees tried to make their newly found freedom less overwhelming.

Especially important after the passage of the Fugitive Slave Act in 1850, which signaled a crackdown on recapturing fugitive slaves, vigilance committees sounded the alarm whenever slave catchers showed up looking for runaways. They spread the word so that fugitives at risk could either flee or hide and, on occasion, even physically interfered with attempted renditions. On one of those occasions, the 1860 attempted arrest of Charles Nalle in Troy, New York, Tubman played a key role.

The first vigilance committee was founded in 1835 in New York City, through the efforts of David Ruggles, a black bookseller and abolitionist. Probably the most active vigilance committee was launched two years later in Philadelphia, a major port of entry for fugitives from Maryland, Delaware, and Virginia. Operating actively for its first five years, the committee spent a year in hiatus after a race riot in 1842 but then resumed operations, with William Still chairing the committee. Under his guidance, hundreds of fugitive slaves were given sanctuary. Still kept a meticulous log of everyone the committee helped. Today, it's one of the most invaluable documents in piecing together the history of the Underground Railroad.

of slavery expressed their jubilation that the Underground "Liberty Lines," worked by both blacks and whites, offered women and men held in bondage an opportunity for freedom. As the popular song "Get Off the Track!" printed in the abolitionist newspaper the *Liberator* on April 19, 1844, put it,

> Ho! the car Emancipation
> rides majestic thro' our nation,
> bearing on its train the story,
> Liberty! a nation's glory.
> Roll it along, thro' the nation,
> freedom's car, Emancipation!

UNDERGROUND RAILROAD ROUTES

Because the successful transportation of slaves along Liberty Lines required secrecy, little precise information is available about routes other than the ones most traveled. At the time, few written records were kept, lest they be found by law officials and used both to incriminate Railroad agents and stationmasters and to bust up routes. The only contemporaneous account to be kept was compiled by William Still of Philadelphia, and he went to great pains to hide his records from authorities. Fearing discovery, he concealed them in an old cemetery building, only retrieving them in 1872, seven years after the Thirteenth Amendment officially outlawed slavery in the United States. Published as a book, Still's record is one of our few eyewitness accounts of the identities and escape strategies of many Underground Railroad fugitives. It's certainly the most exhaustive.

As a general rule, routes north of the Mason-Dixon line were less clandestine than ones in border slave states. Some abolitionist newspapers even proudly announced their locations and boasted about the number of slaves traveling to freedom on them. The presumption was that the further north the route was, the less chance there was of slaves traveling it being captured and taken back to slavery. This confidence was shattered after the passage of the 1850 Fugitive Slave Act, and more than one abolitionist rued the fact that too much was publicly known about the routes. As Frederick Douglass complained, "The practice of publishing every new invention by which a slave is known to have escaped from slavery has neither wisdom nor necessity to sustain it." Most immediately, Douglass was referring to the well-publicized escape of Henry "Box" Brown, who, in 1849, had himself shipped in a wooden crate to the North and freedom. But Douglass also noted that too much newspaper coverage about the Underground Railroad was, in general, risking turning it into an "Upper-ground Railroad" whose agents, safe houses, and routes were exposed for all to see (Douglass 2003, 188).

Most routes followed natural geographical conduits to the North. Generally speaking, there were two main landlines, an eastern and a western one, separated by the Appalachian Mountains. Dozens of auxiliary lines branched off from them. Additionally, there were three water lines: one following the northward course of major rivers; one skirting the Atlantic coast; and one involving the Great Lakes, usually Michigan, Erie, or Ontario but occasionally Huron.

The eastern route served fugitives from the border states of Delaware, Maryland, and Virginia. Nearly all the slaves following this route had Philadelphia as their first stop, where stationmaster William Still recorded their names and either helped them find lodging and work in the area or sent them to Underground Railroad stations further north in New York and New England. In addition to Still's station, prominent ones along this route included Thomas Garrett's in Wilmington, Delaware, and Frederick Douglass's in Rochester, New York.

Still is one of the most pivotal players in the story of the Underground Railroad. Born in New Jersey in 1821, the free son of ex-slave parents, he located to Philadelphia in his mid-twenties and was immediately taken on by the Pennsylvania Anti-Slavery Society as a clerk. Three years later, he became the executive director of the Society's Vigilance Committee, charged with steering fugitives to safety in the wake of the Fugitive Slave Act. It was he who was responsible for coordinating the safe houses and agents along the eastern line, and it was also he who did the bulk of fund-raising from churches, abolitionist societies, philanthropic groups, and wealthy individuals that was necessary to care for fugitives after their arrival in the North. His Philadelphia office was always stocked with clothing and food for newly arrived runaways.

The western route covered a larger land mass and, consequently, had more branches than its eastern counterpart. It primarily served fugitives from the border states of Kentucky and northwest Virginia (now West Virginia) to the south and Missouri to the west. Its major routes ran through Indiana, Illinois, and Ohio on the one hand, and Iowa and Wisconsin on the other. For the western routes, Cincinnati and Detroit were major hubs. Although Philadelphia was probably the single busiest station on the Underground Railroad, a good half of all Railroad passengers escaped to freedom on the western lines.

One of the major obstacles that had to be reckoned with on the western route was the wide, deep, and frequently swift Ohio River that separated the slave state of Kentucky from the free state of Ohio. Reverend John Rankin was one of the many stationmasters along the river who welcomed fugitives who managed to make it across. Another was John Parker, an ex-slave who lived in Ripley, Rankin's town. Whereas Rankin was content to serve as a stationmaster for runaways seeking food, shelter, and rest,

Parker was also a conductor, who for years made nightly trips across the Ohio River to transport fugitives looking for a way to cross. He later estimated that he rowed at least one fugitive a week to safety.

Parker has left us one of the most extraordinary, but not unique, acts of heroism in the annals of the Underground Railroad. One night, a band of fugitives made it to the banks of the Ohio River on the Kentucky side, just ahead of pursuing bloodhounds. Parker couldn't take them all in his boat and had to leave two of the male slaves behind. Just as he started to pull away, a passenger cried out in agony that one of the men left behind was her husband. Then, remembered Parker, "I witnessed an example of heroism and self-sacrifice that made me proud of my race. For one of the single men safely in the boat, hearing the cry of the woman for her husband, arose without a word [and] walked quietly to the [river] bank. The husband sprang into the boat as I pushed off" (Parker 1866, 103).

Getting across major rivers like the Ohio was a daunting task for fugitive slaves, most of whom didn't know how to swim. Even those who could risked their lives in the swift and wide waters that often served as the borders between free and slave states. For slaves in the Deep South, far away from the Mason-Dixon line and the likelihood of a successful overland run for freedom, riverways were the only feasible routes to follow. The Mississippi River was probably the water route most often used by runaways, who either stowed away in boats or were hired out by their masters as crew members. Free blacks who served on the boats so frequently encouraged slaves they encountered at ports along the way to flee that, in 1840, the *St. Louis Gazette* urged river captains to cease hiring them. Jefferson Davis, future president of the Confederacy, complained that too many slaves from his home state of Mississippi were fleeing by river boats and barges. Both he and the *Gazette* probably exaggerated the number of successful escapes, but their comments indicate that at least some Deep South slaves followed the Mississippi River to freedom. Similar, although probably less-utilized water routes existed on the Ohio, Missouri, and Illinois Rivers.

Slaves in the eastern coastal states who were able to bypass the dangers of overland Underground Railroad routes followed a waterline up the Atlantic seaboard. Making their way to port cities such as Baltimore, Norfolk, Wilmington, Charleston, Savannah, and even New Orleans (although in this last case, the Mississippi River route was more likely to be used), slaves stowed away on ships, bribed captains for passage, or posed as free men to travel to northern ports such as New Haven, New Bedford, Boston, and Portland. Frederick Douglass made use of the Atlantic route in his escape, sailing as he did across the "waters of the noble Chesapeake," that "broad road of destruction to slavery," until he arrived in New Bedford (Douglass 2003, 177). The town he arrived at, which hosted thriving whaling and shipbuilding industries, was such a popular destination for escaping slaves that it became known as the "Fugitive's Gibraltar."

One of the Atlantic coast route's most notorious and tragically unsuccessful escape attempts occurred in 1848 aboard the *Pearl*, a schooner captained by Daniel Drayton, a seagoing man with a long history of helping runaway slaves get to the north. Drayton loaded seventy-seven Washington, D.C., slaves aboard his ship as the District was distracted by festivities celebrating the restoration of the French Republic following the overthrow of King Louis Philippe. Drayton's intention was to follow the Potomac River to the Chesapeake Bay, and then head for the free state of New Jersey. But he ran into bad weather, and before the storm cleared long enough for him to get to the Bay, the *Pearl* was overtaken by an armed steamship and escorted back to Washington. Charged with slave stealing, which he proudly acknowledged, Drayton was given an incredibly harsh sentence of twenty years. His slave passengers fared even worse. They were all sold Down South by their angry masters. Drayton was finally pardoned and released after serving four years. He later wrote, "If a man wishes to realize the agony which our American slave trade inflicts in the separation of families, let him personally feel that separation, as I did; let him pass four years in the Washington jail" (Drayton 1855, 119).

Most fugitive-carrying ships that followed the Atlantic coast route understandably steered north. But four years before the Pearl attempt, Captain Jonathan Walker, a Massachusetts slavery opponent who settled in Florida, headed south to the Bahamas with seven fugitives in an open boat. Walker fell ill midjourney, and his sailboat, after drifting aimlessly with its terrified cargo, was eventually captured. It's unclear what the fate of the runaways was, although it's likely to have been unpleasant. Walker was led in chains back to Pensacola, shackled to the floor of his jail cell, and found guilty of slave stealing. Fined an exorbitant sum, which he was unable to pay, he languished for several years in prison before the fine was paid by supporters. He also had the letters "S.S."—"Slave Stealer"—branded onto his right hand. When the Quaker poet and abolitionist John Greenleaf Whittier heard about the punishment, he insisted that the letters stood for "Slave Savior," and he immortalized Walker in a couplet:

> Then lift that manly right hand, bold ploughman of the wave!
> Its branded palm shall prophecy, "SALVATION TO THE SLAVE!"
> (Whittier 1856, 200)

For fugitives whose final destination was Canada, the last leg of their journey was frequently across one of the Great Lakes that bordered it and the United States. Both steam vessels and sailing ships crisscrossed the lakes from U.S. ports such as Racine, Chicago, Detroit, Cleveland, and Buffalo. Refugees who followed the Underground Railroad's western routes typically crossed over Lake Michigan. Runaways following the eastern routes were more likely to sail over Ontario or Erie.

Regardless of which lake they chose, they generally had little trouble finding captains willing to ferry them, either for money or out of sympathy, across to Canada. Many of the vessels were manned by black men, and some ex-slaves became well-known water conductors across the lakes. One of them was William Wells Brown. Born in Kentucky, Brown made his way to freedom in 1834 by traveling up the Missouri River. He worked for the next decade on Lake Erie steamboats, where he led dozens of fleeing slaves to Canadian freedom. An outspoken abolitionist, Brown wrote an autobiography recounting his bondage in gripping detail that, in its day, was as well read and admired as Frederick Douglass's. He also published *Clotel*, the first novel written by a U.S. black, based loosely upon the Thomas Jefferson and Sally Hemmings relationship.

THE ABOLITIONIST MOVEMENT

Agents, stationmasters, and conductors on the Underground Railroad all shared in common a detestation of slavery and the conviction that it needed to be ended. By the 1840s, they were commonly referred to as "abolitionists."

It would be a mistake to assume that all northerners opposed slavery. Most, in fact, either did not or were indifferent to it. After the explosion of cotton production in the South following Eli Whitney's 1793 invention of the cotton gin, northern cloth manufacturers found their fortunes increasingly aligned with those of southerners, whose vast plantations were worked by slaves. Even northerners who disapproved of slavery widely differed in their attitudes about black persons and how the fate of free blacks should be determined.

As early as the late seventeenth century, moral disapproval of slavery began to be voiced. In 1688, Quakers from Germantown, Pennsylvania, issued a condemnation of it. "There is a saying that we shall do to all men like as we will be done ourselves," they proclaimed, "making no difference of what generation, descent or color they are. And those who steal or rob men, and those who buy or purchase them, are they not all alike?" (Hendricks et al. 2012, 1). Five years later, George Keith, another Quaker, published *An Exhortation & Caution to Friends Concerning Buying or Keeping of Negroes,* one of the first antislavery tracts to appear in North America. John Woolman and Anthony Benezet lent their influential voices to the Quaker campaign against slavery, and, by the mid-eighteenth century, most Quakers had freed their slaves and endorsed a policy of gradual emancipation throughout the colonies. In 1775, they also founded the first antislavery organization, cumbersomely named the Society for the Relief of Free Negroes Unlawfully Held in Bondage.

Several luminaries of the Revolutionary War, such as James Otis, Thomas Paine, Benjamin Rush, and Benjamin Franklin agitated for the abolition of slavery, recognizing that the struggle for liberty in which they had participated rightfully should not be limited to persons of European descent. In 1784, Franklin, along with Alexander Hamilton and Chief Justice John Jay, helped establish the Pennsylvania Society for the Abolition of Slavery. The following year saw the founding of the New York Manumission Society. These two organizations would consolidate their efforts by the end of the century.

In the meantime, northern state legislatures were abolishing slavery within their borders. While still a colony, Vermont ended slavery in 1777. By 1804, when New Jersey outlawed it, slavery in New England and the mid-Atlantic states, except for Maryland and Delaware, was a thing of the past.

During this early period, slavery opponents favored gradual emancipation of the existing slave population. The U.S. Constitution required that the importation of slaves into the nation end in 1808. The antislavery faction's hope was that after that period, slave owners could be persuaded through reason and moral conviction to slowly manumit their slaves. Some proposals even called for the federal government to compensate them for the financial loss they would sustain in doing so.

With the possibility of gradual emancipation, a new question, whether free blacks should be allowed to remain in the country, emerged. It wasn't a merely hypothetical one. As we saw in chapter 1, populations of free blacks in both the free north and in border slave states such as Virginia, Delaware, and Maryland were on the rise. Nearly no whites, believing as so many did in the inferiority of blacks, thought that freed slaves should be mainstreamed into U.S. society. Given this, the options were segregation of ex-slaves into all-black enclaves or removing them from the nation completely. In 1816, the American Colonization Society was organized to lobby for sending "ex-bondsmen out of the country, preferably to its African outpost, Liberia" (Walters 1978, 78). Although many prominent whites believed that colonization was a humane strategy, it was understandably resisted by free blacks, who insisted that the United States and not Africa was their homeland and their birthright.

In the early nineteenth century, religious opposition to slavery spread outward from Quakers to include clergy and laity from a number of Christian denominations, and the call for gradual and compensated emancipation transformed to one that demanded immediate freedom for slaves without compensation to their owners. Presbyterian minister John Rankin, mentioned earlier, was one of these new abolitionists who called for immediate emancipation. Run out of the states of Tennessee and Kentucky for preaching against the evils of slavery, he eventually made his way in 1822 to Ripley, Ohio, a river town fifty miles from Cincinnati that was separated from Kentucky by the Ohio River. Purchasing a house on a high bluff overlooking the river, Rankin shone a light in it every night as a beacon to let slaves escaping from Kentucky know that they could find shelter with him. Over the next four decades, he offered hospitality to approximately two thousand fugitives before sending them on their way. He also wrote *Letters on Slavery,* published in 1827, which became one of the most popular antislavery polemics of the day. Curiously, *Letters* was originally written to convert Rankin's slave-owning brother, Thomas.

Although his book was widely read, Rankin exerted an unintended influence on his fellow abolitionists, as well as tens of thousands of Americans, through the medium of the best-selling U.S. novel of the nineteenth century, *Uncle Tom's Cabin.* In 1834, during a synodal meeting of Presbyterians in Ohio, Lyman Beecher and his daughter Harriet were introduced to Rankin. Both of them visited his Underground Railroad station in Ripley—where, incidentally, Harriet met her future husband Calvin Stowe—and heard numerous tales from Rankin about the slaves he'd helped to freedom.

One of the stories involved a young slave woman who fled her Kentucky master in late winter, just as the ice was beginning to thaw on the Ohio River. Cradling an infant in her arms, she jumped from one ice floe to the next, miraculously making the perilous crossing to safety and finding haven in Rankin's home. Her escape was just in time, because the ice on the river had completely broken up by the following morning. Her pursuers, arriving at the river bank, presumed that she and her child had drowned and gave up their hunt. Harriet Stowe was mesmerized by this account, and when she came to write her famous novel nearly two decades later, she included a version of Rankin's story, by having her slave girl character Eliza Harris make a similarly hair-raising escape across treacherous ice floes.

At around the same time that John Rankin began aiding slave fugitives in Ohio, a young Quaker journalist named Benjamin Lundy launched an abolitionist newspaper called *Genius of Universal Emancipation.* (The name seems less odd once one realizes that by "Genius," Lundy simply meant "Spirit.") The paper grew steadily in both subscription and influence, progressing in just a few years from a monthly to a weekly publication. A young abolitionist from Boston, William Lloyd Garrison, collaborated with Lundy on the *Genius* for a couple of years, until he launched his own newspaper, the *Liberator,* which eventually became the nation's leading abolitionist weekly.

THE MARGARET GARNER TRAGEDY

Like Harriet Beecher Stowe, U.S. author and Nobel Laureate Toni Morrison was artistically inspired by a story of attempted escape from bondage. Unlike the slave mother who made it across the Ohio River with her infant, the episode on which Morrison's 1987 novel *Beloved* is based ended tragically.

At the end of January 1856, Robert and Margaret Garner and their three children fled from their Kentucky master, a man given to alternating fits of depression and rage. They made their way across the frozen Ohio River and eventually wound up in Cincinnati, where they hid in the home of one of Margaret's cousins.

In just a matter of hours, their location was discovered. As federal marshals and local law officers closed in, Margaret vowed that she would kill her children before she'd allow them to be taken back to slavery. As her husband fired on the posse storming the house, a distraught Margaret killed her youngest daughter Mary with a butcher knife. She also seriously wounded her other two children before officers broke through the door and took her and her husband into custody.

Federal law mandated that they be rendered immediately to their master. In an effort to keep them in Ohio and free from slavery, a local abolitionist attorney filed to have the two charged with murder, a state offense. Within a month, however, the court ruled that the federal law trumped the state murder charge, and the Garners were returned to Kentucky. Their master immediately sold them to a Mississippi cotton planter. Burdened by the grueling work and, no doubt, grief, Margaret died of typhoid fever in 1858.

Lundy was a proponent of gradual emancipation. He suggested that slaves could "buy" their freedom according to the value of the crops they cultivated and harvested, thus attaining their freedom over a period of time without unduly burdening their owners financially. On a darker note, Lundy also came to advocate compulsory colonization of free blacks and ex-slaves. Both of these positions were unacceptable to Garrison. Although the two men parted on good terms, their fundamentally different approaches to abolitionism made the break between them inevitable.

Garrison came out swinging. In the first issue of his *Liberator*, January 1, 1831, he insisted that gradual emancipation was a "pernicious doctrine," and offered a "recantation" of any endorsement he may have given it in the past. Slavery was a sinful affront to both God and humans and ought not to be countenanced in any way whatsoever. The corollary, of course, was that both slave owners and anyone who advocated slavery, be they private citizens or statespersons, were acting immorally. Consequently, concluded Garrison, the only way to redress the sin of slavery was to emancipate slaves immediately rather than gradually, and to do so without compensating their owners. Why shouldn't immorality be abolished instead of allowed to continue indefinitely? And why should perpetrators of immoral acts be rewarded?

If anyone deserved compensation, it was the victims of the immorality, the slaves, who simply by virtue of their humanity deserved the same kind of consideration afforded to whites. Garrison was one of the few Americans of his day who actually championed racial equality. Most everyone else, including even opponents of slavery, continued to think in terms of white superiority.

Garrison's call for immediate emancipation was a startling repudiation of the antislavery tradition up to that point, and he wanted to make sure that his readers appreciated that, having crossed the Rubicon, he had no intention of turning back. He recognized the inevitability of alarming more moderate abolitionists with what they took to be his extremism, but he was determined to plow ahead. As he wrote in the *Liberator's* inaugural issue,

> I will be as harsh as truth, and as uncompromising as justice. On this subject [immediate emancipation] I do not wish to think, or to speak, or write, with moderation. No! No! Tell a man whose house is on fire to give a moderate alarm; tell him to moderately rescue his wife from the hands of the ravisher; tell the mother to gradually extricate her babe from the fire into which it has fallen; but urge me not to use moderation in a cause like the present. I am in earnest—I will not equivocate—I will not excuse—I will not retreat a single inch—and I WILL BE HEARD.

Garrison realized that convincing his fellow white Americans that slavery was abhorrent to both human reason and Christian faith was an uphill struggle. The strategy he endorsed came to be known as "moral suasion," a steady appeal—although his proslavery enemies considered it an assault—on the consciences of the nation's citizenry to do the right thing. Wielding "carnal weapons" of violence against slavery would only add to the misery it bred. Far better, Garrison argued, to help southern slaveholders admit what he believed they secretly and uneasily knew all along: owning another human being is wrong.

Garrison's pacifism was somewhat uneven. He defended the use of "carnal weapons" in John Brown's raid on the Harpers Ferry arsenal in 1859, for example, writing in the December 16, 1859, issue of the *Liberator* that "as a peace man—an 'ultra' peace man—I am prepared to say, 'Success to every slave insurrection at the South, and in every slave country.' And I do not see how I compromise or stain my peace profession in making that declaration. Whenever there is a contest between the oppressed and the oppressor—the weapons being equal between the parties—God knows my heart must be with the oppressed, and always against the oppressor.

Therefore, whenever commenced, I cannot but wish success to all slave insurrections."

It wasn't long before Garrison was recognized, for good or ill, depending on whether one was a slave owner or slavery opponent, as the nation's leading white abolitionist. In 1832 he helped found the New England Anti-Slavery Society, whose membership was open to both blacks and whites. One year later, he joined with abolitionists from eleven states to found the American Anti-Slavery Society (AASS), whose members pledged "to overthrow the most execrable system of slavery that has ever been witnessed upon earth," to struggle to "secure to the colored population of the United States all the rights and privileges which belong to them as men and as Americans—come what may to our persons, our interests, or our reputations," and to do so peacefully (Ferrell 2006, 152).

The activities of the AASS were largely underwritten by Lewis and Arthur Tappan, Massachusetts-born brothers who settled in New York City and became two of the nation's wealthiest entrepreneurs. Intensely religious, fiercely abolitionist, and indifferent to the fury their positions generated—Lewis's Manhattan home was looted by an enraged proslavery mob in 1834—the brothers provided much-needed funding for abolitionist activities, such as organizing conferences, soliciting speakers, and printing antislavery pamphlets mailed to thousands through the postal system. (Slavery advocates protested so loudly at the mail campaign that President Andrew Jackson's postmaster finally banned abolitionist literature from being delivered through the U.S. postal service.)

The Tappan brothers underwrote another campaign as well: an effort to flood Congress with hundreds of antislavery petitions containing thousands of names. The brothers hired people to collect the names, and then deliver the petitions to Congress, which sympathetic legislators then read into the official record. Southern congressmen, as well as a few northern ones, objected to this campaign, claiming that the petitions were tying up the business of government, and succeeded in pushing through a ban on them that lasted for a full eight years, from 1836 to 1844. It was actions such as these on the part of elected officials that gradually drove Garrison to the conclusion that the laws of the land were corrupt and ought not to be obeyed. In one particularly dramatic moment, he publicly burned a copy of the U.S. Constitution at an 1854 Fourth of July abolitionist rally in Massachusetts. As he struck a match to the document, he shouted to the crowd, "Let the people say, Amen!"

By 1840, the abolitionist movement had splintered into a number of factions. One of the causes of division was disagreement about appropriate tactics when it came to battling slavery. Garrison loyalists continued to advocate for moral suasion and reject political action on the grounds that the laws and government were too corrupted by southern special interests to be reliable agents of change.

Other abolitionists, including ex-slave Frederick Douglass, who had initially thrown his lot in with Garrison but ultimately broke with him over the question of nonviolence, believed that the most effective way to battle slavery was through political action and the courts. Even though the Constitution allowed for slavery, Douglass and his associates believed that the Declaration of Independence's insistence that all men were created equal took precedence. Consequently, headed by Kentucky abolitionist James G. Birney, they founded the Liberty Party in 1840. Birney ran for president that same year, and, even though he fared badly, with less than seven thousand votes, the abolitionist movement now had a political arm. Over the next twenty years, the party drew many slavery opponents from the tottering Whig party, as well as field candidates for political office, but it never succeeded in making much political inroad, and eventually disbanded after the 1860 election of the first Republican president, Abraham Lincoln.

The Liberty Party especially appealed to those opponents of slavery who were sympathetic to the possibility that only coercion, be it political or physical, could put an end to the peculiar institution. This especially appealed to black abolitionists like Douglass, many of whom were ex-slaves who had personally experienced both the cruelty of bondage and the unlikelihood of slave owners' consciences being pricked by moral suasion. As Douglass observed in his abolitionist newspaper the *North Star* on December 3, 1847, "He who has *endured the cruel pangs of Slavery* is the [best qualified] man to *advocate Liberty*" by whatever means it took.

The largely secular approach taken by Liberty Party stalwarts was too much for the evangelical Tappan brothers, who insisted that a religious revival was the key to ending slavery. If they convinced slave owners that their possession of human beings was an affront to Christ's intentions, the brothers believed, the peculiar institution would end overnight. Unlike the die-hard Garrisonians, the Tappans and like-minded abolitionists weren't averse to the possibility of physical coercion; as we'll see in chapter 7, they were two of the underwriters of John Brown's 1859 violent raid on the Harpers Ferry arsenal. Unlike many other abolitionists, the brothers also endorsed racial amalgamation as an antidote to the racism they correctly saw as rampant among both defenders and opponents of slavery. Their advocacy of the creation of a "copper-skinned" United States as a solution to bigotry was, predictably, wildly unpopular.

There was also a splintering of the movement because of differences of opinion about the role of women in abolitionist societies. The Garrisonians lobbied for their full inclusion when it came to administrative and tactical decision making, and it's certainly the case that the movement profited from the stalwart participation of women such as Lucretia Mott, Angelina and Sarah Grimké, Maria W. Child, and Harriet Beecher Stowe.

Other abolitionists, especially ones belonging to the Tappan faction, disagreed.

Despite the splintering of the movement in the 1840s, abolitionists of all persuasions succeeded in raising national awareness about the horrors of slavery and keeping it in the public eye. Probably one hundred thousand persons joined local abolitionist societies in the two decades preceding the Civil War, and thousands more, although eschewing the label of abolitionists, came to have moral reservations about slavery, even if they continued to believe that black persons were inferior to whites.

Interestingly, not all abolitionists were supporters of the Underground Railroad. Some Garrisonians committed to radical nonviolence objected to slaves "stealing themselves" from their legal owners because they reckoned all stealing a form of violence. Others even objected to opponents of slavery buying slaves in order to set them free, arguing that participating in the exchange was an implicit acknowledgment and legitimization of the legal propriety of owning humans as property.

On the other extreme were those abolitionists who were ambivalent about the Underground Railroad because they thought it fell far short of the drastic steps needed to put an end to slavery. Consequently, they believed, the agents, stationmasters, and stockbrokers who invested their time and resources to it should devote themselves to the eradication of the peculiar institution itself rather than expend energy in the piecemeal rescue of slaves.

In 1840, for example, one of them complained that abolitionists should be "for abolishing slavery itself, not by aiding [slaves] to run away, but so that slaves need not run away to get their liberty" (Gara 1996, 74). Abolitionist Maria Chapman agreed, worrying that building Underground Railroad networks turned a blind eye to "tyranny" instead of "defying it" (Gara 1996, 76). Thomas Wentworth Higginson, a Massachusetts clergyman who would later command black troops in the Civil War and befriend Tubman, believed that the Underground Railroad was a "necessary evil." Writing in 1857, he insisted that it "makes cowards of us all. It makes us think and hesitate and look over our shoulders, and listen, and wonder, and not dare to tell the truth to the man who stands by our side" (Gara 1996, 77).

Still, these criticisms of the Underground Railroad were not widely endorsed in abolitionist circles. Opponents of slavery generally recognized that it was a mistake to downplay or condemn individual escapes from bondage out of misguided fidelity to a high-minded conviction that slavery as an institution was wicked and ought not to be tolerated. Most abolitionists combined idealism with pragmatism; they believed with all their hearts that slavery was an affront to God and humans, and they also believed that any tactic that chipped away at it should be welcomed. In their minds, the Underground Railroad was one of those tactics.

5

Return to the Jaws

Glory to God and Jesus too,
one more soul is safe!
Oh, go and carry the news,
one more soul got safe!

—Joe Bailey (Bradford 1869, 34)

STRANGER IN A STRANGE LAND

When conductors and agents on the Underground Railroad finally deposited Tubman in Philadelphia, her first response, as we saw in chapter 3, was jubilation. "I felt," she said, "like I was in Heaven" (Bradford 1869, 19). Then came the stark and sobering realization that she was all alone. Everyone she knew and loved, as well as the lifestyle and surroundings by which she had oriented herself for nearly three decades, were gone, left behind on the Eastern Shore.

"I had crossed the line," she recalled. "I was free; but there was no one to welcome me to the land of freedom. I was a stranger in a strange land; and my home, after all, was down in Maryland; because my father, my mother, my brothers, and sisters, and friends were there." She felt, she said, like a man who had been imprisoned for twenty-five years, all the while dreaming of his homecoming. When finally released, he discovers, to his dismay that "his old home is not there. The house has been pulled down, and a new one has been put up in its place; his family and friends are gone nobody knows where; here is no one to take him by the hand, no one to welcome him" (Bradford 1869, 19–20).

It wasn't only the absence of family or comfortingly familiar landmarks that discombobulated Tubman. The very freedom that she had wanted for so long was dizzying. In just the space of a few days, she was transported from a rural setting in which most black persons were enslaved to a city with a large and vibrant free black community. As a consequence, Tubman, feisty and headstrong though she had been as a slave, felt out of her depth. It took her a while to adjust herself to the new and heady reality of living as a free woman.

The Philadelphia she arrived in was one of the nation's largest cities, with a population of slightly over 120,000. Some twenty thousand of them were free blacks who worked at any number of occupations: laborers, longshoremen, mariners, barbers, nursemaids, cooks, domestic help, milliners, and so on. Moreover, most of them lived relatively comfortable lives. By 1850, the city's black population owned real estate with a total value of over half a million dollars and had established their own insurance societies and building-and-loan banks.

The City of Brotherly Love had always been a refuge for blacks fleeing slavery, partly because it was so close to the slave states of Maryland and Delaware, but also because the city's Quakers had long condemned the peculiar institution and made Philadelphia a safe haven for runaways. In fact, one of the oldest abolitionist organizations in the nation, the Pennsylvania Society for the Promotion of the Abolition of Slavery, whose first president was none other than Benjamin Franklin, was headquartered there.

Tubman quickly and joyfully discovered that the city held a number of churches with all-black congregations in which she could worship freely and without anxiety. Bethel African Methodist Episcopal (AME) Church, the most famous of the early Republic's black churches, opened there in 1794. Although Tubman worshiped with various denominations throughout her life, her final years in Auburn saw her as an active participant in that city's AME Church.

Additionally, and astoundingly to her, Tubman discovered that the city's public sidewalks and gardens, as well as cultural events like public lectures were open to her, an unthinkable opportunity for slaves and even freedmen back on the Eastern Shore.

But there was a dark side to her newly found freedom: the jarring presence of an ugly racism. Hatred of blacks was nothing new to Tubman, nor to any other person who had been a slave in the South. But its cheek-to-jowl presence with a broadening of opportunities for black persons created a disturbing dissonance in an escaped slave trying to adjust to new surroundings.

Ironically, but perhaps predictably, the more the city's free blacks worked to improve their economic status, the more the white population resented them. The hostility was motivated by several factors, but two obvious ones were dislike of seeing supposedly inferior blacks succeed and fear that upwardly mobile blacks deprived whites of job opportunities. As historian Catherine Clinton documents, despite the relative health of Philadelphia's black community, the city was rife with racial tension that periodically erupted in overt acts of individual or group violence. Race riots broke out at least four times in the two decades immediately prior to Tubman's arrival, one of them culminating in the 1838 arson of the newly built Pennsylvania Hall, as well as assaults on Bethel AME, and a black orphanage (Clinton 2004, 50–51).

THE AFRICAN METHODIST EPISCOPAL CHURCH

The African Methodist Episcopal (AME) Church, whose mother house, Bethel AME, Tubman attended in Philadelphia, was an offshoot of the largely white Methodist Episcopal Church. Its origins went back to November 1787, when Richard Allen and several other black members of St. George Methodist Episcopal Church left in protest during a church service.

St. George was under renovation, and worship space was at a premium. As a consequence, many black members, who were already expected to stand while white congregants sat, were forcibly evicted. Allen, who became the first AME bishop in 1816, collaborated with fellow blacks throughout the middle Atlantic states to form a denomination that supported racial equality in word and deed and, hence, was especially attractive to blacks, who often felt unwelcome in white congregations. Throughout the antebellum years, AME congregations actively participated in local vigilance committees, abolitionist societies, and relief agencies. Led by Allen, the AME Church vigorously opposed the aims of the American Colonization Society.

The AME has always been known for its strong advocacy of good works, with a special emphasis on the so-called works of mercy listed in the Gospel of Matthew: feeding the hungry, clothing the naked, nursing the sick, sheltering the homeless, and visiting the imprisoned.

After the Civil War, the AME became the church of choice for many freed southern slaves and was in the forefront when it came to offering educational and skill-training opportunities to them. In her postwar years in Auburn, Tubman was a loyal member of the local AME church, frequently organizing bazaars for the relief of ex-slaves in the South. By the mid-nineteenth century, AME membership had mushroomed to a quarter million. Tubman's dream of opening a home for indigent blacks was salvaged by the AME Church when the plan fell on hard times. It continues to own Tubman's original property, now an historical museum site.

Given all this, Tubman quickly found out that the freedom she'd won for herself had to be exercised cautiously. In this strange new land in which she found herself, this was at least one thing that was all too familiar. She may have escaped bondage and even attained some level of standing when it came to rights, but in the eyes of many white Philadelphians, she and her fellow blacks were still disdained and often despised as second class.

"I WAS FREE, AND THEY SHOULD BE FREE"

One of the hardest sacrifices slaves who fled to freedom had to endure was leaving loved ones behind, both those who remained enslaved and freedmen who, like Tubman's husband, John, refused to accompany them. After their escape, many ex-slaves sought ways to bring their family members north. Their usual strategy was to save money in the hope of buying their loved ones' freedom. Not surprisingly, their efforts were usually unsuccessful, both because they rarely saved sufficient funds and because their former masters, still seeing them as property, refused to have any commercial dealings with them that risked recognizing the ex-slaves' newly won status as human beings rather than chattel property.

Tubman, who was always extremely close to her own family, resolved to bring her parents and siblings to freedom, and she hoped to persuade John to join them. Unlike most other refugees, she determined that she would personally rescue them, even though it meant putting herself in danger of capture. The very moment she crossed over the Delaware-Pennsylvania border, she began working toward that goal. "I was free, and they should be free," she told biographer Sarah Bradford. "I would make them a home in the North and bring them there, God helping me" (Bradford 1869, 20).

First, however, she needed money, both to keep body and soul together and to save for future rescue operations. So Tubman took whatever jobs she could find, largely domestic work—cleaning and cooking, and perhaps childminding—in Philadelphia and, in the summer, at Cape May, a popular holiday spot then and now.

Tubman had been in the North just over a year when she was contacted by someone from Dorchester County with the alarming news that her niece Kessiah, who had just barely escaped being sold two years earlier, was slated once again for the auction block. Despite the ongoing lawsuit against her right to own the children of Ben and Rit Ross, Eliza Ann Brodess had decided that her financial situation was too dire to worry about legal niceties. So Kessiah, as well as her two young children, Alfred and Araminta, were to be sacrificed.

The sale was scheduled for December 1850. Tubman and Kessiah's free husband, John Bowley, hatched a daring scheme to rescue his wife and children from under the auctioneer's very nose.

On the day of the sale, Kessiah, Alfred, and Araminta endured the humiliation of being paraded in front of the country courthouse like beasts of burden so that prospective buyers could examine them for possible defects. Then the bidding commenced, and when an offer was made that John Brodess, who was representing his mother, found acceptable, the three slaves were declared sold. The auctioneer, accompanied perhaps by Brodess, took a refreshment break before collecting money from the buyer. When the two men returned to finalize the sale, the buyer, who they then discovered was John Bowley, had disappeared. Furious at what they assumed was a delaying tactic on Bowley's part, they sent for Kessiah and the children to put them up for auction again. But by then they'd disappeared, secreted away to a friendly home not far from the courthouse.

Just prior to the sale, Tubman had left Philadelphia for Baltimore to await their arrival there. Bowley rowed his wife and children in a log canoe up the Chesapeake to Baltimore, braving the December weather in a boat that was less than stable. When they arrived, Tubman, probably working with agents of the Underground Railroad who had helped her in her own flight to freedom a year earlier, found hiding places for them until she could have them transported to Pennsylvania. She also likely helped them out financially.

Kessiah and her family were barely settled in their newfound freedom when Tubman returned to Baltimore in the spring of 1851, this time to escort her brother Moses, along with two other unnamed slaves, to Philadelphia. In less than a year-and-a-half after her own escape from bondage, she had aided the successful flight of no fewer than four family members. It was just the beginning.

The details of these first two rescues—and, indeed, of all subsequent ones—are murky. For obvious reasons, helping slaves escape from bondage was a business that had to be shrouded in secrecy. Underground Railroad routes, stations, and agents would have been seriously compromised had their locations and identities been revealed. Not only did actual participants in escapes remain closed-mouthed about their adventures, but, except in a very few cases, written records weren't kept. Thomas Garrett, the Quaker abolitionist who operated a station in Wilmington, Delaware, was open about his eagerness to give assistance to escaped slaves, and William Still, a Philadelphia-based black abolitionist and Underground Railroad stationmaster, kept meticulous records, safely hidden until the end of the war and of slavery, of fugitives who arrived on his doorstep. But they were exceptions to the rule.

Still's record of fugitives is voluminous, largely because of the huge number of Maryland slaves who made it to Pennsylvania. In 1850 alone, there were 259 successful escapes from Maryland, more than from any other slaveholding state. Additionally, there were probably dozens of unsuccessful ones. Several factors contributed to the high number: Maryland's physical proximity to a free state, an abundance of overland and water routes to freedom, and a large state population of free blacks who were willing to help refugees along their way. Had Tubman and her family been born in Virginia, much less in states situated further south, it's doubtful that she could have pulled off as many successful rescue operations as she did. As things turned out, she made as many as thirteen trips to the Eastern Shore to rescue a total of seventy to ninety slaves. As in the cases of her niece Kessiah and brother Moses, she also abetted the escapes of perhaps as many as fifty more without personally leading them to freedom. This is a remarkable record.

In the fall of 1851, several months after meeting her fugitive brother in Baltimore, Tubman decided it was time to venture back to the Eastern Shore. Her goal was to persuade her husband, John, to join her in the North.

The very fact that Tubman felt it necessary to return to Dorchester County, a place in which she was in danger of being recognized, captured, and sold down south, suggests two things. The first is that she desperately missed her husband, from whom she had been separated a full two years. The second is that John was as reluctant to leave his home in 1851 as he had been in 1849. Given her connections on the Eastern Shore, Tubman surely must have sent word to him on more than one occasion about her whereabouts, asking him to join her, and perhaps even sending him money for the journey. As a free man, John would have had no trouble in packing up and moving on had he wanted to go. In fact, the journey northward would have been much easier had he gone on his own than if he returned with Harriet via the circuitous Underground Railroad route they would have had to follow in order to keep her safe. It's reasonable to conclude, then, that John had resisted earlier efforts on Tubman's part to convince him to join her. Out of desperation, she decided to travel south to fetch her husband, carrying with her a new suit of clothes for him.

What Tubman discovered when she arrived in Dorchester County confirmed what she must have suspected all along: John had no intention of going with her. He even refused to meet with her upon receiving word of her return. In her absence, he had married again, a free woman named Caroline, and was in the process of starting a family with her. Perhaps one of the reasons he abandoned Tubman was because in all the years they had been together, she had failed to conceive. Whatever the reason, however, he was content with his new life and had no intention of abandoning it.

Tubman was crushed by her husband's betrayal and so recklessly furious that she initially intended to go to his house and raise a ruckus, even at the risk of drawing attention to herself and getting captured. But she soon steeled herself to accept the fact that their relationship was over, and the future she'd hoped for with him would never be. Swallowing the brutal truth that he could do without her, she in turn resolved to "drop him out of her heart" (Larson 2003, 91). She not only didn't give way to grief but defiantly took the opportunity of her trip to the Eastern Shore to lead several slaves north to freedom. This was Tubman's first on-site rescue.

FUGITIVE SLAVE LAW

It was these fugitive slaves, eleven in number, whom the ex-slave and abolitionist Frederick Douglass remembered sheltering. Douglass had settled in Rochester, New York, in 1847, where he edited the abolitionist newspaper the *North Star* and ran an Underground Railroad station. He records in his memoir offering hospitality in 1851 to "eleven fugitives at the same time under my roof." They were headed to Canada, and Douglass was charged not only with providing them shelter but also scrounging up sufficient funds to get them over the border. "It was the largest number I ever had at any one time," he recalled, "and I had some difficulty in providing so many with food and shelter." Still, the refugees were grateful for whatever he could do for them—"a strip of carpet on the floor for a bed, or a place on the straw in the barnloft" (Douglass 1882, 329). This assembly of fugitives would have been put on trains (individually, so as to not attract unwanted attention) from Philadelphia to New York City, then on to Albany, and finally Rochester.

Most likely included in this Canada-bound group were Tubman's niece Kessiah Bowley, along with her husband and children. They had determined that Philadelphia was no longer a safe haven for the same reason that Tubman was escorting the fugitives to Canada: the passage of the 1850 Fugitive Slave Act, called by its many critics the "Bloodhound Law."

Back in 1793, Congress passed a federal law, also known as the Fugitive Slave Act, that mandated the return of runaway slaves to their masters. The law was a concession to southern slaveholders who believed, with some justification, that northerners violated the constitutionally guaranteed property rights of slave owners by not ensuring the return of fugitives. This first Slave Act did little to calm their resentment, however, because legislators and officers of the court in free states too often refused to enforce it. Simmering at what they considered to be an injustice, southerners closely followed the progress of an 1842 Supreme Court case, *Prigg v. Pennsylvania*, which challenged northern noncompliance. The Court upheld the law—a victory for slave owners—but refused to rule on whether northern state officials were obliged by it to cooperate in the capture of slaves. So the resentment continued to simmer.

In 1850, a national crisis paved the way for a new piece of legislation regarding fugitive slaves that had more teeth in it. It was part of an omnibus

ABOLITIONIST NEWSPAPERS

Beginning in the second decade of the nineteenth century and continuing to the end of the Civil War, several newspapers devoted to the abolitionist cause were printed in the United States. By far the three most influential were Benjamin Lundy's *Genius of Universal Emancipation,* William Lloyd Garrison's *Liberator,* and Frederick Douglass's *The North Star.*

Lundy's *Genius* ran from 1821 to 1839, although issues in its final five years appeared only sporadically. The paper's editorials and general position, advocating a peaceful and gradual emancipation of slaves, reflected Lundy's Quakerism. An important feature in the *Genius* was Lundy's willingness to publish essays and verse written by women correspondents, the most frequent one being Elizabeth Margaret Chandler, a Philadelphia Quaker who moved to the Michigan frontier and, from there, contributed a regular column.

Garrison served an apprenticeship with Lundy but broke with him in 1831 to found the *Liberator,* which quickly became the nation's longest-running and best-known abolitionist newspaper. Like Lundy, Garrison was a pacifist who believed that the best tool against slavery was "moral suasion's" appeal to the conscience. But he was a fierce defender of immediate and uncompensated emancipation, and became an ardent critic of the U.S. government, insisting that it was complicit in the sin of slavery by not outlawing it. The leading abolitionists of the antebellum period, men and women and blacks and whites, eagerly contributed to the *Liberator.*

Financed in part from the royalties from his autobiographical *Narrative,* the *North Star* was founded in 1847 in Rochester, New York, by ex-slave Frederick Douglass. Named after the stellar compass of fugitives on the Underground Railroad, the newspaper's motto was "Right is of no Sex—Truth is of no Color—God is the Father of us all, and we are all Brethren."

Unlike the editorial position adopted by the *Liberator,* the *North Star* called for a political solution to emancipation. Although an early ally of Garrison's, Douglass came to believe that moral suasion was ineffective in the battle against slavery. Instead, he believed that political action—and, if need be, armed resistance—was called for. The newspaper defended this position throughout its entire printing run.

In 1851, Douglass merged *The North Star* with the *Liberty Party Paper,* the organ of the abolitionist political party with which Douglass was associated, to form *Frederick Douglass' Paper.* It ran until 1860.

bill brokered by Kentucky Senator Henry Clay in an effort to hold together a nation that was already beginning to splinter over slavery. The Compromise of 1850, as it was called, held back the dogs of war for another decade, but just barely.

The crisis that the compromise sought to address was precipitated by debate over whether slavery should be extended to the vast territories annexed in 1848 at the conclusion of the Mexican War. Thousands of square miles in size, the huge area included the current states of California, Nevada, and Utah, most of Arizona, and large portions of Colorado and New Mexico.

Up until then, Congress had striven to maintain a numerical parity between free and slave states as a means of keeping the peace between them. By 1849, free-soil Democrats and Whigs controlled Congress. They wanted the California and New Mexico territories admitted as free states, even though that would upset the delicate balance of senatorial representation. Surprisingly, they were supported by President Zachary Taylor, even though he himself was a southerner and a slave owner. Legislators from slave states were furious at what they saw as a gambit to minimalize their influence, and debates in the Senate and House were so heated that they sometimes erupted in actual physical scuffles. These brawls reflected the mood of the nation.

In an attempt to keep a lid on things, Clay struggled for months to pull together support for a patchwork bill that he hoped would mollify all parties. To placate northerners, the bill allowed California to enter the nation as a free state. The New Mexico territory was allowed to determine for itself whether or not to embrace slavery. This grant of "popular sovereignty" was a concession to the slaveholding South, even though the geography and climate of the territory didn't really lend itself to agricultural slave labor.

Given that the concession to the South seemed rather paltry, Clay added a provision to his omnibus that replaced the earlier Fugitive Slave Act with a new one. It stipulated that state officials were required not only to aid federal officers in the pursuit and return of fugitive slaves, but also to cooperate with extralegal private slave catchers hired by slaveholders to track down their runaway property. Failure to do so was criminalized, with each offense carrying the extraordinarily steep fine of $1,000.

Additionally, the new Fugitive Slave Act required private citizens, under pain of the same penalty, to assist officers of the law and slave catchers in their endeavors. Harboring fugitives or conveying them from station to station on the Underground Railroad was also prohibited, and defenders of the bill assured lawbreaking Americans that they would be punished. There would be no more looking away when it came to runaway slaves.

Nor was that all. Claimants of runaway slaves weren't required to offer any documentation establishing their legal right to the fugitives. All that was needed was an affidavit swearing as much. To make matters worse, justices of the peace and officers of the law were offered bounties for nabbing and returning refugees, thus establishing an almost irresistible motive for taking ownership claims by southerners at face value. Finally, apprehended blacks weren't allowed to make statements on their own behalf. They were rendered mute, as properly befit property.

Congress passed Clay's Compromise of 1850 in September of that year. Two months later, Millard Fillmore, who succeeded to the presidency on Taylor's unexpected death, announced that the bill represented "a settlement in principle and substance—a final settlement of the dangerous and exciting" issue of extending slavery. He predicted that the "final and irrevocable" new legislation had rescued the nation "from the wide and boundless agitation" that had been brewing for years. And, in an ominous reference to the Fugitive Slave Act, he assured the nation that he would "shrink from no responsibility" in discharging his "solemnly imposed" duties to uphold the law of the land (Richardson 2007, 5, 80, 93) For his part, Henry Clay was delighted at his success in pushing the bill through Congress. He was convinced it would "pacify, tranquillize, and harmonize the country" (Bordewich 2012, 358).

It didn't. Moderates on either side of the issue might have felt some degree of relief that yet another crisis over the issue of slavery had been averted, but fire-breathing secessionists on the one hand and ardent abolitionists on the other were infuriated by what each saw, although for different reasons, as a betrayal of the causes they endorsed.

Georgian Herschel Johnson sneered that the new Fugitive Slave Act was "a fecund box of nauseous nostrums," while one southern editor responded to it by fuming that he despised the Union and the North every bit as much as he loathed hell itself. The governor of Mississippi sputtered that his state's only realistic recourse was to withdraw from the Union. Only slightly less dramatically, South Carolina's James "King Cotton" Hammond predicted that Clay's compromise would inevitably lead to secession (Schott 1988, 136).

For their part, abolitionists were quick to condemn the Fugitive Slave Act as a danger to every black man, woman, and child living in free states. Charles Francis Adams, the most recent star in a distinguished U.S. dynasty that included two presidents, denounced it as "the consummation of the iniquities of this most disgraceful session of Congress" (Hamilton 2005, 167). Abolitionist William Lloyd Garrison bitterly accused northern congressmen in the *Liberator* (March 15, 1850) of "bending the knee" to the South.

Exercised as militant whites on either side of the slavery issue were about the Fugitive Slave Law, northern-dwelling blacks were terrified. Both those who had fled for freedom and those born free had long known that living in a border free state, they risked being kidnapped by slave catchers and dragged into bondage. But those who lived or had migrated further north felt relatively safer because of their distance from the Mason-Dixie line. That all changed with the passage of the 1850 law. Now blacks realized that, despite living in free states, they could be legally apprehended and shipped to the South simply on the unsubstantiated word of a white man or woman. Frederick Douglass expressed their fear and anger well: "There is no valley so deep, no mountain so high, no plain so extensive, no spot so sacred to God and liberty in all this extended country," he wrote, "where the black man may not fall prey to the remorseless cupidity of his white brethren" (Blassingame 1982, Series 1, 2: 295).

Henceforth, cognizant of her white brethren's cupidity, Tubman would make sure that the slaves she rescued didn't stop until they arrived in Canada.

RESCUING BROTHERS

After leaving Frederick Douglass's home, Tubman lead her eleven fugitives to St. Catharines, a town just across the U.S. Canadian border that was becoming a point of entry for a growing number of runaway slaves. One northern journalist who visited the town in 1855 to investigate how the nearly one-thousand-member black community fared was enthusiastic about what he saw there. "Refuge! Refuge for the oppressed!" he exulted. "Refuge for Americans escaping from abuse and cruel bondage in their native land! . . . Rest for the hunted slave! Rest for the travel-soiled and footsore fugitive" (Drew 2008, 214).

Canada offered safety from the dreaded Fugitive Slave Law. But runaways born and raised in temperate southern states often found its cold climate something of a shock, and supplying them with adequate clothing as well as food and shelter was a problem, at least before black refugee communities were better established. Tubman remained with her eleven fugitives during the winter of 1851 to 1852 to help them adjust to their new surroundings. As her early biographer Franklin Sanborn wrote, the runaways "earned their bread by chopping wood in the snows of a Canadian forest; they were frost-bitten, hungry, and naked. Harriet was their good angel. She kept house for her brother [Moses], and the poor creatures boarded with her. She worked for them, begged for them, prayed for them . . . and carried them by the help of God through the hard winter" (Bradford 1869, 77). As soon as spring arrived, Tubman returned to Philadelphia and Cape May to cook, clean, and save money. She was determined to return to the Eastern Shore. Even if John Tubman had scorned her, she had other family members who would welcome the opportunity to head north to freedom.

Tubman wouldn't make another foray to Maryland until spring 1854. During those two years, she made contact with leading abolitionists of the day such as William Still, Thomas Garrett, and Lucretia Mott. She also cared for her grandnephew James Bowley, son of Kessiah and John, who stayed for a few months in Philadelphia with her after she led his parents to Canada. Tubman devoted half her weekly earnings to paying for James to go to a school that catered to black youth. When he finally rejoined his parents in Canada, he was fully literate. Following the war, James returned south, eventually settled in South Carolina, and became a respected teacher, judge, and state legislator.

In early 1854, Tubman traveled to Dorchester County to bring out her brothers Henry, Ben, and Robert, all of whom were still owned by Eliza Ann Brodess. William Still recorded brief descriptions of them after their escape. Henry, he wrote, was a "smart" twenty-two-year old man of chestnut color; Ben, twenty-eight, also of chestnut color, was intelligent and of medium height; and Robert, Tubman's oldest brother, was thirty-five, likewise of chestnut color (Still 2007, 158–159).

All three brothers had attempted to escape bondage on several occasions. Henry and Ben had accompanied Tubman on her initial flight to freedom. The three of them had eventually returned, even though it's likely that Tubman turned back only because the other two lost their resolve. Since her departure, the three brothers had longed to join her and their brother Moses in freedom and had set out on at least three different occasions. Each time, they turned back, unable to find a way off the Eastern Shore without being detected.

Tubman was unable to bring them out in the spring of 1854, even though she did take a young slave named Winnibar Johnson back north with her. She also left instructions about stations along the Underground Railroad route to help another slave, Sam Green, make his way to freedom in August of that year. She returned to Dorchester County in December after she heard that Brodess intended to sell her brothers over the Christmas holiday. Given that they'd proven so troublesome, it was a near certainty that they would be sold down south rather than to buyers on the Eastern Shore who were aware of their history of escape attempts. Tubman realized that if she didn't rescue them quickly, she'd never see them again.

Remembering the abortive first effort to rescue them in the spring, she wanted to make sure things went more smoothly this time. First, she had to let her brothers know that she was coming for them. She arranged for someone in Philadelphia to write a coded letter to Jacob Jackson, a freedman in Dorchester Country. Because he could read and write, Jackson was most likely a communications channel between runaways who had settled in the north and the families they'd left behind.

The letter Tubman dictated to Jackson purported to be from his adoptive son William Henry, who, as a free man, had traveled northward some years earlier. In it, "William Henry" asked his "father" to "read my letter to the old folks, and give my love to them." Then came the coded message, a quote from a black spiritual well known to slaves, that Tubman wanted conveyed to Harry, Ben, and Robert: "Tell my brothers to be always watching unto prayer, and when the good old ship of Zion comes along, to be ready to step aboard" (Bradford 1869, 57).

A decade earlier, Tubman's letter might not have aroused official suspicion, but given the large numbers of successful runaways in recent years, Dorchester authorities had taken to reading all incoming letters addressed to blacks. They were immediately puzzled by the letter, because it was well known that William Henry had no brothers. When they called in Jacob Jackson for an explanation, he employed the strategy that so many canny blacks did when dealing with white authorities: he feigned a simple-minded bewilderment. "That letter can't be meant for me, no how," he told them. "I can't make head nor tail of it" (Bradford 1869, 58). Then he promptly took off to alert Tubman's brothers of her imminent arrival.

Probably traveling by water from Baltimore, Tubman arrived at the Eastern Shore on Christmas Eve, which fell that year on a Saturday. Because slave owners in the area generally gave their slaves a few days off at Christmas, she probably assumed she had a largish window of opportunity to secret away her brothers. But on her arrival, Tubman discovered that Eliza Ann Brodess was wasting no time: she intended to sell Henry, Ben, and Robert on Monday, the day after Christmas. Tubman had to act quickly.

She arranged to meet her brothers and hike with them under cover of darkness to their father's home in Poplar Neck, where they would rest a bit before beginning the trek northward. What she couldn't have known is that Robert's wife, Mary, was just about to give birth, and he couldn't bear to leave her until the baby was born. His two brothers, who were joined by Ben's fiancée, Jane Kane, a twenty-two-year old slave who had been regularly abused by an extremely harsh master, set out with Tubman for Poplar Neck, while Robert stayed behind long enough to see his baby girl come into the world. Then, without telling Mary his plans or saying farewell to his two sons, he took off, hoping to catch up with his brothers and sister. It was a heartbreaking decision, but he hoped that after winning his own freedom, he could somehow manage the liberation of his family.

As we'll see in the next chapter, one of the secrets of Tubman's success as an Underground Railroad conductor was her steely discipline. She tolerated no delays unless they were necessary for the safety of herself and the refugees she was guiding to freedom. That same rule applied even to her kin. When the delayed Robert failed to meet the rendezvous deadline she had set, she determined to leave without him. So with her other two brothers and Jane Kane, who was disguised as a man, she set out for her father's place some miles distant from the rendezvous point. Somewhere along the way, they were joined by two more slaves, John Chase and Peter Jackson.

When Robert finally caught up with the party on Christmas morning, he found them hunkered down in a corncrib near their parents' cabin. It was raining heavily, and the band decided to stay where they were until darkness, hoping that the weather would break.

Tubman hadn't seen her mother in six years, and being so close without communicating with her must have been painful. To make matters worse, she soon spotted Rit peering out of the cabin on the lookout for her sons, who she thought were coming home for Christmas. "The poor old woman had been expecting the boys all day, to spend Christmas with her as usual. She had been hard at work, had killed a pig, and put it to all the various uses to which sinner's flesh is doomed, and had made all the preparations her circumstances admitted of, to give them a sumptuous entertainment." Every so often, Rit would step out of the cabin into the rain "and, shading her eyes with her hand, take a long look down the road to see if her children were coming, and then they could almost hear her sigh as she turned into the house, disappointed" (Bradford 1869, 60–61).

The reason for keeping Rit in the dark was fear that if she knew "of their being in her neighborhood, or of their intentions, she would have raised such an uproar in her efforts to detain them with her, that the whole plantation would have been alarmed" (Bradford 1869, 20). Apparently they thought Ben a safer bet, or perhaps it was just that they were increasingly hungry and cold as they crouched in the damp and windswept corn crib. At any rate, Tubman eventually sent John Chase and Peter Jackson to her parents' cabin to let Ben in on what was happening. He managed to bring them some food without Rit suspecting anything and checked in on them several times throughout Christmas Day. When darkness fell and they began their journey northward, he even accompanied them for a few miles before bidding them farewell.

Curiously, however, he never laid eyes on his children during this whole time. Ben had assiduously refused to look at Tubman and her three brothers when he delivered food to the fugitives. Moreover, when he accompanied them, he blindfolded himself and had to be guided along the way by a son on either side. He only removed the blindfold after the party had left him and he could no longer hear their footsteps. His reason for this strange behavior was to avoid having to lie to the officials if they came questioning him after the three brothers' absence was noticed. He could tell them truthfully that he hadn't "seen" Henry, Ben, or Robert. It's not clear, however, what the motive was. Was it fear of punitive measures if he was caught in a lie to authorities, or was it a moral scruple about lying that prompted him? Perhaps a bit of both.

At any rate, Ben seems to have been worried about the repercussions of so many of his family members fleeing bondage. Beginning with Tubman's escape in 1849, four of his sons and a granddaughter and her family had fled. As the father and grandfather of so many fugitives, suspicion would have naturally fallen on him as being either a collaborator or an acquiescent observer. That things were getting uncomfortable is evidenced by the fact that he went out of his way six months after Robert, Ben, and Henry fled to file notice in the Dorchester County courthouse that he had bought his wife Rit from Eliza Ann Brodess for twenty dollars. The purchase had apparently been made some earlier time, but Brodess had failed to have the bill of sale officially recorded. Ben must have felt the need to ensure his and Rit's ability to leave Dorchester County, and he could do so only if she no longer belonged to Brodess. Rit still remained a slave; since she was well over forty-five years of age, Maryland law disallowed her manumission. But at least now she legally belonged to Ben, and, as a consequence, he could relocate with her whenever he wished. This would uncomplicate matters if he discovered that the law was closing in on him, thereby making a hasty exit from the Eastern Shore advisable.

It's unknown what route Tubman and her charges traveled, but it took them four days to cover the hundred miles that lay between Poplar Oak and Wilmington, Delaware. Once there, they made contact with Thomas Garrett, who wrote a letter that same day—the first documented reference to Tubman as an Underground Railroad operative—describing their arrival. He noted that he sent Tubman, six men, and one woman on to a local agent "to be forwarded across the country to the city." The identity of the sixth man, if there was one (perhaps Garrett misremembered), is unknown. The fugitives' journey northward had obviously been a hard one. "Harriet, and one of the men had worn their shoes off their feet, and I gave them two dollars to help fit them out." Seeing the weariness of the fugitives, Garrett also hired a carriage to convey them to their next stop (Sernett 2007, 44).

The city to which Garrett sent them was Philadelphia, where they were greeted by William Still, who recorded his description of the brothers. Still also transcribed new names for them, ones they selected. Henceforth Henry would be William Henry Stewart; Ben, James Stewart; and Robert, John Stewart.

Supplied with funds by Still and directed to a series of stations along the Underground route, Tubman and her party traveled first to New York City, then Albany, and then across the border to St. Catharines. The following year, Ben—James Stewart—traveled west to join John and Kessiah Bowley, who had relocated to Chatham, Canada, where a community of ex-slaves was forming. Robert—John Stewart—and Henry—William Henry Stewart—chose to remain in St. Catharines, where they established a foothold by hiring themselves out as laborers. John eventually became a coachman and William Henry a farmer.

As she had when she rescued the Bowleys three years earlier, Tubman wintered in St. Catharines with her brothers, undoubtedly feeling a responsibility to make sure they adjusted to their new surroundings before she headed back to the United States. In the spring of 1856 she was once again in Philadelphia. There were more Eastern Shore slaves to rescue, and first and foremost among them were her parents, Ben and Rit.

6

Small-Scale Guerrilla Warfare

The whites can't catch Moses 'cause you see she's born with the charm. The Lord has given Moses the power.

—William Wells Brown (Larson 2003, 137)

FROM BAD TO WORSE

The passage of the 1850 Fugitive Slave Law convinced Tubman that neither she and her family members nor any other black person north of the Mason-Dixon line were safe so long as they stayed in the United States. As she said, "I wouldn't trust Uncle Sam with my people no longer, but I brought 'em clear off to Canada" (Bradford 1886, 39). For the next few years, Tubman and her rescued family members would think of Canada as their permanent home base, even though she spent a good part of each year working in Philadelphia and Cape May before slipping into Maryland, sometimes for extended stays, to affect more rescues.

In the meantime, the sectional debate about the morality and political consequences of slavery intensified, despite Henry Clay's hope that his 1850 omnibus would pacify the nation. Proponents of human bondage remained furious about what they saw as northern officials dragging their heels on enforcing the Fugitive Slave Act, and abolitionists were equally furious in their resistance to it. Moreover, a number of polemical books exacerbated the growing divide by stirring up the general populace.

On the slavery side, George Fitzhugh's 1854 *Sociology for the South*, which purported to be a scientific study of how bondage affected slaves but, in actuality, was a pretty transparent apology for slavery, argued that the average slave was "as happy as a human being could be" (Fitzhugh 1854, 246). That same year, Boston-based clergyman Nehemiah Adams's *A Southside View of Slavery* appeared. Adams traveled throughout the South and discovered, he told his readers, that abolitionist descriptions of slave owners were perniciously misleading. Far from being monsters, they were "the guardians, educators, and saviors of the African race in this country," fulfilling, according to Adams, both the physical and spiritual needs of slaves (Adams 1854, 9). The assumption underlying Fitzhugh's and Adams's claims was that blacks, like children, were incapable of taking care of themselves and were consequently in need of caretaking and firm—and sometimes stern—supervision. As Fitzhugh put it, "The negro is improvident [and] will not lay up in summer for the wants of winter" (Fitzhugh 1854, 82).

On the antislavery side, undoubtedly the most influential book was Harriet Beecher Stowe's *Uncle Tom's Cabin* (1852), to which both Fitzhugh and Adams were responding. A fictional depiction of slavery, with gripping descriptions of the brutal treatment of slaves by masters and overseers and the extreme danger slaves braved to make their way to freedom—a desperate Eliza clutching her baby and fleeing bloodhounds became an iconic image in the midcentury United States—Stowe's book was an instant bestseller. Its purple passages pulled at the heartstrings of white middle-class northerners even as it infuriated southern defenders of slavery who saw it, correctly, as an assault on their way of life.

In direct response to Adams's *Southside View of Slavery*, a young journalist named Benjamin Drew published *A North-Side View of Slavery. The Refugee: or the Narratives of Fugitive Slaves in Canada* in 1856. Drew traveled to Canada to interview runaway slaves who had fled to St. Catharines and other towns and settlements north of the U.S. border. Some of those he interviewed were Tubman and her brothers; rather surprisingly, given her ongoing rescue work, Tubman apparently gave Drew permission to use her real name in his account of their conversation. The story Drew received from ex-slaves differed dramatically from Fitzhugh's and Adams's accounts of contented and fulfilled slaves. His interviewees' testimonies convinced him that Stowe's novel, despite its melodrama, was truer to reality than the supposedly scientific and empirical claims defended by the two apologists for slavery.

In the midst of the increasingly bitter national debate about slavery, what began as a scheme to open up new territory for railroad lines exploded in the space of two years into a piece of legislation that prompted a small-scale civil war preceding the larger and deadlier one that erupted in 1861.

In 1852, several congressmen from Illinois, Missouri, and Iowa proposed that the federal government ratify as states of the union a huge landmass, ranging from the Indian Territory (now Oklahoma) to the Canadian border, that was the northern remnant of the Louisiana Territory purchased from France in 1803. Their motive was to cash in on what they knew would be the lucrative business of railroad-building once states were carved out of the vast territory.

There was, however, a problem with their scheme. According to the Missouri Compromise of 1820, an early deal brokered by Henry Clay to keep peace between free and slaveholding states, slavery was banned north of the 36-30 parallel, which included the landmass under consideration. Southerners immediately saw that if the territory was divided into states, the congressional balance between slave and free states would tip against them in favor of the North. This was a possibility they refused to tolerate.

Illinois senator Stephen Douglas was a big proponent of the railroad deal, both because it would benefit Chicago, his state's primary metropolitan area, but also because the value of his own real estate holdings in the city would be enhanced. After months of searching for a solution that would advance his goal while satisfying those on either side of the squabble over extending slavery, Douglas appealed to one of the provisions of the 1850 Compromise: the permission given to New Mexico to decide for itself whether it would allow or outlaw slavery. Using popular sovereignty as his wedge, Douglas proposed federal legislation, subsequently called the Kansas-Nebraska Act, which explicitly repudiated the Missouri Compromise; created two new states, Kansas and Nebraska, out of the territory; and gave the residents in each the right to vote for or against slavery. The assumption was that congressional parity would be maintained de facto, since the expectation was that the northernmost proposed state, Nebraska, would reject slavery, and the southernmost one, Kansas, would accept it. Douglas was confident that his solution would satisfy everyone.

Instead, it raised a fresh storm. Within twenty-four hours of its introduction in the Senate, the bill provoked powerful opposition led by Ohio senator Salmon Chase. He and his coalition minced no words in their condemnation of Douglas's bill, calling it "a gross violation of a sacred pledge"—the limitation on the extension of slavery mandated by the Missouri Compromise—a "betrayal of sacred rights"; and "part and parcel of an atrocious plot to exclude from a vast unoccupied region immigrants from the Old World and free laborers from our own States, and convert it into a dreary region of despotism inhabited by masters and slaves" (Gienapp 2001, 72).

Congress and the U.S. public at large wrangled over the bill for weeks. It finally passed the Senate in early March, after a half-drunken Douglas harangued his colleagues from the floor for a full four hours, spewing "violence and vulgarity," as one journalist put it, that was impossible to "convey but a faint idea" of in print (Nevins 1947, 143). Nine senators, recognizing that a vote either way was a political liability for them, abstained.

The bill still had to get through the House of Representatives, and that took another three months of acrimonious debate. Alexander Stephens, Georgia representative and future vice president of the Confederacy, was the floor manager for the bill, and he refused to call for a vote until he was confident of success. Even so, when the decision finally came on May 22, it squeaked by on a 114 to 104 vote. President Franklin Pierce signed it into law a week later, killing the Missouri Compromise and replacing it with the doctrine of popular sovereignty.

Douglas's bill set in motion a chain of events that embroiled the northern territory in a mini-civil war between proslavery and free soil settlers, each wanting to create a majority in the region to push for the legalization or prohibition of human bondage. Encouraged by a homesteading provision in the bill granting one hundred sixty-acre tracts to anyone willing to move to the territory, hundreds of men from the eastern and southern states packed up and relocated to the future state of Kansas. Some came for a fresh start in life or out of conviction one way or another about slavery. Many were adventurers who recognized that the region would soon be rendered lawless as pro- and antislavery militias took shape and fought one another.

William Seward, New York senator and future Secretary of State to Abraham Lincoln, clearly saw what was at stake. "Come on then, gentlemen of the Slave States," he grimly declared. "Since there is no escaping your challenge, I accept it in behalf of the cause of freedom. We will engage in competition for the virgin soil of Kansas, and God give the victory to the side which is stronger in numbers as it is in right" (*Congressional Globe*, 769). Massachusetts senator Charles Sumner saw the impending danger with less romantic eyes. Douglas's bill, he lamented, "annuls all past compromises with Slavery, and makes all future compromises impossible. Thus it puts Freedom and Slavery fact to face, and bids them grapple. Who can doubt the result?" (Donald 1960, 260–261).

TUBMAN'S WAR

The result was a mini-civil war that earned the future state the sobriquet of "Bleeding Kansas." It was one in which John Brown, one of Tubman's later associates and admirers, took part. In the meantime, the drama being played out in Kansas was paralleled by what one of Tubman's biographers called her own "small-scale guerrilla warfare" (Sernett 2007, 61).

Her struggle against bondage wasn't provoked by the congressional debates over the extension of slavery into the territories. Being unable to read, she knew nothing except by hearsay of the intellectual skirmishes between authors such as Fitzhugh, Adams, and Drew. Nor was she exercised, as so many white northerners were, by fictional treatments of slavery like *Uncle Tom's Cabin*. Offered the opportunity to see a stage production of Stowe's novel, Tubman declined. "I haven't got no heart to go and see the suffering of my people played on the stage," she said. "I've heard some of *Uncle Tom's Cabin* read, and I tell you Mrs. Stowe's pen hasn't begun to

---

UNCLE TOM'S CABIN

Harriet Beecher Stowe's famous novel, an example of the sentimental literature genre so popular in the mid-nineteenth-century United States, was serialized in *The National Era* beginning in June 1851 before it was published as a book the following year. No other volume except the Bible sold as well at the time, and it wasn't long before Stowe's novel was translated into several languages. Its depiction of slavery outraged southerners but galvanized thousands of northern readers, especially women, into opposition to the peculiar institution.

The novel's impact is difficult to exaggerate. When President Lincoln was introduced to Stowe, he reportedly remarked, "So you're the little woman who wrote the big book that started this great war." The story is probably apocryphal, but its appraisal of the novel's influence isn't far wrong.

Stowe based many of the incidents in her book on actual events she'd read about. After the novel's appearance, in response to critics who insisted that she offered a distorted portrait of slave life, she published a compendium of the primary sources from which she had pulled her story. Her *A Key to Uncle Tom's Cabin* appeared in 1853.

Although the name of the novel's eponymous hero has since taken on a negative connotation, the character Uncle Tom embodied the Christian virtues so dear to Stowe, who was the daughter, sister, and wife of clergymen. Uncle Tom remains kind and gentle under the most adverse of circumstances, a genuine Christlike figure, in stark contrast to the brutal Simon Legree. Stowe's intention was to put the lie to southern claims that slave owning was compatible with Christianity. But—and this is surely one of the novel's strengths—she resisted painting all slave owners as one-dimensional villains. Legree's daughter, Eva, whom Uncle Tom befriends, is depicted as innocent and charitable. Stowe's point was that even if some slave owners like Legree are inherently wicked, many, like Eva, aren't. It's just that their active or passive participation in the sin of slavery morally implicates them.

paint what slavery is as I have seen it at the far South. I've seen the real thing, and I don't want to see it on no stage or in no theater" (McGowan and Kashatus 2011, 53).

The guerrilla warfare Tubman waged against slavery—her return, again and again, to the "enemy territory" of the Eastern Shore to disrupt and subvert the slavery system by leading fugitives to freedom—was fueled, as she suggested in her remark about Stowe's novel, by firsthand knowledge of just how horrible involuntary servitude is. Having both personally endured its cruelties and witnessed the suffering it inflicted on acquaintances and family members, Tubman was convinced that it was an evil affront to God. No more succinct statement of what motivated her can be found than something she said to Benjamin Drew when he traveled to Canada to interview her. "Now I've been free," she told him, "I know what a dreadful condition slavery is. I have seen hundreds of escaped slaves, but I never saw one who was willing to go back and be a slave . . . I think slavery is the next thing to hell. If a person would send another into bondage, he would, it appears to me, be bad enough to send him into hell, if he could" (Humez 2003, 25).

By its very nature, guerrilla warfare is covert. Consequently, we have only a few details about Tubman's strategies for getting slaves away from their masters and evading slave catchers long enough to push through to freedom. Some of them come from Sarah Bradford's biographies of Tubman, others from anecdotes Tubman told throughout her long life before audiences and in private conversations, and still others from the recollections of Underground Railroad collaborators like Thomas Garrett. Piecing them together gives us a general idea of her mode of operation, while, at the same time, leaving tantalizingly blank spaces.

She generally planned her rescue operations for the winter months. Although this meant colder and wetter weather, it also made for longer nights, thereby enabling Tubman's nocturnal-traveling fugitives the opportunity to cover ground more swiftly than they could have in the shorter summer nights. Whenever possible, she preferred to set out on Saturday night. Because most slaves had Sundays off, they wouldn't be missed until sometime Monday at the earliest. It would take at least another day for word of the escape to circulate in newspapers and public notices.

It's unclear how often Tubman sent word of her arrival on the Eastern Shore ahead of time via the slave grapevine, as she did when she dispatched the coded letter to Jacob Jackson in preparation for rescuing her brothers, or how often she simply showed up and attracted potential refugees by word of mouth. Either tactic was risky, but the second especially so. As a safeguard, Tubman often gave false information about her whereabouts until she was confident that the slaves who had expressed interest in fleeing were in earnest. She also rarely stayed with the same families during her visits.

She almost never actually ventured into slave houses on plantations. The risk was simply too great that she might be recognized or betrayed. Instead, she designated a particular time and place for refugees to meet her, usually in a secluded woodland or some other deserted place.

Still, there was always the possibility, given the number of people Tubman had worked for as a slave, that she would run across whites who had known her. She became adept at disguises. Sometimes she wore silk dresses (although most likely ones that had seen better days) to give the impression that she was one of Dorchester County's many middle-class free blacks. Although still young, she often disguised herself as a shambling, bent old woman. Occasionally she even posed as a man to throw off suspicions.

On at least three occasions, she ran into previous masters, once without any apparent disguise at all. Remarkably, however, the white man, probably Dr. Thompson, didn't recognize her. Thomas Garrett implausibly surmised that this was because Tubman's skin color had lightened as a consequence of her no longer being a field slave exposed to the hot sun (Larson 2003, 124). It's more likely that Thompson's belief that Tubman was long gone from the Eastern Shore prevented him from actually seeing her for who she was.

On another occasion, Tubman, disguised as an old woman, had just bought a couple of live chickens when she saw one of her past masters walking toward her in the marketplace. She shook the chickens, which she was holding by their legs, so that they began to squawk and flutter, thereby throwing up a noisy smokescreen. As Sarah Bradford put it, the ex-master "went on his way, little thinking that he was brushing the very garments of the woman who had dared to steal herself, and others of his belongings" (Bradford 1886, 35).

Another time, Tubman, spying a white man who could recognize her, grabbed a newspaper and held it in front of her face as if she were reading it. When she told the story years later, she chuckled that for all she knew, given her illiteracy, she could have been holding it upside down. But the ruse worked nonetheless (Larson 2003, 125).

Once Tubman set out on the road to freedom with refugees in tow, she was grimly no-nonsense. She recognized that the slightest misstep could result in discovery and capture, which, at least in her case, would certainly result in being sold to a cotton or rice planter in the Deep South, imprisonment, or even execution. So she insisted on absolute obedience, even resorting to physical threats to either intimidate stubborn fugitives or stiffen timid ones. A single faint-hearted refugee, especially one who wanted to turn back and give himself up, could put the entire group at risk, and that was something Tubman wouldn't tolerate.

Tubman was as hard on herself as she was on the people she led to freedom. She willingly endured hunger, cold, and weariness to get them to safety, recognizing that she was the one person in the group who simply couldn't afford the luxury of relaxing vigilance for even a second, despite occasionally suffering temporary narcoleptic spells during her rescues. Her grit was especially evident when, in one of her rescue operations, suffering from a toothache, she used the butt of the pistol she carried to knock out her top row of teeth. One can only imagine the reaction of her refugees to such an action.

Because a single black woman attracted less attention than several black men and women traveling together, Tubman often hid her fugitives while she scouted out possible routes. If the coast was clear, she sometimes summoned them by singing verses from slave spirituals that signaled them to come forward. She had an uncanny ability to sense danger and never hesitated to abruptly change course if she believed that she and her wards were in danger of discovery. When asked to account for her highly tuned gift for intuiting threats, she remarked that she had inherited it from her father. "When danger is near," she said, "my heart goes flutter, flutter" (Clinton 2004, 92).

It wasn't just second sight inherited from her father that Tubman believed guided her. She was also convinced that God traveled with her and her wards and protected them from slave catchers. One of her acquaintances put it like this:

> She could elude patrols and pursuers with as much ease and unconcern as an eagle would soar through the heavens. She "had faith in God"; always asked Him what to do, and direct her, "which," she said, "He always did." She would talk about "consulting with God," or "asking of Him," just as one would consult a friend upon matters of business. (Clinton 2004, 91)

As Tubman remarked, God never deceived her. Or, as one of her friends said of her during this period, she was born with the "charm" (Larson 2003, 137).

In steering her wards to northern freedom, Tubman generally followed the Choptank River, often seeking refuge along the way at the homes of friendly free blacks such as the Reverend Samuel Green or Underground Railroad stations in Delaware towns such as Odessa, Camden, and Wilmington, from where Thomas Garrett would send her and her fugitives on to Philadelphia and freedom. She got into the habit of carrying daguerreotypes of Railroad agents to help her distinguish genuine well-wishers from posers looking to alert slave catchers. On more than one occasion, she refused hospitality from persons, possibly legitimate agents, because she didn't recognize them.

Before the 1850 Slave Act, runaways either settled in the greater Philadelphia area or traveled northward, frequently by train, veering west for upper state New York or east for the Atlantic seaboard. After 1850, Tubman generally escorted fugitives all the way to Canada. Once there, she frequently stayed throughout the winter to help them find their bearings in their new homeland.

RESCUES

Although many of the details of Tubman's rescue operations are murky, some specifics are known. In December 1855, for example, she escorted an Eastern Shore slave named Henry Hooper to Philadelphia. Either that same month or in early January, she returned to Maryland for her brother William Henry's wife and son. It might have been on this same trip that she tried, unsuccessfully, to rescue her sister Rachel and Rachel's children. Apparently it was impossible to gain access to the children, and Rachel was understandably unwilling to leave them behind.

Tubman, determined as ever to get as many family members to freedom as she could, made another attempt to rescue Rachel in May 1856. That she chose to return to the Eastern Shore in spring rather than wait until winter indicated just how eager she was to liberate her sister from bondage. Once again, however, she failed, although she did get four men to Philadelphia and eventually to Canada. But she paid a steep price.

In getting her four Underground Railroad passengers out of Maryland, she experienced one of her intuitive warnings of impending danger that convinced her to change her planned route. In doing so, she came upon an unexpected stream of tide water. In the absence of a boat, there was no way to cross it but to plunge in. The men accompanying Tubman couldn't swim—nor, for that matter, could she—and they refused to enter the water. So Tubman, partly to reassure them but mainly to escape the captors she feared closing in on them, waded in. The water came up to her shoulders, but she managed to get to the other side, motivating the four men, considerably taller than she, to follow.

It wasn't long before they had to cross more water. Soaked to the skin and shivering with cold, they finally made their way to the home of a free black family, where they dried off and rested. Tubman was so grateful for the hospitality that she gifted her hostess with her petticoats. But when she and her companions arrived at Thomas Garrett's place in Wilmington, he found her quite ill. By the time she made it to Canada, she likely had pneumonia, and it took her all summer to recover. Garrett was so alarmed at her condition that he worried she risked becoming an invalid. He feared, he wrote, that her pneumonia would "permanently settle on her lungs" (McGowan and Kashatus 2011, 68).

During the years in which Tubman ventured south to bring slaves to freedom, no one was a closer collaborator in both spirit and deed than

Thomas Garrett, a deeply committed Quaker credited with helping some 2,700 slaves attain their freedom. He was one of Tubman's earliest supporters. Without his financial and emotional support, her success might have been much less than it was.

Garrett was born in Upper Darby Township, west of Philadelphia, in 1789, into a well-off Quaker family, which, like many other Philadelphia members of the Society of Friends, had abolitionist sympathies. Garrett's early dislike of slavery was on full display by the time he was in his early twenties. A free black who was a family servant was snatched by a gang of slave catchers who planned to sell her into slavery. Garrett followed the kidnappers to the Philadelphia Navy Yard and rescued her before she was hauled aboard the ship for the trip south.

Garrett left Upper Darby for Wilmington in his early thirties, with the deliberate intention of providing safe haven for runaway slaves. He started a prosperous iron and hardware business, liberally using his profits to fund his antislavery activities. Because Delaware was a slave state, Garrett's opposition, which he made no attempt to keep secret, aroused a good deal of local animosity, and he was more than once threatened with physical violence.

His abolitionist work got him into legal trouble in 1848, when he was sued in federal court for slave stealing. Garrett, who was unapologetic during the proceedings, was found guilty and hit with such a massive fine that it bankrupted him. The misfortune might have crushed the spirit of a less committed man, but Garrett's response was that he was grateful for the publicity the trial and conviction had brought him, because now even more fugitives would know about his willingness to help them. "Garrett," warned the judge upon sentencing him, "let this be a lesson to you, not to interfere hereafter with the cause of justice, by helping off runaway negroes." "Judge," Garrett replied, "thee hasn't left me a dollar, but I wish to say to thee, and to all in this court room, that if anyone knows of a fugitive who wants a shelter, and a friend, send him to Thomas Garrett, and he will befriend him!" (Whyman 1896, 112). At the age of sixty, practically penniless, he began a new business, which, thanks to his industriousness, soon prospered as much as his old one had. And he was as good as his word to the court, continuing to aid runaway slaves whenever he could.

Garrett met Tubman in the mid-1850s, and worked with her until the coming of the Civil War. He was clearly intrigued by her deep conviction that God had recruited her for her rescue work and admired her fearlessness in carrying it out. "I never met with any person of any color," he once noted, "who had more confidence in the voice of God, as spoken direct to her soul" (Clinton 2004, 91). In writing to a member of the Ladies Emancipation Society of Edinburgh, Scotland, he described her as "a noble woman," and he meant it (Larson 2003, 123). Even though Tubman's somewhat imperious demands for his help at times irritated him, Garrett had a genuine and deep affection for her.

So he was delighted when she showed up again on his doorstep in September 1856, recovered from her illness and ready to resume her guerrilla war. Even though her landlady in Philadelphia had sold her personal belongings and rented out her room, Tubman was in good spirits. As usual, she boldly asked Garrett for money, telling him that her immediate plans were to travel to Baltimore to bring two slave children to Philadelphia, and then to try once more to bring her sister Rachel up from the Eastern Shore. "God tells me," she asserted, "you have money for me." Garrett, taken aback, asked Tubman how much she needed, to which she responded twenty-three dollars. It just so happened that Garrett had been sent five pounds from Scottish abolitionists—nearly twenty-five dollars—which he gladly handed over to Tubman, marveling at what struck him as an obvious example of divine providence.

Tubman may have made two trips to Baltimore that September, or Garrett may have been confused about her plans, because it's not clear that she rescued two children around that time. But she did bring up from Baltimore a young woman named Tilly, the fiancée of a runaway slave who had waited in Canada for her for eight long years. Hearing that Tilly was about to be sold into the Deep South, the young man asked Tubman to retrieve her and gave her some money to aid in the rescue. The way in which Tubman went about saving Tilly was, in the judgment of Garrett, "remarkable" and displayed "great shrewdness" (Larson 2003, 131).

As a safety precaution before setting out, Tubman armed herself with a certificate that testified she was a free Philadelphian. She landed safely in Baltimore and located Tilly without any trouble. The problem was how to get her to Philadelphia without arousing suspicion. Two black women traveling on their own in a slave state invited suspicion. So Tubman, who somehow managed to obtain a fake travel pass for Tilly, booked passage for the two of them on a steamboat that was headed south instead of north. It was a shrewd move indeed.

Arriving at Seaford, Delaware, the two women checked into a hotel—an audacious step in itself—intending to take a train the next morning to Camden. Tilly was understandably nervous and became positively frightened when she and Tubman were confronted by a suspicious slave catcher the following day. Tubman showed him her certificate and Tilly's forged travel pass, and he let them be. Finally arriving in Camden, a carriage took them the final fifty miles to Thomas Garrett's place in Wilmington. Although she hadn't shown it at the time, not wanting to rattle Tilly even more, Tubman was clearly worried during this rescue, even though she insisted, when asked by Garrett, that she hadn't been frightened. As she later more honestly confessed, she prayed throughout the night at the

Seaford hotel, "Oh, Lord! You've been with me in six troubles"—that is, six slave rescues—"don't desert me in the seventh!" (Larson 2003, 133).

Tilly was sent on to her fiancé in Canada, unaccompanied by Tubman. With the cash given her by Garrett in hand, Tubman returned to the Eastern Shore that November, determined to finally rescue her sister Rachel. Once more she failed, again because Rachel refused to leave her children behind and there was no way to retrieve them from their master, who was different from Rachel's, without arousing suspicion. Tubman intended to return at Christmas, hoping that then Rachel and the children would be together, but she was unable to follow through with the plan.

While on the Eastern Shore, however, several slaves learned of her presence and asked her to lead them to freedom. Two brothers, Josiah (Joe) and Ben Bailey, Peter Pennington, and Eliza Manokey joined up with her in mid-November. Their rescue proved to be one of the most daunting ever undertaken by Tubman.

Ben Bailey was owned by a man named John Campbell Henry. His brother Joe was owned by William Hughlett, who, all together, possessed some forty slaves. Hughlett had paid top price for Joe, nearly $2,000, and gave him the responsible position of supervising Hughlett's business of cutting and hauling timber. As a consequence, Joe and his brother were acquainted not only with black shipmen who came to collect the wood for Baltimore shipyards, but also with Tubman's father Ben Ross, who was also a timberman. Joe had told Ben that he wanted to be notified the next time Tubman returned to the area because they wanted her to guide them north.

Joe sought out Ben because Hughlett, immediately upon purchasing Joe, had whipped him. As Tubman told the story to Sarah Bradford, Hughlett approached Joe with "a strong new rawhide in his hand" and ordered, "Now, Joe, strip and take a licking."

The surprised Joe tried to protest. "'Master,' said he, 'haven't I always been faithful to you? Haven't I worked through sun and rain, early in the mornin' and late at night; haven't I saved you an overseer by doin' his work? Have you anything to complain agin me?'"

Hughlett's reply was brutally impersonal. "'No, Joe, I have no complaint to make of you. You're a good nigger, an' you've always worked well. But you belong to me now; you're my nigger, and the first lesson my niggers have to learn is that I am master and they belong to me, and are never to resist anything I order them to do. So I always begin by giving them a good licking. Now strip and take it'" (Bradford 1886, 40–41).

Joe submitted to the lash, but promised himself that it would be his last. That night, he made his way to Ben Ross's house to leave his message for Tubman. By the time she arrived, he'd convinced his brother Ben, Pennington, and Eliza Manokey to flee with him.

The journey northward was a particularly hard one, doubling what was normally a travel time of less than a week to nearly two. The weather was wet and cold, but what really slowed the group down were the numerous slave catchers on the lookout for them in order to collect the bounties on their heads. Hughlett was offering an enormous reward of $1,500 for Joe, and Turpin Wright, Pennington's master, had put up $800 for his capture. Ben's master was only willing to post a $300 reward for his return. But the apprehension of all three would net the slave catchers a tidy sum.

As a consequence of the extensive manhunt, the forever cautious Tubman was even more so. At times, she and her wards hid in potato holes within mere feet of roaming slave catchers. At other times they had to separate, each going to a different hiding place. All of them were helped with disguises by friendly free blacks, including the Reverend Samuel Green. They were passed on from one Underground Railroad station to the next, until they finally arrived at the outskirts of Wilmington, not far from Thomas Garrett's welcoming home.

To their dismay, they discovered that the masters of Ben, Joe, and Peter, foreseeing that the fugitives would try to make their way to Wilmington, were already there, nailing reward notices up around town and encouraging both bounty hunters and officers of the law to be on the lookout. Local blacks were doing their best to tear down the notices, but word spread of the large reward anyway. The only thing for the fugitives to do was to go into hiding until some way could be found to get them into Wilmington undetected. It was a dilemma, because the only route into town, a bridge that spanned the Christiana River, was well guarded.

When Thomas Garrett learned of their arrival, he came up with a pretty shrewd plan of his own to get them across the river and into town. He hired a couple of wagons, filled them with black bricklayers, and sent them across the bridge as if they were going to a job. According to Bradford's account,

> This was a common sight there, and caused no remark. They went across the bridge singing and shouting, and it was not an unexpected thing that they should return as they went. After nightfall (and, fortunately, the night was very dark) the same wagons recrossed the bridge, but with an unlooked-for addition to their party. The fugitives were lying close together on the bottom of the wagons; the bricklayers were on the seats, still singing and shouting; and so they passed the guards, who were all unsuspicious of the nature of the load contained in the wagons, or of the amount of property thus escaping their hands. (Bradford 1886, 45)

Once across the bridge and in Garrett's home, the refugees had only a few hours to recuperate. They were quickly packed off to Philadelphia, and, by the end of November, they were in New York City and on their way via

Albany, Syracuse, and Rochester, to the Canadian border, which they planned to cross over via the suspension bridge at Niagara Falls.

Joe Bailey was described as "a noble specimen of a negro, enormously tall, and of splendid muscular development" (Bradford 1886, 39). Clearly, Hughlett was impressed enough by his steadiness and leadership skills to purchase him at an unusually high price, and then make him a foreman. But the days of anxiety as he and the others avoided slave catchers, vigilantes, and civil authorities wore on his nerves. He suffered something of an emotional crisis when they arrived in New York City because the agent, a man named Johnson, who had been tasked with sending them on to Albany, immediately recognized him. "'Well, Joe,' the agent said, 'I am glad to see the man who is worth $2,000 to his master.' At this, Joe's heart sank. 'Oh, Master, how did you know me!' he panted. 'Here is the advertisement in our office,' said Mr. Johnson, 'and the description is so close that no one could mistake it'" (Bradford 1886, 46).

Joe's anxiety only increased when he asked to look at a map and discovered to his horror how much terrain there remained between him and the Canadian border. It was at that moment that he appeared to give up hope. Previously, he had been cheerful enough, despite his anxiety. He'd even joined in singing gospels and hymns of thanksgiving and praise. But after seeing the map, "from that time, Joe was silent; he talked no more; he sang no more; he sat with his head on his hand, and nobody could 'rouse him, nor make him take any interest in anything" (Bradford 1886, 48).

Throughout the entire journey through New York state, Joe remained despondent, "sitting silent and sad, always thinking of the horrors that awaited him if recaptured" (Bradford 1886, 49). Even as their train crossed the suspension bridge linking Canada and the United States, Joe couldn't bring himself to celebrate or even to raise his head, despite Tubman's encouragement, to view the majestic falls. When their carriage had crossed the mid-span, which meant they were officially in Canadian territory, Tubman shook Joe and excitedly said to him, "Joe, you're in Queen Victoria's dominions! You're a free man!" (Bradford 1886, 51).

It was only then that Joe Bailey allowed himself to believe that he was well and truly liberated. He jumped up, tears streaming down his face, and began singing in a loud and joyful voice.

> Glory to God and Jesus too,
> One more soul got safe;
> Oh, go and carry the news,
> One more soul got safe.
> (Bradford 1886, 51)

Nor did his joy end when he disembarked from the train. At the station he continued shouting and singing, attracting a large crowd of white men

CANADIAN EMANCIPATION

England ended slavery within its dominions in 1833, but for forty years prior to that, Canada opened its doors to U.S. slaves seeking refuge. Canadian asylum was especially crucial after the 1850 Fugitive Slave Act rendered it unsafe for fugitives to remain even in free states.

In 1793, the legislature of Upper Canada (the southern portion of Ontario) agreed on an Emancipation Act, pushed by Lieutenant Governor John Graves Simcoe, which, for all practical purposes outlawed slavery. A few days later, the legislature of Lower Canada (the southern portions of Quebec and Labrador) passed a similar bill. Both laws forbade the importation of new slaves into Canada and mandated that the children of current ones be freed when they reached the age of twenty-five.

Canadian opposition to slavery had been building for some time, despite the objections of slaveholding U.S. loyalists who had fled to Canada following the American Revolution. The tipping point was the highly publicized fate of a slave girl, Chloe Cooley, owned by William Vrooman, a loyalist New Yorker who had settled on the Canadian side of Niagara Falls.

In March 1793, probably getting word that the Emancipation Act was in the offing, Vrooman took Chloe to the U.S. side of the Niagara River and sold her. The slave girl went unwillingly and created a ruckus that attracted wide attention and elicited much sympathy for her fate. Following the passage of the Emancipation Act, official Canadian policy was to welcome refugees and refuse demands by angry ex-owners for their extradition. Attorneys for the owners tried to work around the asylum by insisting that the fugitives were common criminals guilty of self-stealing, but Canadian officials found this ludicrous. As Lieutenant Governor Sir Francis Bond Head noted in 1837, "Surely a slave breaking *out* of his master's house is not guilty of the burglary which a thief would commit who should force the same locks and bolts in order to break *in*" (Winks 2008, 170).

and women curious to discover what all the ruckus was about. "Thank the Lord," Joe proclaimed. "There's only one more journey for me now, and that's to heaven!" (Bradford 1886, 53). Tubman wryly replied, "You might have looked at the Falls first and then gone to Heaven afterwards" (Larson 2003, 136).

BEN AND RIT

After Tubman and her four fugitive slaves left Garrett's home on their way to Canada, he didn't hear from her for several months. By March 1857, he was getting worried. For all he knew, she had ventured into Maryland again and had been captured. In all likelihood, she had told him of her plans to return to the Eastern Shore in December to try, once again, to rescue her sister Rachel. Garrett was concerned about her personal well-being but also recognized how devastating to the cause it would be to lose her. As he wrote to a fellow abolitionist, "it would be a sorrowful act if such a hero as she, should be lost from the Underground Railroad" (Larson 2003, 137).

Garrett needn't have worried. It appears that Tubman spent the winter months in Canada and didn't venture southward again until the beginning of April. It may have been that she was having trouble raising or earning money for future rescues. Even working round the clock as she did as a cleaner, cook, and childminder, she often had little cash left after helping out family and friends. If it hadn't been for generous donations from abolitionists, her rescue operations would've been seriously curtailed.

At any rate, when spring came, she made her way to New York City, where she went to its branch of the American Anti-Slavery Society and refused to leave until she'd been given sufficient funds to get her back to the Eastern Shore. She was determined to rescue her parents because, as bad as the Fugitive Slave Act had made things, recent events made them even worse. She feared that if she didn't get her parents out of Maryland soon, she'd be unable to.

What prompted her alarm was a serious crackdown in the state when it came to slaves itching to make a dash for freedom, as well as free blacks suspected of aiding and abetting them. There had been long-standing concern among Marylanders about the "self-thievery" of slaves. But a dramatic escape in early March, occurring at just about the time Garrett was expressing his concern for Tubman's safety, was the immediate cause of the crackdown.

A Dorchester County slave named Henry Predeaux, who feared that his master was planning to sell him, headed off for freedom with seven companions. Their masters, furious at the audacity of their slaves, offered a huge reward for their capture. By the time the fugitives reached Dover, Delaware, word about the reward was widespread. It proved irresistible to a free black man who, posing as an Underground Railroad stationmaster, convinced the runaways that the local sheriff was sympathetic to their plight and had offered them the jail as a place to rest and recuperate before continuing their journey to the north and freedom.

It didn't take long for the eight to recognize that they'd been duped once they arrived at the jail, and a furious fight erupted. When the sheriff tried to put them in chains, Predeaux flung a shovelful of red-hot embers around the room to distract him. Then he held him off with a poker while his companions broke through a window and escaped into the night. Predeaux followed them, and sooner or later, along several different routes, all eight made it to freedom. Their courageous resistance made them heroes to abo-litionists but shameless scoundrels to defenders of slavery. The escape of the Dover Eight, as they soon came to be called, determined Eastern Shore slave owners to put their heads together in order to find ways to safeguard their property. Vigilante groups were organized to roam the countryside on constant lookout for runaways, and spies were enlisted to report back to slave owners any rumors of discontent and potential runs to freedom.

But that wasn't enough. Eastern Shore slave owners were positive that the Dover Eight had been assisted by free blacks, and their suspicions immediately turned to the Reverend Samuel Green, the fifty-five-year-old friend of Tubman's who had often assisted runaways in the past. Less than a month after the Dover Eight escaped, his house was searched by local deputies for incriminating evidence. They found railroad schedules for trains traveling to New Jersey, a map of Canada, and a copy of *Uncle Tom's Cabin*. It's difficult to know which of these more angered the local authori-ties, who immediately arrested Green.

The official charge against him was that he violated a Maryland law, which stated that merely owning "any abolition handbill, pamphlet, news-paper, pictorial representation or other paper of an inflammatory charac-ter" was sufficient cause to assume an intention of creating "discontent" or "stirr[ing] up to insurrection the people of color of this State." The Cana-dian map and railroad timetables weren't enough to convict Green, but the possession of Stowe's novel proved to be a red flag. The novel, claimed the authorities, had seduced Green, who "had lived quietly and contentedly in the community in which he was born," until it fell into his hands. So for the crime of "having in his possession a certain abolitionist pamphlet [sic] called Uncle Tom's Cabin," Green was punished with ten years in the state penitentiary. He was released after serving half the sentence on the condi-tion that he leave Maryland (Larson 2003, 143).

Tubman learned about Green's fate, as well as the increased vigilance on the Eastern Shore, and realized that her parents, Ben and Rit, were likely in peril. Neither of them was in danger of being sold South. Ben had been free since 1840, and he had purchased Rit in 1855, thereby protecting her from the auction block. But the authorities had suspected for some time that Ben had aided escaping slaves, and the exploits of his daughter, who was already being called "Moses" by admiring slaves, not to mention the escape to freedom of so many of his children, made him a predictable target of the law. There was also reason—good as it turned out—to believe that he had sheltered the Dover Eight. So his arrest was imminent, so much so that his former master, Dr. Anthony Thompson, even advised him to leave Maryland.

In late May, Tubman came for them. In their seventies and no longer in the best of health—Ben, especially, suffered from rheumatism—her parents were understandably reluctant to pack up and leave the area in which they'd lived their whole lives. But Tubman was determined that they depart. Realizing that their age and infirmities made it impossible to take them out of Maryland by foot, she arranged to haul them during the nights in a rickety, jerry-rigged wagon drawn by a broken-down nag wearing a straw collar. Crotchety to the end, the old folks complained about leaving behind their possessions, but their daughter allowed them to bring only a featherbed-tick, which Rit insisted on, and Ben's broadax, which he couldn't bear to leave behind.

By June 4, the three arrived at Garrett's house. Delighted to see that Tubman was safe and sound, he gave them enough money to get them to Philadelphia. William Still sent them on to New York City, Rochester, and finally St. Catharines, where they joined their sons and grandchildren already settled there.

For once, though, Tubman didn't stay with her family in Canada. Returning to Philadelphia after seeing her parents safely to Rochester, she collected funds and made her way back to the Eastern Shore to rescue Rachel and her children, Angerine and Ben. Although she stayed there for several weeks that summer, it once more proved impossible to get her sister, niece, and nephew to freedom. Rachel simply wouldn't desert the children, and it was impossible to get all of them together at once.

Three of Tubman's siblings had been sold "down south" and hence out of her reach, but she had rescued five of them, as well as her mother and father in several daring "small-scale guerrilla warfare" raids into enemy territory. She grieved, of course, for her absent family members, and she would try one more time to save Rachel. But her achievement was impressive.

7

The Struggle Widens

She exposed herself to the fury of the sympathizers with slavery, without fear, and suffered their blows without flinching.

—Martin I. Townsend, Esq. (Bradford 1869, 102)

A NEW PHASE

Following the 1857 rescue of her parents, Tubman's "small-scale guerrilla warfare" against slavery entered a new phase. She returned to the South a couple more times to lead slaves to freedom, but her struggle against the peculiar institution broadened in several ways.

She came out of the shadows, where her work on the Underground Railroad had necessarily kept her, to begin speaking publicly in the North about her travails as a slave and her subsequent rescue missions, becoming one of abolitionism's most exciting spokespersons. She enthusiastically supported John Brown's plans to spark a slave insurrection in Virginia, raising money and recruits on his behalf and, at least for a while, planning on joining him. She physically participated in the dramatic rescue of a fugitive captured by slave catchers and threatened with rendition back to bondage, suffering "blows without flinching" and displaying the same determination and courage that had fueled her many trips southward to rescue slaves. All the while, she tirelessly scrambled to find ways to materially support both her own family members and others, whom she had already led to freedom and settled in Canada.

MATERFAMILIAS

Fugitive slaves who migrated to Canada following the passage of the 1850 Fugitive Slave Act tended to congregate, at least initially, in towns that were close to the U.S.-Canadian border. Eventually, several black settlements were established, the most notable of which were Wilberforce, Dawn, and Elgin (Walters 2012, 109–117). In the earliest years, towns such as St. Catharines and, a bit further west, Chatham, were the primary destination points. Tubman's relatives settled in both. Tubman and her parents resided in St. Catharines.

The town, located just twelve miles from Niagara Falls, had a black community at the time of nearly one thousand, many of them escapees from Maryland's Eastern Shore. Clustered for the most part on several blocks of North Street, they made their livings as best they could as day laborers in a variety of jobs including cooking, waiting tables, cleaning, and blacksmithing.

Chatham, just across the border from Detroit, also boasted a large ex-slave community, comprising a full one-fifth of the town's population. Although they lived apart from the white residents and maintained separate churches and schools, their presence was keenly felt. As one of the locals said in 1855, runaway slaves were "as thick as blackbirds in a corn-field" (Drew 2008, 22).

Canada offered legal refuge to U.S. slaves as well as all the legal rights enjoyed by Canadian residents. In 1793 and again in 1800, the country had passed laws restricting the importation of slaves and mandating the freedom of all slaves already in Canada when they reached the age of twenty-five. By 1833, when the United Kingdom abolished slavery in all its holdings, Canada had already acquired the reputation, applauded by U.S. abolitionists but scandalous to proponents of slavery, of being the "New Canaan" for runaways. One journalist who visited the refugee community in St. Catharines gushed that Canada offered "Refuge! Refuge for the oppressed! Refuge for Americans escaping from abuse and cruel bondage in their native land! . . . Rest for the hunted slave! Rest for the travel-soiled and foot-sore fugitives!" (Drew 2008, 41).

But in fact things weren't quite as rosy as the journalist imagined. In the first place, many of the fugitives found the Canadian winters nearly unbearable. Already discombobulated by being thrown into unfamiliar surroundings and separated from everything they'd once known, and often not having sufficient clothing to protect them from the elements, refugees suffered from bronchitis and pneumonia at alarming rates. Tubman's own parents, especially her mother Rit, complained bitterly about the cold.

Additionally, refugees discovered that the racial prejudice they'd endured in the United States was present in Canada as well, despite the fact that they were protected under the law. When the Chatham resident observed that resettled slaves were as thick in his town as "blackbirds in a corn-field," he was complaining, not neutrally describing. The presence of blacks was often resented by native Canadians, doubtlessly one of the reasons that refugees tended to congregate together in communities. Locals looked upon them as lazy, shiftless, and dishonest. It's not unusual for refugees to be greeted with suspicious wariness by natives. For slave fugitives, the problem was compounded by racial prejudice.

Both these factors, but especially the harsh climate—by the spring of 1858, Rit was insisting that another northern winter would kill her—prompted Tubman to begin seeking a more hospitable home for her parents. That meant moving them south, back into the United States. Although the Fugitive Slave Act was still a threat for runaways, both Ben and Rit were, under the law, immune from it. As we've seen, Ben was a freedman and Rit, technically, was his slave, since he had purchased her a few years earlier.

Tubman eventually settled on Auburn, an abolition-friendly town in western New York State, home to many Underground Railroad supporters, including Martha Coffin Wright, Lucretia Mott's sister, and William and Frances Seward. Some refugees from the Eastern Shore had settled in Auburn, and Tubman was familiar with their community there. But what decided the matter was William Seward's offer, sometime in late 1858 or early 1859, to sell her a house and seven acres of land on quite reasonable terms. The property was a small part of what Seward had inherited from his father-in-law Elijah Miller, one of Auburn's leading and wealthiest lawyers.

Seward, whose father had been a slave owner, moved to Auburn when he married and practiced law there for a few years with his father-in-law. But his heart was in politics. In 1849, the same year that Tubman made her run for freedom, he was elected to the United States Senate and made a name for himself almost immediately in a maiden speech lambasting the Fugitive Slave Act that came to be known as the "Higher Law" oration. In it, Seward argued that even if southern slaveholders were legally correct in their interpretation that the Constitution granted them the right to extend slavery throughout U.S. territories, a "higher" law ordained by "the Creator of the Universe" forbade the practice of human bondage. The American Anti-Slavery Society, founded by William Lloyd Garrison in 1833, was so impressed by the speech that it printed and distributed thousands of copies.

SEWARD'S HIGHER LAW SPEECH

William Seward had the reputation of being a pretty bad public speaker. He usually read his speeches in a monotone voice, and, if he used hand gestures at all, they tended to come off as rather wooden. So when he rose on March 11, 1850, to give his maiden speech as the freshman senator from New York, not many of his colleagues seated in the chamber paid much attention.

But the nation did. In short order, one hundred thousand pamphlets of his oration, the "Higher Law Speech," were printed, and Seward became a household name, applauded by opponents of slavery and vilified by its supporters.

Seward delivered his speech in the midst of a raucous congressional and national debate over whether the peculiar institution ought to be extended to U.S. territories and soon-to-be states such as California. Seeking to avert a national crisis, New England's Daniel Webster, considered then, and now, to be one of the nation's greatest political orators, rose in the Senate on March 7 to insist that slavery was a purely legal matter, not a moral one. The only pertinent question was whether the Constitution allowed for its spread, and the only proper answer, declared Webster, was a resounding yes. Webster clearly thought that debating the morality of slavery only muddied the issue before Congress.

Seward's Higher Law Speech was a direct response to Webster. He allowed that the Constitution referred to slavery without explicitly condemning it. But he insisted that when there is a clash between conscience and the law of the land, the "higher laws" of morality must supersede mere human laws. The Constitution, insisted Seward, gives Americans "stewardship" but not "arbitrary authority" over the "national domain." That which properly regulates human authority comes from "a higher law than the Constitution," and that higher law condemns treating human beings as if they were chattel. With this "higher law," there can be no legitimate compromise.

Eight years later, around the time he sold the property to Tubman, Seward made the second great speech of his life, warning in Rochester, New York, that an "irrepressible conflict" between slave and free labor was quickly diminishing the likelihood of peaceful coexistence. Joining the fledging Republican Party, Seward hoped to be its nominee in the presidential race of 1860. His uncompromising denunciation of slavery proved too threatening to delegates, and the nomination went to Abraham Lincoln, who also disliked slavery but hadn't made as much noise about it as Seward.

Seward's sale of the small holding to Tubman was remarkable for several reasons. The easy terms that he offered her—she had to pay only $25 down and make quarterly payments of $10—testified both to his conviction that slavery was a great evil and his desire to do whatever he could to help fugitive slaves. Moreover, the fact that he sold to a woman in a day and age when it was unusual for women to own property in their own names was in itself unusual. Finally, the transaction was technically illegal. The Dred Scott decision of 1857 had stripped slaves of human rights, including the right to own property. Because Tubman was still legally a slave, she had no legal claim on the farm that Seward sold her. The fact that Seward entered into the transaction may have been a deliberate act of defiance to a Supreme Court decision that he considered unjust. It's also surely the case that Seward, always politically ambitious, must have been aware that going out of his way to help Tubman would enhance his standing in the abolitionist community.

After moving her parents and her brother John to the Auburn property, Tubman faced the problem of keeping up the mortgage payments and providing for household needs. In the past, she had never been reticent about soliciting funds from others to support her rescue trips to the Eastern Shore or to buy supplies for refugees in Canada. Now she began asking for personal help in the form of cash or supplies, and, as usual, the many friends and acquaintances she'd made over the past decade of work on the Underground Railroad came to her aid. She soon realized that charity wouldn't be enough to cover her expenses, so she began traveling throughout the northern states, especially New York and Massachusetts, giving popular lectures and speeches about her life as a slave and her adventures as an Underground Railroad conductor. Since she was still a slave, she was occasionally introduced under a false name—"Harriet Garrison," apparently after William Lloyd Garrison, was sometimes used—but her audiences knew perfectly well who she was. The honoraria she received, often in the form of collections gathered from the people who came to hear her, were intended to pay down the mortgage and provide for her parents and brother. It wasn't unusual for Tubman, whom her patrons often considered generous to a fault, to share the money she received with ex-slaves down on their luck or with relief agencies that helped them. In her later years, well-meaning but patronizing white acquaintances, worried about her tendency to give away what little money she had, tried to manage her finances.

Tubman was, by all accounts, a thrilling speaker. When she walked onto the stage or platform, many in the audience, primed by secondhand stories about the exploits of the "Moses of her people," were surprised by her diminutive stature, her plain clothes, and her missing front teeth. But the moment she began recounting her life story, they were enthralled, first because hearing speeches from female ex-slaves was so uncommon at the time—Tubman and Sojourner Truth were far outnumbered on the lecture circuit by male ex-slaves—and second because Tubman knew how to spin a good tale. "She has great dramatic power," recounted one of her admirers. Listening to her, "the scene rises before you as she saw it, and her voice and language change with her different actors" (Larson 2003, 169). Her ability to captivate audiences was especially surprising given that she had no previous experience of public speaking. For obvious reasons, during her active years on the Underground Railroad, she'd remained in the background to ensure anonymity.

Ben and Rit Ross, the parents of Tubman and her siblings, were technically the heads of the family. But from a functional perspective, Tubman had been the de facto materfamilias ever since she'd rescued her first relative from slavery. That most of her family was free was entirely attributable to her courage and determination, and once she got them to the North, she labored tirelessly to support them. Her dedication to family was always paramount in her life, second only to her devotion to God, and it gradually led her to take on the mantle of family elder. But her competence and reliability unintentionally encouraged an overdependence on her from her relatives, one that bred a certain amount of passivity on their part and only added to her burden.

At the beginning of November 1859, for example, her elder brother John sent a letter to her that positively reeks of helplessness. Tubman was on the lecture circuit at the time, raising money, while John was in Auburn with their parents. In the letter, he almost immediately complains about not hearing from her, and then launches into a litany of grievances. Their father wanted to return to Canada to retrieve some of his belongings. What did Tubman think? "Please write as soon as possible and not delay." Ben and Rit were getting old and feeble, and John had no one to help him care for them. A man who promised the household a stove hadn't delivered it. More of the Tubman clan wanted to leave Canada for Auburn. The quarterly mortgage payment to Seward hadn't been paid. "Write me particularly what you want me to do." Throughout the entire letter, it's clear that the one person whom the entire family depended upon to answer questions, make decisions, fix problems, avert crises, and provide material support was Tubman. It's a role she willingly accepted, despite its frequent thanklessness.

Given her devotion to family, it's reasonable to assume that not having any children of her own was a source of personal sadness for Tubman. It's not clear why she remained childless. But shortly after her purchase of the Auburn homestead, she finally became a mother, albeit not a biological one, under circumstances that remain mysterious to this day.

On a return from a clandestine trip to the Eastern Shore, probably in late spring or early summer of 1859, Tubman was accompanied by an eight- or nine-year-old light-skinned black girl named Margaret, subsequently called either Margaret Tubman or Margaret Stewart. As an adult, Margaret claimed that she was Tubman's niece, one of a set of twins fathered by one of Tubman's brothers, whom she referred to as a free man wealthy enough to own a carriage driven by a pair of chestnut horses. She went on to say that Tubman had stolen her away, and that she only stopped weeping at being separated from her mother and twin brother when she and Tubman traveled North by steamboat. Margaret's daughter Alice Lucas, who was born in 1900, repeated her mother's story.

It's a strange tale that just doesn't fit known facts. There's no evidence that Tubman had a brother, free or otherwise, left in Maryland by the time she returned to Auburn with Margaret. Moreover, there's no record of twins among her known brothers' children, much less why, if Margaret did in fact have a twin brother, Tubman didn't rescue him as well. Finally, it seems completely out of character that Tubman would kidnap an unwilling child from her family. Alice Lucas tried to exonerate Tubman's seizure of her mother by saying that Tubman "knew the joys of motherhood would never be hers and she longed for some little creature who would love her for her own self's sake" (Clinton 2004, 119). But there were plenty of black children in the North, orphaned and living in dire poverty, who Tubman could have adopted in order to know the "joys of motherhood."

Because Alice Lucas asserted that her mother bore a physical resemblance to Tubman, some historians consider the possibility that Margaret might have been Tubman's natural daughter (Clinton 2004, 121; Larson 2003, 199). But there's no reason to take this hypothesis seriously. In 1896, when applying for a pension for her wartime service, Tubman denied having any children. Moreover, photographs of Margaret as an adult don't reveal the similarity that Alice claimed to see.

Whatever the truth behind the relationship between Tubman and Margaret, the rest of the Tubman/Stewart clan not only never accepted her as a bona fide member of the family, but even displayed animosity toward her that continued into successive generations. Perhaps this is one reason why Tubman eventually asked Florence Seward to take Margaret into her household. Tubman's intention was probably that Margaret would act as a servant to the Sewards, but Florence and her widowed sister Lazette Worden raised the girl as one of their own.

The trip south in which Tubman picked up Margaret wasn't her final journey to the Eastern Shore. In late November 1860, she ventured there to try one last time to rescue her sister Rachel and Rachel's two children. Unknown to her, Rachel had died a few months earlier, and Tubman failed once more to retrieve the two children. She later intimated that she could have bribed an overseer to release them to her, but she didn't have the $30 he demanded. So she settled for guiding to freedom a family that was unrelated to her. But Rachel and her children were lost.

GENERAL TUBMAN

In April 1858, about a year before buying the property in Auburn, Tubman met John Brown. The two were immediately impressed by one another. They shared much in common. Both despised slavery. Both were profoundly religious and prone to sometimes apocalyptic visions. Both were willing to use violence in their struggles against human bondage. And both were intensely admired and even adulated by abolitionists, and just as fiercely loathed by slavery's supporters.

Brown probably learned about Tubman earlier in the year during a three-week sojourn in Frederick Douglass's Rochester, New York, home. The two men had known one another for a full decade and had attended the 1855 inaugural meeting of the Radical Abolitionist Party, a short-lived political venture. Tubman, on the other hand, surely would have known about Brown long before she actually met him because of his highly publicized exploits—some called them atrocities—in the "Bleeding Kansas" conflict of the 1850s.

Brown, born in 1800, was a son of New England who never quite seemed to know his place in the world until he became an abolitionist. Married at twenty and widowed at thirty-two, he tried his hand at a number of occupations, including tanning and farming. By the time he reached middle age, he was loaded down with debt and, having remarried, a household of children.

Things came together for him in 1837, following the murder of Elijah Lovejoy, an antislavery journalist whose Illinois newspaper office was destroyed by a proslavery mob. The violent act shocked opponents of slavery throughout the land, but Brown was especially affected. At a public meeting shortly after the outrage, he committed himself publicly to the struggle. "Here, before God, in the presence of these witnesses," he proclaimed, "from this time, I consecrate my life to the destruction of slavery!" (Clinton 2004, 126). After meeting him in 1847, Frederick Douglass declared that Brown's empathy for the plight of slaves was so deep that it was as if his white "soul had been pierced with the iron of slavery" (Oakes 1970, 63).

From the earliest days of his 1837 "consecration" to abolitionism, Brown dreamed of fomenting and leading a slave insurrection in the southern states. For a while, he published bellicose articles in abolitionist periodicals. But then, in 1849, he moved his family to a mixed community—a quite unusual thing at the time—on land in the Adirondacks donated by the New York millionaire and abolitionist Gerrit Smith. For a few years, he seemed content to farm his few acres and dream his dreams.

The Kansas-Nebraska Act of 1854 stirred Brown to action. As we saw in chapter 6, the law sponsored by Stephen Douglas was intended to quell the escalating tension between free and slave states about the spread of slavery into U.S. territories. As a compromise, Douglas proposed that the people residing in the territories of Kansas and Nebraska, both of which had applied to Congress for admission as states, could decide by "popular sovereignty" whether or not to allow slavery within their borders.

THE LOVEJOY RIOT

On November 7, 1837, a tragedy occurred in the town of Alton, Illinois, which shocked opponents of slavery. Abolitionist Elijah P. Lovejoy was murdered by a proslavery mob.

Lovejoy, a native of Maine and a graduate of Waterville (now Colby) College and Princeton Theological Seminary, had located to St. Louis, Missouri, to found a church and edit an abolitionist newspaper, *The Observer*. After his printing press was destroyed in two separate incidents, he decided to relocate across the Mississippi River to Illinois, a free state, and set up shop in Alton. His views on slavery incited anger there as well, however, culminating in the riot that left him dead.

Abolitionists back east deplored his murder, but followers of pacifist abolitionist William Lloyd Garrison were also ambivalent about its circumstances. It turned out that Alton police, unable to provide Lovejoy with the protection he requested from them, had armed and deputized him as a bona fide militia member. During the riot, Lovejoy had fired into the mob, killing one man and, in turn, had been shot himself, dying instantly.

Garrison insisted that the mob's violence was an assault on freedom of the press that had to be resisted by everyone, regardless of where they stood on the issue of slavery. One month later, upward of five thousand people packed into Boston's Faneuil Hall to condemn Lovejoy's murder and defend journalistic freedom. The violence to which Lovejoy had resorted remained a thorn of contention in the abolitionist community, with many concluding, as Garrison put it, that because of his use of firearms, Lovejoy may have died a martyr, but not a Christian one.

Far from resulting in what Douglas hoped for, the policy of popular sovereignty proved to be disastrous. Pro- and antislavery constituencies began pouring into the Kansas territory, each hoping to swell their numbers sufficiently to sway the vote. The inrush led to guerrilla warfare between the two factions so fierce that it amounted to a small-scale civil war. "Bleeding Kansas" became an omen of the mayhem into which the entire country would plunge in 1861.

Brown saw the Kansas conflict as an opportunity to take his crusade against slavery to a new level. Putting together a small band of recruits, several of which were his sons, he left his New York farm, traveled to Kansas, and joined the fray, engaging exuberantly in a number of skirmishes with proslavery settlers and militia. The intensity of his conviction that he was God-appointed to be the scourge of slavery, as well as his willingness to resort to violence to fulfill that sense of mission, became all too apparent on the night of May 24, 1856. Near a creek named Pottawatomie, Brown and his men dragged five proslavery settlers from their beds and massacred them with broadswords and axes. Three months later, at Osawatomie, they fought a heated battle with proslavers bent on vengeance for the murders. Brown and his men soon fled, but the two events earned him a reputation as someone who was unafraid to shed blood in the abolitionist cause. As Brown himself unequivocally stated, "I will die fighting for this cause" (Oakes 1970, 171).

Brown returned east to cash in on his reputation as a man of action—not for himself personally, but to gather support for his decades-old scheme to foment a slave insurrection in the upper Alleghenies. His plans had grown to include the establishment of an insurrectionist state, and much of his sojourn in Douglass's home in 1858 was devoted to drafting a constitution for it. Realizing that he would need money with which to recruit soldiers and purchase weapons, Brown subsequently traveled to Boston in search of underwriters. He quickly found six of them—Gerrit Smith, Thomas Wentworth Higginson, Samuel Gridley Howe, George Stearns, Theodore Parker, and Franklin Sanborn. These sponsors, who both donated their own money and solicited contributions from others, later became known as the "Secret Six." All of them were eager to support Brown from behind the scenes, although none of them was willing to join him on the front lines.

Brown, accompanied by Jermain Wesley Loguen, an ex-slave who became a bishop in the AME Zion Church, traveled to St. Catharines that spring to meet Tubman. His purpose was to recruit her to his cause and ask her to persuade others from the expatriate black community in Canada to join him. Knowing of her skills in navigating fugitives to safety and evading pursuers, he was confident that she would be a good resource when he launched his insurrection.

Upon being introduced to Tubman, Brown did something strange but not out of keeping with his rather unpredictable and sometimes bizarre prophetic behavior. As a witness described it, Brown "shook hands with her three times, saying 'The first I see is General Tubman, the second is General Tubman, and the third is General Tubman." At the conclusion of their meeting, he repeated his three-part salutation (Humez 2003, 34). It's not clear what his intent was. Perhaps he was merely trying to impress upon Tubman his confidence in her as a military collaborator, or perhaps there was a religious symbolism, significant only to Brown, in thrice calling Tubman a general. Whatever the reason, he had clearly made up his mind about her caliber before actually meeting her, and their conversation together only affirmed his original opinion. He would refer to her on several later occasions as "General Tubman," underscoring his confidence in her leadership by referring to her with masculine pronouns.

Tubman must have caught her breath in surprise when she first laid eyes on Brown, because she realized she'd seen him before—in a dream. Her biographer Sarah Bradford recorded Tubman's recounting of the vision.

She thought she was in "a wilderness sort of place, all full of rocks and bushes," when she saw a serpent raise its head among the rocks, and as it did so, it became the head of an old man with a long white beard, gazing at her "wishful like, jes as ef he war gwine to speak to me," and then two other heads rose up beside him, younger than he, and as she stood looking at them, and wondering what they could want with her, a great crowd of men rushed in and struck down the younger heads, and then the head of the old man, still looking at her so "wishful." This dream she had again and again, and could not interpret it; but, when she met Captain Brown, shortly after, behold, he was the very image of the head she had seen. (Bradford 1869, 82–83)

One month after meeting with Tubman, Brown arrived in Chatham, Canada, to convene a sort of constitutional convention for the insurrectional government he hoped to establish in the Alleghenies after his slave revolt. Posing as a gathering intent on forming a local Masonic lodge, Brown and the attending delegates, just short of fifty black men, discussed and unanimously ratified his constitution. Conspicuous by their absence were Frederick Douglass and Harriet Tubman. It's not clear why Tubman wasn't an attendee, but Douglass had begun to have second thoughts about the feasibility of Brown's plans. Later, in August 1859, he told Brown to his face that the hoped-for slave revolt was a fantasy.

Brown felt ready to launch his raid immediately following the Chatham convention. He had sufficient financial backing from the Secret Six and he'd managed to recruit, probably with Tubman's aid, several fugitive slaves from the St. Catharines area. One of them, surprisingly, was Joe Bailey, the desperately frightened refugee whom Tubman had been forced to threaten during his rescue to keep him from returning to bondage or, worse, giving the entire party of fugitives away. Brown soon learned that news of his plans had somehow been leaked to government officials. Sensing danger of federal intervention (which probably wasn't in the offing), he postponed the raid and returned to Kansas.

In the meantime, Tubman was making the rounds in New England, speaking to different groups of abolitionists to solicit funds for both herself and Canadian refugees. It was during this time that she met Franklin Sanborn, one of the Secret Six, as well as the author of the first newspaper biography of her, which Bradford later incorporated verbatim in her own biographies of Tubman. At the time they met, Sanborn, although still in his twenties, was a rising star in antislavery circles and knew everybody who was anybody among the abolitionists. It was through him that Tubman was introduced to New England luminaries like Ralph Waldo Emerson, Henry David Thoreau, and Bronson Alcott, as well as to a woman named Ann Whiting who tried, without success, to teach Tubman to read. Sanborn also arranged many speaking engagements for her, helping to make her exploits more widely known. The funds that such engagements brought her became pressingly important to Tubman after her purchase of the Seward property.

Brown, now back in the east, met with Tubman on several occasions in the spring and summer of 1859. She urged him to launch his insurrection on July 4, believing that the propitious date would highlight the second war for independence that Brown hoped to spark. Brown hesitated again, believing this time that he was insufficiently prepared.

Brown and Tubman might have met more frequently that summer but for the fact that she had a busy speaking schedule, especially in Massachusetts. On the Fourth of July, the same day she had hoped Brown's slave revolt would launch, she appeared before the Massachusetts Anti-Slavery Society. One of its leading members, Thomas Wentworth Higginson, a clergyman who went on to command a black brigade in the Civil War, introduced her as a conductor on the Underground Railroad but declined out of concern for her safety to tell the audience her name. He simply referred to her as Moses. A reporter for William Lloyd Garrison's *Liberator* wrote in the July 18, 1859, issue that following Tubman's talk, Higginson made an appeal for funds. "This brave woman," Higginson told the audience, "had never asked for a cent from the Abolitionists." Instead, "all her operations had been conducted at her own cost, with money earned by herself." But now, Higginson went on to say, she needed funds to support her aging parents and to pay the mortgage on property she'd purchased for their old age. Until she had secured their future, he said, she would be unable to "resume the practice of her profession!"—namely, rescuing slaves. Higginson's veiled warning worked, and Tubman collected nearly $40.

The following month, Tubman spoke at the New England Colored Citizens' Convention. It was a lively and defiant gathering whose members voted to censure the Dred Scott decision, the 1850 Fugitive Slave Act, and the American Colonization Society. When it was Tubman's turn to address the assembly—she was introduced as Harriet Garrison—she told a parable, recorded in the *Liberator* (August 26, 1859), that she would repeat many times in the years before the war. A farmer, she said, had sown onions and garlic on some of his land to increase the output of milk from his dairy cows. But the two herbs made the butter he processed too strong to stomach, and so he planted clover in the pastures to tone down the flavor. It was too late, however, because the wind had blown onion and garlic seeds over all his fields. "Just so," Tubman told the convention delegates, "the white people had got the 'nigger' here to do their drudgery, and now they were trying to root 'em out and send 'em to Africa. But they can't do it; we're rooted her, and they can't pull us up."

In late summer, Brown set out for Harpers Ferry, Virginia, where he'd decided his revolt would begin, to scout out the lay of the land. Tubman

remained in Massachusetts. Brown apparently tried to contact her by letter and word of mouth to let her know that he intended to strike in October, but it seems that Tubman did not get the news until the last minute,
if at all. She had taken ill while in New Bedford, most likely from the
effects of her old head injury but, in October, was recovered enough to
head for New York City, possibly, if she knew about his plans, with intentions of joining Brown. By then, it was too late. The raid had already been
launched.

It was ridiculously bungled from start to finish. On the morning of
October 16, Brown cut telegraph lines connecting Harpers Ferry with the
outside world and seized the small town's federal arsenal. His assumption
was that slaves in the surrounding areas would immediately rise up on
hearing of his action and join him. They did not, and Brown quickly found
himself and his men bottled up inside the arsenal building with no chance
of escape. They were quickly surrounded by marines commanded by
Lieutenant Colonel Robert E. Lee and a young subordinate named J. E. B.
Stuart. After a forty-eight hour battle, in which ten of Brown's men, including two of his sons, were wounded or killed, Brown tried to negotiate his
way out of his predicament. The marines stormed the building, capturing
the wounded Brown and six of his companions. Five of his ill-fated band,
who were not in the arsenal, escaped, including another of Brown's sons, as
well as the only black man from Canada who finally wound up joining the
plot. Several members of the Secret Six, panicked that their involvement in
the failed raid would be made public, started packing for Canada.

Still recovering from his wounds, Brown, sometimes so weak he could
barely stand, was tried for treason ten days later. His trial lasted less than a
week, and the jury deliberated for less than an hour before sentencing him
to death. He was hanged a month later.

On the morning of the botched raid, Tubman, hundreds of miles north
of Harpers Ferry, sensed that something was wrong but couldn't put her
finger on the source of her unease. She finally got enough clarity to conclude that Brown was in danger's way. After she received word of the
unsuccessful raid that killed two of his sons, she recalled the dream she'd
had about the serpent with Brown's face. It was then that she understood
the significance of the dream's two younger snakes being struck down. It
had been, she concluded, a prophetic vision of the raid at Harpers Ferry.

Tubman never lost her admiration for John Brown, nor her grief at his
violent death. Years later, when she founded a shelter in Auburn for indigent blacks, she insisted on calling it the John Brown Hall. She remarked at
least once that Brown's willingness to die for the sake of others made him
a Christ-like figure (Sanborn 1863). His death, she told a friend, accomplished more than "100 men would in living" (Larson 2003, 177). Tubman
also believed that Brown's martyrdom portended the inevitability that

slavery would be swept away during her own lifetime, a conviction that few other ex-slaves shared.

Had "General Tubman" actually accompanied Brown to Harpers Ferry, it's almost certain that she would have met her death. Either she would have been slain in the fighting at the arsenal, or she would have been captured afterward. Given her notoriety as a "stealer" of slaves, as well as the bounty that furious Eastern Shore slave owners had put on her head, it's likely that she would have been hanged, either alongside Brown in Virginia or back in Maryland.

"AFRICAN FURY" IN TROY

The Secret Six weren't the only ones who fled to Canada in the wake of Brown's disastrous raid. So did Tubman and her parents. Southern congressional legislators were pushing for a full investigation into Brown, his backers, and possible collaborators, and Tubman's name was mentioned several times in papers Brown indiscreetly had left behind. In mid-January, a U.S. marshal arrived in Auburn, probably looking for Tubman. By then, however, she and her parents had already returned to St. Catharines.

By early spring 1860, Tubman, leaving Ben and Rit in Canada for the time being, was back in New York lecturing. Learning she was back in the country, Gerrit Smith invited her to speak to an abolitionist gathering he planned to host in Boston. On her way eastward at the end of April, Tubman stopped in Troy, New York, to visit her cousin John Hooper. There she participated in—and by some accounts, led—the rescue of the fugitive slave Charles Nalle.

It had been five months since Brown's execution, and during that time, Tubman's grief and anger had settled deeply within her. The ferocity with which she acted in the Nalle rescue was surely fueled by a resolution to honor the memory of John Brown by living up to his faith in her as a warrior. Her participation must have given her a good deal of satisfaction. It also, incidentally, served as a dress rehearsal for her later career as a Union scout and spy in the Civil War.

Charles Nalle had fled his Virginia slave master, a man named Blucher Hansbrough, less than two years earlier. Taking his wife and six children with him, he initially settled with them in Columbia, Pennsylvania, a town nestled on the left bank of the Susquehanna River not far from the Maryland border. Feeling unsafe there, Nalle headed north to find work and a new home for his family, leaving behind his pregnant wife and his children, and promising to send for them once he got settled. He felt relatively comfortable doing this because his wife was a free woman and safe, so he thought, from slave catchers.

He was mistaken. Mrs. Nalle was arrested soon after his departure to the north, not because she was a fugitive herself but on the grounds that she had aided in the escape of her husband. Perhaps her arrest was intended as a lure to draw Nalle back to captivity. At any rate, she was thrown into a Washington, D.C., jail cell. It's unknown who took charge of the Nalle children.

When he received word of his wife's incarceration, Nalle, by this time working as a coachman in Troy, sought out a lawyer. Illiterate himself, he wanted the attorney, Horace Avril, to write letters both to his wife and others who might assist in getting her out of jail. Whether out of a sense of duty to obey the 1850 Fugitive Slave Act or (more likely) in the hope of collecting a bounty, Avril instead got in touch with Bulcher Hansbrough, who promptly requested a warrant for Nalle's arrest. The fugitive slave was seized by Troy officers of the law on April 27 and taken to the State Street office of the U.S. commissioner to await his hearing before a local judge, who would be bound by law to immediately order his return to bondage.

Word of Nalle's arrest spread quickly among Troy's black community, thanks in large part to the efforts of William Henry, a black grocer and abolitionist with whom he was boarding. As local attorney Martin Townsend scurried to obtain a writ of habeas corpus, Henry gathered a large and increasingly agitated antislavery crowd in front of the building in which Nalle was a prisoner. Alarmed town officials, seeing that trouble was brewing, may have been unpleasantly reminded of rescue attempts elsewhere that had ended in violence. There had been several of them since the passage of the Fugitive Slave Act.

On September 11, 1851, nearly a year to the day that Congress approved the Act, a riot broke out in the Pennsylvania village of Christiania between runaway slaves and the white posse members who came to recapture them. Led by Edwin Gorsuch, the Marylander from whom the slaves had escaped, the band of slave catchers demanded their surrender. Christiana's vigilance committee, headed by an ex-slave named William Parker, had offered them asylum and refused to give them up. "Where do you see it in Scripture," Parker demanded, "that a man should traffic in his brother's blood?" Gorsuch, infuriated by the question, retorted, "Do you call a nigger my brother?" Parker defiantly answered in the affirmative, and then shots rang out (Parker 1866, 285). Gorsuch was killed and the posse retreated without their quarry. Three years later, a federal jury deliberated for only twenty minutes before acquitting the slaves and their white supporters on the charges of murder and treason.

Less than a month after the Christiana riot, another one broke out in Syracuse, New York. A fugitive by the name of William "Jerry" Henry (some newspapers at the time called him "McHenry") had been captured. As he was being led to the U.S. commissioner's office, he slipped away and disappeared into a crowd that had gathered to protest his arrest. Recaptured, he was taken to the city jail, which was then pelted with stones and bricks by the angry crowd. An ex-slave and minister, Samuel Ringgold Ward, called for immediate action to rescue Jerry. "Fellow citizens," he shouted, "upon us, the voters of New York State, to a very great extent, rests the responsibility of this Fugitive Slave Law. It is for us to say whether this enactment shall continue to stain our statute books, or be swept away into merited oblivion!" (Ward 2010, 65). Urged on by Ward, the crowd broke through the jail doors and whisked Jerry away to safety.

The rescue attempt that especially drew the nation's attention was unsuccessful. It occurred in May 1854 in Boston. Anthony Burns, a young Virginia slave who had made his way to freedom by stowing away on a northbound ship, was captured by federal commissioners and ordered back to his master. A mass protest meeting was held in Faneuil Hall, after which a mob of men, led by Thomas Wentworth Higginson, rushed the nearby courthouse where Burns was being held, in a bid to rescue him. During the melee, a deputy marshal was killed, prompting Boston's mayor to call up four companies of marines, complete with artillery, to maintain peace and order. The courthouse was also encircled by heavy harbor chains to hold the crowd back. Burns was marched to the docks surrounded by armed marines. Along the way, an estimated ten thousand Bostonians lined the streets in protest, and black mourning crepe was draped from windows and on doors. Afterward, it came to light that the government had spent at least $20,000 to return a slave who was subsequently sold by his angry master for $962.00. Opponents of slavery condemned the whole affair as scandalously immoral, but even slavery proponents found it ludicrous.

These and similarly dramatic acts of resistance to the recapture of fugitive slaves demonstrated the antipathy many northerners felt for the Fugitive Slave Act. It was certainly a motive in the rescue of Charles Nalle.

Attracted by the commotion, Tubman joined the crowd and concocted a plan with William Henry to scout out the situation from the inside. Posing as a somewhat dim-witted and aged food vendor, Tubman—not yet forty years of age—made her way into the building. She was present when the inevitable judgment to return Nalle to Virginia was made. Upon hearing it, a desperate Nalle broke away and balanced himself on a window ledge as if he intended to jump. Bailiffs quickly dragged him back and manacled him.

This was when Tubman acted. Surprising everyone in the room by her sudden transformation from an old woman into a frenzied younger one, she grabbed hold of Nalle and began dragging him, still manacled, down the stairs toward the crowd surrounding the building. According to the account she later told Bradford, Tubman "seized one officer and pulled him down, then another, and tore him away from the man [Nalle]; and keeping her arms about the slave, she cried to her friends: 'Drag us out! Drag him to the river! Drown him! But don't let them have him!' They were knocked down together, and while down she tore off her sunbonnet and tied it on the head of the fugitive," apparently hoping to confuse authorities (Bradford 1869, 90).

The crowd succeeded in grabbing the by now half-conscious and bloody Nalle away from the officers. They carried him bodily down to the Hudson River, where they loaded him and a few hundred supporters, including Tubman, onto a ferry away from his pursuers. Additional officers of the law were waiting on the West Troy side of the river, and, when the ferry docked, they seized Nalle a second time and marched him off to a judge's office. Tubman rallied the crowd to storm the building and, according to the April 27 issue of the *Troy Whig*, the door was finally pulled open by "an immense Negro" who was immediately stunned by the blunt end of a hatchet wielded by a deputy sheriff. In falling, he blocked the door from being shut again, and "when the men who led the assault upon the door of Judge Stewart's office were stricken down, Harriet and a number of other colored women rushed over their bodies," grabbed Nalle, threw him in a wagon, and whisked him away to Canada (Bradford 1886, 127). Tubman later boasted that she hoisted Nalle "acrossed my shoulder like a bag o' meal and took him away out of there" (Larson 2003, 182).

The next day, the *Troy Times* praised the courage of the men and women, but especially the blacks, who had pulled off the rescue. "The rescuers numbered many of our most respectable citizens—lawyers, editors, public men and private individuals. The rank and file, though, were black, and African fury is entitled to claim the greatest share in the rescue" (American Anti-Slavery Society 1861, 62).

It was this same "African fury" that John Brown had hoped to ignite by his raid on Harpers Ferry. It must've gratified Tubman to have acted in his spirit in helping to rescue Nalle.

GENERAL TUBMAN GOES TO WAR

Following the dramatic rescue of Nalle, Tubman proceeded on to Boston, where she spent the summer months giving talks to various antislavery gatherings. One of the persons who heard her there was Louisa May Alcott, who, at twenty-seven, hadn't yet achieved the reputation she later enjoyed as the author of *Little Women*. One of Tubman's twentieth-century biographers speculates that she was the inspiration for a character in Alcott's 1873 novel *Work: A Story of Experience* (Humez 2003, 42).

On the Fourth of July, Tubman was a featured speaker at a suffrage meeting in Boston. The following day, William Lloyd Garrison reported her speech in the *Liberator*, calling her "a colored woman of the name of Moses." His praise infuriated Philadelphia-based proslavery author John Bell Robinson, who attacked Tubman's admirers. "What could be more insulting," he demanded, "after having lost over $50,000 worth of property by that deluded negress, than for a large congregation of whites and well educated people of Boston to endorse such an imposition on the Constitutional rights of the slave States[?]" (Clinton 2004, 143).

Despite a lively speaking schedule, Tubman was feeling strapped for cash. Most of the money she earned went to support her parents and Canadian refugees. She kept back for herself just barely enough to meet her own needs. She was also putting aside as much money as she could for what proved to be her last rescue mission to the Eastern Shore. As a consequence, she was way behind in her mortgage payments to Seward, who fortunately seemed not to be bothered by the delinquency.

As mentioned earlier, this final trip was Tubman's last attempt to rescue Rachel and her children from bondage. Unbeknown to Tubman, Rachel had died a few weeks earlier, and once Tubman was back in Maryland, it again proved impossible to save the children. Instead, Tubman led the Ennals, a family of six (some accounts say seven), three adults and three children, to freedom. The journey northward began sometime in November. The party arrived at Thomas Garrett's on December 1, and then proceeded all the way to St. Catharines.

It was an arduous rescue, probably the most difficult one Tubman made, mainly because the Underground Railroad routes leading out of the Eastern Shore had been disrupted and seriously compromised by the increased surveillance of slave owners in Dorchester County who were alarmed by the number of successful slave escapes.

Tubman ran into difficulties almost from the get-go. As Sarah Bradford told the story,

> Harriet came, just as morning broke, to a town, where a colored man had lived whose house had been one of her stations of the under-ground, or unseen railroad. They reached the house, and leaving her party huddled together in the middle of the street, in a pouring rain, Harriet went to the door, and gave the peculiar rap which was her customary signal to her friends. There was not the usual ready response, and she was obliged to repeat the signal several times. At length a window was raised, and the head of a white man appeared, with the gruff question, "Who are you?" and "What do you want?" Harriet asked after her friend, and was told that he had been obliged to leave for "harboring niggers." (Bradford 1886, 53–55)

Sensing danger, she immediately led her party into the cold waters of a nearby swamp. The white man apparently alerted authorities, because the party of runaways, crouched down on a bit of dry land in the swamp, could hear the sound of search parties. One of the Ennal children was an infant (Bradford says there were two infant twins) whom Tubman had to drug with laudanum to keep quiet until the patrols were out of earshot.

Tubman and her wards lay in hiding, hungry and freezing, all day long. "They were truly in a wretched condition, but Harriet's faith never wavered, her silent prayer still ascended, and she confidently expected help from some quarter or other" (Bradford 1886, 56). Around dusk, her prayer was answered. Tubman spied a man "dressed in Quaker garb" walking along the edge of the swamp, talking to himself. As he got closer, she realized that he was telling her that she would find a horse and provision-filled wagon in a nearby barn. Thanks to this guardian angel, they made their way out of the swamp and to the next Underground Railroad station up the line.

After that, the going remained slow and hard. Tubman and the refugees found little food along the way and less warmth. By the time they reached safety in Canada, Tubman was exhausted and had frostbite in both of her feet. She was in such bad shape that her relatives in St. Catharines insisted that she spend the rest of the winter months with them to recuperate from her ordeal.

It was just as well that she did. Slave catchers were roaming around Syracuse and Auburn looking for fugitives, and it's likely that one of their targets was Tubman, especially after Garrison had drawn attention to her in the *Liberator*. There was another reason to remain safely on the other side of the border: the drift toward civil war following Abraham Lincoln's election to the presidency in November 1860. Tubman's benefactor, William Seward, had been appointed Lincoln's Secretary of State, and he was doing everything he could to dissuade fire-eating secessionists from leading their states out of the Union. Tubman's abolitionist friends were afraid that Seward would be tempted to offer her up as one way of mollifying them. Given Seward's record on the slavery question, it was an unjust suspicion, and Tubman seemed not to share it. She nonetheless remained in Canada, although probably traveling back and forth a few times between Auburn and St. Catharines, until the war Sumner dreaded erupted in April with the attack on Fort Sumter and Lincoln's mustering of seventy-five thousand state militia volunteers.

Sometime that summer, Tubman traveled to Virginia's Fortress Monroe, located where the James River empties into the Chesapeake Bay, with General Benjamin Butler's Massachusetts volunteer brigade. In all likelihood, she went as an unpaid volunteer to help the hundreds of fugitive slaves or "contrabands of war," as Butler styled them, who flooded into Fortress Monroe seeking asylum.

By late fall, she was back in Boston for a meeting with Massachusetts governor John Andrew, a staunch abolitionist who wanted to enlist her in the Union war effort. In November, Union forces had captured South

Carolina's Port Royal, a barrier island just south of Charleston, giving them control of broad swathes of the rich Lowcountry. Hundreds of slaves, owned by cotton and rice planters, deserted to the Union stronghold. The army was ill-equipped to take care of them, even though it was more than willing to put them to work. So northern relief agencies began preparing, in cooperation with the U.S. Treasury Department, to send people and supplies to Port Royal to help the ex-slaves adjust to their new lives. The agency volunteers soon became known as "Gideon's Army."

Governor Andrew asked Tubman to join the New England Freedman's Aid Society, whose members intended to focus on educating Port Royal slaves and training them in self-supporting skills. Tubman readily agreed; because she was illiterate, she was designated a teacher of "domestic arts." After arranging for her parents to be cared for in her absence, she sailed with ninety other volunteers to South Carolina, the only person of color in the cohort.

Why did Tubman agree to Andrew's invitation? A simple explanation is that she believed that the war was the beginning of the end to slavery and

NEW ENGLAND FREEDMEN'S AID SOCIETY

Tubman departed for Port Royal, South Carolina, under the auspices of the New England Freedmen's Aid Society (NEFAS), a regional branch of the more extensive Freedmen's Aid Society (FAS). Founded in 1861 as an auxiliary of the American Missionary Association, the FAS' mandate was to send volunteers to the South during and after the Civil War to offer material assistance, skills training, and education to ex-slaves.

The New England branch of the FAS, initially called the Educational Commission, was organized in 1862, and charged with the "industrial, social, intellectual, moral, and religious education" of newly liberated slaves. Tubman was a member of the first group it dispatched to Port Royal, South Carolina. Although she was illiterate, commission leaders believed she could be of great benefit in earning the trust of fugitive slaves and teaching them life skills. She was paid $10 a month for her services by the commission, which officially changed its name to NEFAS in 1864.

The work of the NEFAS was largely underwritten by Methodist, Presbyterian, and Congregationalist churches, although the U.S. Treasury contributed some financing. It continued its work in the postwar South, opening dozens of schools and training scores of black educators before disbanding in 1874.

The society officially recognized Tubman's contributions in its journal, the *Freedmen's Record,* in March 1865, when Ednah Dow Cheney wrote an account of her life. In it, Cheney not only praised Tubman but also appealed to readers to offer financial assistance to her so that she could continue her relief work.

wanted to be part of it in any way she could. Teaching domestic arts wasn't exactly what John Brown had in mind for her when he called her "General Tubman," but if it furthered the Union cause, she was ready to accept the assignment.

Years afterward, however, Tubman told at least two persons that Andrew had something entirely different in mind in sending her south. Given her years of experience in dodging slave catchers and scouting out secret pathways, he believed that she would be a perfect spy for the Union forces stationed at Port Royal. As a black woman, she could explore behind enemy lines without raising suspicion. As an ex-slave, she could be more persuasive than a white soldier when it came to persuading Lowcountry slaves to flee from their masters or possibly even revolt.

As things turned out, at least as Tubman remembered them, her clandestine mission was scrapped at the last minute, and she was asked instead to distribute clothes to contrabands. If this is what happened, it's unknown from what source the countermand to Andrew's instructions came. But it wasn't long before the Union Army was glad to accept more martial services from General Tubman.

8

"This Black Heroine"

The good Lord has come down to deliver my people,
and I must go to help him.

—Harriet Tubman (May 2013, 406)

TUBMAN HEADS SOUTH

In May 1862, Tubman sailed down the Atlantic seaboard, traveling further south than she'd ever been. Her ship docked at Port Royal, an island off the South Carolina coast.

The landscape of coastal South Carolina—the Lowcountry, as it's called—would have looked somewhat familiar to her from her Eastern Shore days: wooded areas, swamps, jagged peninsulas, scattered islands, and lots of marshland. What she couldn't have anticipated was just how dreadfully hot and humid the area would become as summer progressed. It was an ideal climate for growing rice. Memories of her sisters who, years earlier, had been sold down south to labor in its sweltering heat must have crossed her mind.

Federal forces had captured Port Royal, one of the South's most important harbor islands, just six months earlier. Troops stationed in Beaufort, the island's primary town and Tubman's ultimate destination, were assigned to the rather ambitiously named Department of the South, comprised of South Carolina, Georgia, and Florida. They were literally surrounded to the north, south, and west by pockets of Confederate forces and on the east by the Atlantic Ocean. But they were in no danger. Despite the fact that some of the richest and most powerful southern families owned vast plantations in the Lowcountry, Confederate military presence in the region was minimal because marshes and swamps made an overland assault by Union troops impracticable. To make up for the relative absence of manpower on the ground, the navigable riverways leading into the plantations were plentifully mined with torpedoes, explosive devices fixed just below the waterline.

The Department of the South was commanded by Major General David Hunter, a West Pointer who arrived in South Carolina just nine months before Tubman. He was known as "Black Dave," partly because of his swarthy complexion but mainly because of his unabashed championing of slave abolition.

When Hunter arrived at his post, he discovered that he had hundreds of ex-slaves on his hands who had lived and labored in the coastal areas taken by the Union Army back in November. Contrabands, as slaves freed by the fortune of war were called, always grew in numbers as Union forces penetrated deeper into the South. But for sheer quantity of them this early in the war, the Department of the South took the prize. Feeding, clothing, and sheltering them proved to be an immense logistical problem.

Hunter was charged not only with extending Union-controlled territory but finding a way to make the liberated slaves useful to the Union cause. To help offset this difficulty, the Treasury Department helped fund what came to be known as the Port Royal Experiment. Northern teachers, nurses, and missionaries were recruited to travel to Beaufort to organize schools, medical clinics, churches, and vocational training. Their goal was to help freed slaves become self-sufficient enough to farm their own tracts of land and contribute materially to the federal war effort by supplying produce, cash crops, and labor.

As an abolitionist, Hunter found the work of the Port Royal Experiment exciting. As a soldier, it wasn't enough to satisfy his desire to integrate ex-slaves fully into the war effort as fighting soldiers. Two months after he took command of the Department of the South, he issued General Order number eleven, which declared that all slaves residing in the three states that comprised the Department were "forever free" (Pearson 1906, 341). He then promptly went about recruiting ex-slaves to serve as Union soldiers. When contrabands didn't enlist as eagerly as he'd expected they would, he took to drafting them. In mid-May, about the time Tubman arrived at Port Royal, Hunter ordered all able-bodied male slave refugees between the ages of eighteen and forty-five to come to his headquarters at Hilton Head and be mustered into the army. This created a high level of tension and resentment between ex-slaves and military authorities. As one of the Port Royal Experiment teachers observed, "The thing [ex-slaves] dread is being made to fight" for "Hunter's pet idea, a regiment of blacks" (Pearson 1906, 340).

Both Hunter's general order and his recruiting of blacks took Abraham Lincoln by surprise. Lincoln wasn't ready to declare a general abolition of slavery, fearing that doing so would alienate slaveholding border states, like Maryland and Kentucky, which had remained loyal to the Union. Moreover, he and most northern whites had grave reservations about the ability of blacks, especially ex-slaves, to serve as soldiers. Still, anyone familiar with Hunter's hatred of slavery shouldn't have been surprised by his actions because he'd made his position crystal clear as early as 1861. If given a military command in the Union forces, he promised, "I would advance south, proclaiming the negro free and arming him as I go. The Great God of the universe had determined that this is the only way in which this war is to be ended, and the sooner it is done the better" (Miller 1977, 67).

Lincoln, who at least in mid-1862 had a difference of opinion with the Great God of the universe when it came to emancipation, voided Hunter's declaration just a week after he issued it. He also ordered Hunter to disband the regiments of black troops he was enthusiastically training. Lincoln's response could have been much harsher. Hunter's critics in Congress and the northern press had called for his firing. Humiliated and angered by the president's public rebuke, Black Dave complied with Lincoln's orders—mostly. He kept one of the black regiments intact and continued drilling its members in the art of war.

Hunter's wasn't an entirely maverick move. Unknown to Lincoln, his secretary of war, Edwin Stanton, was in favor of enlisting blacks, and had, in fact, authorized the financing of Hunter's recruitment efforts. When Lincoln ordered Black Dave to cease and desist training ex-slaves as soldiers, Stanton remained silent, neither explicitly endorsing nor disagreeing with Lincoln's decision. But his silence was an implicit go-ahead, or at least that's how Hunter read it.

Tubman was taken aback by what she encountered in Beaufort. To begin with, she was one of the first northern blacks to arrive as part of the Port Royal Experiment, and this tended to isolate her from her mainly white coworkers, many of whom were willing enough to help ex-slaves but had no wish to socialize with black persons. Moreover, she found it difficult to get accustomed to the accents and Gullah patois spoken by many of the South Carolina refugees. At least initially, her time in Beaufort was lonely. That the town was chaotically packed with contraband ex-slaves with nothing to do and no place to go didn't make things any easier for her. Finally, she arrived just in time for the sickly season, which usually lasted from May until the first cool weather in October or November. The number of illnesses that struck down white soldiers and civilians alike during the sweltering months of summer was staggering. Dysentery, typhus, yellow fever, cholera, typhoid, pneumonia, smallpox, fever, and malaria decimated the ranks of troops stationed in the Department of the South. Throughout the Civil War, three out of every five soldiers died of disease unrelated to wounds. In the areas around Port Royal, the mortality rate was even higher.

Once she got her bearings, Tubman rolled up her sleeves and, with her usual determination, threw herself into work. She wound up doing a bit of everything. Her initial assignment was to manage a Beaufort house that the YMCA had organized as a center for the distribution of food and bibles to soldiers. Her primary focus quickly shifted to the contraband population, and she went to work in a hospital that had been set up for freed slaves. Her duties included bathing and feeding the sick and serving as a factotum for whatever nursing tasks needed done. She also used the woodlore she'd acquired over the years to search out medicinal herbs and plants.

GULLAH

When Tubman arrived at Port Royal, she encountered Gullah among the slave fugitives who streamed in from the Low Country of South Carolina. They were the descendants of Africans snatched from the west "rice coast" nations of Angola (the name Gullah may be an adulteration of Angola) and Sierra Leone, areas that were known as large rice producers. The Gullah were especially valued by Low Country rice planters for their expertise in growing the crop and their resistance to the humid climate and diseases associated with it.

Because Gullah were primarily concentrated in the Low Country of South Carolina and Georgia, they remained largely isolated from more assimilated slave cultures and thus retained many of their African customs, conventions, and language. One of the reasons Tubman found it so difficult to understand them is that the Creole they spoke was a combination of English and African similar to Sierra Leon's Krio. Unsurprisingly, whites as well as non-Gullah slaves took the Creole as a sign of savagery. As one planter wrote in the 1850s, "These low country negroes, living through generations of small contact with whites have hardly learned to speak intelligibly" (Blassingame 1979, 29).

The Gullah were particularly eager to serve the Union cause, and many of them fought with distinction in the 1st South Carolina Volunteer Infantry Regiment, an all-black unit commanded by Thomas Wentworth Higginson, the Massachusetts abolitionist and Tubman friend. Intrigued by their language, Higginson compiled lists of expressions and words, many of which are still spoken today by Gullah who remain in the Lowcountry and Sea Islands.

Her knowledge of them and her skill in concocting potions from them were so impressive that her aid was frequently requested by Union officers faced with dozens of laid-up soldiers.

She was especially helpful when an outbreak of dysentery among white soldiers stationed on the Georgia-Florida border threatened to lay low an entire regiment. The officer who asked for her help worried that his men were "dying off like sheep" before they ever saw action in the field (Bradford 1886, 51). Tubman recalled that she prepared a medicine from "roots which grew near the water which gave the disease." The unit's doctor, who was also down with dysentery, was her first patient. After drinking her concoction, "the disease stopped on him. And then he said, 'give it to the soldiers.' So I boiled up a great boiler of roots and herbs, and the General told a man to take two cans and go round and give it to all in the camp that needed it, and it cured them" (Telford in Larson 2003, 224–225).

In keeping with the spirit of the Port Royal Experiment, Tubman also sought ways to help the refugee slaves become more self-reliant. One of her schemes was the establishment of a laundry, which she hoped would provide them with a steady income from washing the clothes of northern soldiers and civilians. The building of the laundry was subsidized by a $200 grant from the Treasury Department. In exchange for her labor, Tubman, who never received a regular military salary, was also allowed to collect government rations.

It wasn't long before what ex-slaves perceived as her unfair privileges caused resentment on their part. Tubman, realizing that her work on their behalf would be for naught if they didn't trust her, relinquished her claim to government rations and began finding ways to support herself. So after putting in long days nursing the sick, she spent a good part of her nights washing linen, making root beer, and baking bread to earn money for her own upkeep and to send to her aging parents back in Auburn. Her capacity for hard and sustained physical labor was astounding.

Nor did Tubman's work stop there. There's evidence to suggest that she was also an advocate for ex-slaves when they were abused or taken advantage of by Union soldiers. William Wells Brown noted that once Union officers in Beaufort learned that Tubman was the famed Underground Railroad "Moses," they "never failed to tip their caps when meeting her" (Brown 1874, 536). Respect for her didn't always extend to other blacks. Predictably, many Union enlisted men—and perhaps some officers as well—were more than willing to mistreat refugee slaves, using them as unpaid servants or even sexually assaulting them. One of the army physicians stationed in Beaufort complained about the "brutal lusts" displayed by soldiers, and reported that some black women had actually been shot by their assailants for resisting unwanted advances (Clinton 2004, 158). On several occasions, Tubman protected vulnerable women, and even arranged for one of them to escape licentious advances by relocating to the North.

General Rufus Saxton arrived at Port Royal in the summer of 1862 to serve as military governor of the Department of the South (as distinct from its military commander, the post held by Hunter). Like General Hunter, Saxton was an advocate for enlisting black troops to fight for the Union. Unlike Hunter, however, he was more successful in doing so. By August, Lincoln had softened on the idea of black troops, and Stanton directed Saxton to raise five full "colored" regiments. The first to be formed was, appropriately, called the First South Carolina Volunteers, and Saxton recruited Thomas Wentworth Higginson, who had traded in a clergyman's pulpit and an author's pen for a warrior's sword, to command it.

Higginson had been active in abolitionist circles throughout the 1850s and was one of the Secret Six who funded John Brown's raid on Harpers Ferry in 1859. He knew Tubman and was delighted to learn on his arrival in South Carolina that she was there. Tubman, whom he described in a letter home as "a sort of nurse and general caretaker," greeted Higginson warmly and asked him to convey her greetings to his mother back in Cambridge, Massachusetts (Looby 2000, 250).

THE COMBAHEE RIVER RAID

It was pretty clear that a major reason Tubman wanted to head south was to help defeat rebels. Her support of John Brown's harebrained scheme to launch a slave revolt in Virginia, as well as some of her escapades as an Underground Railroad conductor, indicated that she was ready and willing to fight if given the opportunity.

Lincoln's hesitancy to emancipate, train, and arm free slaves as part of the war effort continuously rankled Tubman. She found his reluctance both witlessly impractical and ungodly. The North, she worried, would soon be depleted of young white men to fight the war. She was convinced that God wouldn't allow victory as long as Lincoln allowed the sin of slavery to continue. As she said to Massachusetts abolitionist Lydia Maria Child,

> They may send the flower of their young men down South, to die of the fever in the summer, and the ague in the winter . . . They may send them one year, two years, till they are *tired* of sending, or till they use up all the young men. All no use! God's ahead of master Lincoln. God won't let master Lincoln beat the South till he does *the right thing*. Master Lincoln, he's a great man, and I am a poor negro; but the negro can tell master Lincoln how to save the money and the young men. He can do it by setting the negroes free. Suppose that was an awful big snake down there, on the floor. He bite you. Folks all

scared, because you die. You send for a doctor to cut the bite; but the snake, rolled up there, and while the doctor doing it, he bite you *again*. The doctor dug out *that* bite; but while the doctor doing it, the snake, he spring up and bite you again; so he *keep* doing it, till you *kill* him. That's what master Lincoln ought to know. (Larson 2003, 206)

Saxton's eagerness to muster black troops, Stanton's go-ahead to do so, and the arrival of Higginson, an abolitionist dear to her heart, gave Tubman hope that the snake's day finally had come. When Lincoln issued his Emancipation Proclamation on January 1, 1863, Tubman was guardedly optimistic. Freedom was given only to slaves living in the rebellious states, not the ones that remained loyal to the Union. For Tubman, this was unacceptable. Only an end to slavery everywhere would satisfy her. But the Proclamation was better than nothing.

She was still chaffing to be more directly involved in the war effort. After nearly a year of nursing and feeding soldiers and contraband, she was eager to take on duties for which her experience as a slave rescuer on the Eastern Shore suited her. Higginson's arrival had given her an ally with direct access to Saxton. In early 1863, another military officer arrived at Beaufort who supported her desire to extend the scope of her activity. He was Colonel James Montgomery.

Unlike the well-bred and educated Higginson, Montgomery was a roughhewn man of action who had few inhibitions when it came to fighting the Confederates. He'd made a name for himself as a Jayhawker, a member of one of the free-state guerrilla bands that had fought proslavery ones in the Kansas Territory prior to the Civil War. As zealous—some would say fanatical—in his hatred of slavery as John Brown, and apparently motivated by similar religious zealotry, Montgomery was convinced that the only way to end human bondage was to throw out the rule book and hit the Confederates in any and every possible way. When he arrived in Beaufort, he was given command of the Second South Carolina Volunteers. Like Higginson's command, the Second South was a colored regiment.

Higginson had reservations about Montgomery from the start, correctly fearing that the Jayhawker's style and discipline was less conventional than his own. But he also recognized that Montgomery had actual battlefield experience, an advantage over Higginson. As Governor Andrew of Massachusetts astutely put it, although Higginson was a proper gentleman, he had never seen action. Montgomery had.

With Higginson and Montgomery as her sponsors, the range of Tubman's activities finally widened. She was given the authority (although never either appropriate official rank or pay) to recruit scouts from local refugee slaves who could guide and accompany her throughout the marshy

Lowcountry in search of rebel outposts and navigable routes. Provided with a small sum of money to bribe slaves who still lived in Confederate-held territory and fed information by her team of scouts, Tubman quickly got a good idea of the lay of the land to the north, south, and west of Port Royal.

Because of her appearance, Tubman was easily able to pass as a local slave during her expeditions had she been questioned by suspicious southerners. But she was also given a military pass, personally issued by General Hunter, for unimpeded movement within federal-held territory. The way in which he wrote it testified to the esteem in which he held Tubman: "Pass the bearer, Harriet Tubman, to Beaufort and back to this place [Hilton Head, Hunter's headquarters], and wherever she wishes to go; and give her free passage at all times, on all Government transports. Harriet was sent to me from Boston by Governor Andrew, of Massachusetts, and is a valuable woman." Hunter ended by pointing out that Tubman was "a servant of the Government" (Bradford 1886, 11). The fact that he felt it necessary to be so effusively complimentary of Tubman suggests that as a black woman, she may have run into some pushback by Union troops.

The Department of the South's primary military responsibility was to defend and hold the Sea Islands in the vicinity of Port Royal, thereby depriving the South of an important port; to push back whatever Confederate troops might be still holed up in the Lowcountry; and to seize contraband, both goods and slaves, from plantations in the region. As already noted, the marshy terrain of the Lowcountry made the overland movement of large bodies of troops impossible. Tubman's efforts in mapping out alternative routes, locations of rebel strongholds, and the whereabouts of working plantations for the Union army was especially invaluable.

Higginson and Montgomery were eager to test their colored regiments on the battlefield, but they proceeded cautiously. As dry runs for larger campaigns, both regiments engaged in small excursions. At the beginning of 1863, Higginson led his First South Carolina in a raiding foray up St. Mary's River, where his men came under fire for the first time. He reported that they conducted themselves admirably, insisting that "nobody knows anything about these men who has not seen them under fire" (Grigg 2004, 52).

Two months later, both the First and Second Volunteers engaged in a campaign to capture and occupy Jacksonville, Florida. Montgomery's men were still in training, and most of them hadn't even been supplied with rifles yet. They were nonetheless loaded onto federal gunboats that sailed down the coast until reaching Jacksonville. The written orders given the two colonels were both open-ended and grandiose: "to carry the proclamation of freedom to the enslaved; to call all loyal men into the service of the United States; to occupy as much of the State of Florida as possible with the forces under your command; and to neglect no means consistent with the usages of civilized warfare to weaken, harass, and annoy those who are in rebellion against the Government of the United States" (Higginson 1984, 108).

Upon arriving on the outskirts of Jacksonville and setting up camp, Montgomery's men, who had finally been given rifles, were set to drilling. Suddenly attacked by Confederate cavalry, the Second South Carolina, aided by Higginson's troops, defended themselves courageously, until they were forced back to the protection of the gunboats. Eventually artillery routed the Confederates, and the town of Jacksonville was secured. Both this campaign and the earlier one on St. Mary's River demonstrated that colored troops were more than capable of standing their ground and fighting. As one of the Second South Carolina's captains exuberantly wrote, Jacksonville Confederates had learned to their dismay "that a black man could stand up and pull a trigger and that a bullet from his rifle was as deadly a thing to receive as if a white man had fired it" (Grigg 2004, 54).

Both Higginson's and Montgomery's units remained in northern Florida until the end of March, venturing out on at least two more local expeditions. Eventually Hunter, desperately short of troops, recalled them both to Port Royal. The colored troops returned with a confidence that they couldn't have felt when they journeyed to Florida a month earlier, when they were green and untried recruits. By the time they returned home, they were soldiers who, in the parlance of the day, had "seen the elephant"— that is, had been in battle.

It's not known if Tubman accompanied either the St. Mary or Jacksonville expeditions. She very well could have, however, as either a scout or cook or even a nurse. What is certain is that she played a central role in a major military operation for which the earlier campaigns had prepared the black troops: a raid up the Combahee River in June 1863.

The Combahee is a meandering tidal river that serves as the dividing line between two Lowcountry counties. At the time of the raid, it was bordered on either side in many places by marshes, thereby making the river the best transportation highway for the plantations in the area.

These were some of the wealthiest and oldest plantations in all of South Carolina. Most of their owners—the Middleton, Heyward, Lowndes, and Nicol families—made their fortunes from rice, a crop so lucrative that it was known as "Carolina gold." Their lands were located upriver, where the tidal flow switched from salt to fresh water. Marshland along the river had been ditched and diked to grow rice. Downriver planters' primary cash crop was cotton, grown well away from the salt marshes created by Combahee overflow. Both rice and cotton required extensive cultivation, and that meant that hundreds of slaves lived and worked on the plantations.

There were also a number of Confederate batteries scattered along the Combahee, remnants of the larger Confederate presence in the Lowcountry before the arrival of the Union Army. The number of troops manning the batteries and outposts was so small that their main purpose was to keep lookout for federal incursion upriver. Their presence was also intended to discourage slaves who knew of the proximity of the Union Army from getting restless.

The purposes of the Combahee raid were to rout remaining Confederates; seize what could be taken and destroy anything left; liberate slaves; and, in general, punish the wealthy slave owners in the area, who also just happened to be some of the most enthusiastic supporters of the Confederacy.

On the night of June 2, Colonel Montgomery, his Second South Carolina Volunteers, and Tubman boarded three army transports for the journey upriver. Two of the boats were armed with Parrott guns and howitzers. The unarmed one was more of a nuisance than an asset, running aground shortly after the small flotilla got underway.

Montgomery's plan was to proceed north on the river, halting to seize every available landing in quick, surgical strikes. Thanks to Tubman and her scouts—they were in the lead boat with Montgomery during the operation—the pilots knew exactly where the landings were to be found, as well as the places in the river that the Confederates had mined. She had also been able to find out the locations of barns where rice harvests, animals, and equipment were stored. Much of her intelligence had been gleaned from slaves who were promised freedom for information. Through them, she conveyed word to other slaves on the plantations to get themselves to landings on the night of the raid so that they could be picked up and carried to Beaufort and liberation. Montgomery would signal to them by having the boats blow their whistles as they approached the landings.

Thanks to Tubman's thorough scouting as well as the well-trained performance of the black troops under Montgomery's command, the raid was a smashing success. Large stores of warehoused rice and other crops were confiscated or burned, as were residences and outbuildings. Floodgates that regulated the flow of water into the rice fields were smashed, flooding and destroying the crop. Horses, cattle, and sheep were rounded up and driven on board. The few remaining Confederate soldiers quickly scattered after firing off a few token shots. The plantation families had already fled upon getting news of the flotilla coming toward them.

Everywhere there were slaves running toward the landings, sometimes excited to the point of hysteria at the prospect of "Mr. Lincoln's army" coming to rescue them from bondage. One of the white officers on the raid wrote about the exhilaration of the liberated slaves. "They rushed toward us running over with delight, and overwhelming us with blessings. 'Lord bless you, Mass,' they would cry, often with tears running down their dark cheeks and cling to our hands, knees, clothing, and weapons. 'De Lord bless you. We been expecting you and prayin' for you this long time! Oh Massa, thank de Lord you come at last!'" (Grigg 2004, 74).

Tubman left an even more vivid description of the joyful hubbub.

> I never see such a sight. We laughed, and laughed, and laughed. Here you'd see a woman with a pail on her head, rice a smokin' in it just as she'd taken it from the fire, young one hanging on behind, one hand round her forehead to hold on, t'other hand digging into the rice-pot, eating with all its might; hold of her dress two or three more; down her back a bag with a pig in it. One woman brought two pigs, a white one and a black one; we took 'em all on board; named the white pig Beauregard, and the black pig Jeff Davis. Sometimes the women would come with twins hangin' round their necks; 'pears like I never see so many twins in my life; bags on their shoulders, baskets on their heads, and young ones taggin' behind, all loaded; pigs squealing, chickens screaming, young ones squalling. (Bradford 1886, 53)

The general uproar reminded Tubman, she later said, of a biblical story dear to her heart, of "the children of Israel, coming out of Egypt" (Telford in Larson 2003, 214).

It might have been at this point in the raid that Tubman had her own misadventure. "In coming on board the boat," she recalled, "I was carrying two pigs for a poor sick woman, who had a child to carry, and the order 'double quick' was given, and I started to run, stepped on my dress, it being rather long, and fell and tore it almost off, so that when I got on board the boat, there was hardly anything left of it but shreds" (Telford in Larson 2003, 219). There and then, she decided that long dresses were utterly unsuitable in such circumstances, and vowed to instead wear bloomers.

At one point, panic broke out among the slaves waiting on the riverbanks to be picked up by oar boats and transported to the larger vessels. Terrified that they would be left behind, they overcrowded the boats, risking capsizing them. Seeing what was happening, Montgomery called upon Tubman to help calm the crowd. "I didn't know what to say," she recalled. But then she remembered how useful singing had been during her Underground Railroad days to both communicate and soothe. "I looked at them about two minutes, and then I sung to them." The slaves on the banks began singing with her and shouting "Glory!" Eventually order was restored and all of them were taken aboard (Bradford 1886, 53).

The two transport boats, loaded with some seven hundred fifty rescued slaves (the exact number is uncertain), endured a violent storm on the way back to Beaufort. By any reckoning, the mission had been a success, thanks largely to the efforts of Tubman and her informants. As a bonus to everything else the raid accomplished, nearly two hundred of the rescued slaves signed on as soldiers under Montgomery.

A reporter from the *Wisconsin State Journal* happened to be in Beaufort when the Second South Carolina disembarked, and he filed a story on the raid that praised in high tones "this black heroine" who guided the soldiers up the Combahee. As a scout for the Union Army, Tubman, he wrote, "courageously penetrated the enemy's lines" to discover their "situation and condition." Then, in a sentence whose praise suggested the depth of his admiration for her, he declared that "in patriotism, sagacity, energy, ability, and all that elevates human character, she is head and shoulders above the many who vaunt their patriotism and boast their philanthropy." He even suggested that the "cuticle" or skin—meaning white—in which these braggarts swaggered was what gave them their mistaken sense of superiority (Larson 2003, 216).

In the meantime, Tubman dictated a letter to Franklin Sanborn, abolitionist, member of the Secret Six supporters of John Brown, and editor of Boston's *The Commonwealth* newspaper, whom she had met in her Underground Railroad days. Surely, she said, the Combahee River raid would show the white world that "we colored people are entitled to some credit for that exploit" (Larson 2003, 219). In July, Sanborn published her letter as well as a biographical sketch of her, the first ever written. In addition to telling her story, part of his motive was to solicit public assistance for her parents, for whose welfare Tubman continuously worried, and to pay down the mortgage on her Auburn home. It worked. Donations rolled in. There was an unexpected consequence, too. Sanborn's article made Tubman's name known to a wider audience than abolitionist circles.

Flush with their success on the river raid, Montgomery and his men were eager for their next venture, which was the capture of Darien, Georgia. Tubman sat this one out, remaining in Beaufort to work with the new refugees collected from the Combahee plantations. Traveling down the coast with the Second South Carolina was a newly arrived colored unit, the Massachusetts Fifty-Fourth, commanded by Colonel Robert Shaw. Upon arriving in Darien, Montgomery reverted to the guerrilla tactics he'd employed in Bleeding Kansas years earlier and ordered the entire town burned, giving free rein to his soldiers to loot. When Shaw, disgusted by what he considered to be a war crime, objected, Montgomery swept his concerns to one side. Rebels, he replied, had to be made to feel the consequences of provoking a real war (Clinton 2004, 175).

Shaw wasn't the only white officer disturbed by Montgomery's way of waging war, including his scorched earth pattern of destruction during the Combahee River raid. Higginson was also troubled by it, calling them detestable and complaining that he was working hard "to coerce him into my notions of civilized warfare" (Looby 2000, 158).

The dismay and even disgust felt by some of Montgomery's fellow Union officers was nothing compared to the outrage voiced by the Southern press.

In a June 19 article in *The Charleston Mercury*, the Combahee raid was condemned as "subversive of every custom of war since the time of the Crusades, and is in violation of every law which governs the conduct of nations towards each other." Montgomery's scorched earth "violation of the laws and customs of all civilized nations is gross, palpable and indisputable," concluded the *Mercury*, and was just another indication that the North would use any unscrupulous means possible to vanquish the South.

Tubman, however, was not one of Montgomery's detractors. She wholeheartedly agreed with his conviction that God approved of harsh measures against slaveholders. Slavery was an abomination, and slave owners evil men and women whom the righteous were called to smite, just as Moses did Pharaoh and Jesus the money changers.

JAYHAWKERS

Colonel James Montgomery served as a Jayhawker in the guerrilla warfare that erupted in 1856 in Kansas and Missouri between opponents and proponents of slavery. Although the origin of the term is uncertain, antislavery fighters were generally referred to as Jayhawkers, and proslavery ones as Border Ruffians or Bushwackers.

Kansas became a battleground after the Kansas-Nebraska Act of 1854 determined that the U.S. territories of Kansas and Nebraska should determine for themselves whether or not to allow slavery within their borders. The assumption was that the northernmost part of the region, Nebraska, would vote to become a free state. Kansas, bordered by the slave state of Missouri, was up for grabs, and, in short order, hundreds of pro- and antislavery families flooded the border to influence the referendum.

The migration also brought in militia-like groups of men who claimed to be defending one side or the other in the slavery debate. The abolitionist John Brown and his sons were some of the fighters who traveled to Kansas for that purpose. All too often, these men were simple brigands who took advantage of the volatile situation to rob and ransack under the pretense of ideology. Jayhawkers and Border Ruffians alike were often brutal in their methods and indiscriminate in their violence.

When the civil war that had been going on in Kansas erupted into a nationwide conflict, many of the Jayhawker and Border Ruffian militia were mustered into the Union and Confederate armies. But their reputations for violence endured. After becoming an army officer, James Montgomery participated, for example, in a short-lived reign of terror against proslavery families in western Missouri, and he continued to employ scorched-earth tactics in the South Carolina Low Country. Although his tactics were distasteful to regular army officers as well as principled volunteers such as Thomas Wentworth Higginson and Robert Shaw, they were adopted by General William Tecumseh Sherman during his infamous March through Georgia.

CRIMSON CROP

The young colonel who objected to what he referred to as Montgomery's "Indian style of fighting," Robert Gould Shaw, came from a Boston Brahmin family (Duncan 1999, 42). Born into wealth, educated in Europe and at Harvard, and connected either through blood or society with the leading lights of New England culture, Shaw's immediate family members, especially his mother, were ardent abolitionists. So when he enlisted in the army at the start of the war, he was moved by a dislike of slavery as much as by patriotism. He saw action at Antietam, sustaining a serious wound that required a goodly period of recovery back in Boston.

Governor John Andrew, another zealous opponent of slavery who had arranged for Tubman to go to Beaufort, wanted to put together an all-black Massachusetts regiment, and he took advantage of the twenty-five-year-old Shaw's Boston convalescence to recruit him as its commander. After months of training, Shaw and his unit, the Massachusetts Fifty-Fourth, arrived in Beaufort on June 3. Two days later, they accompanied Montgomery to Darien, Georgia.

Humiliated by his presence at the town's burning, Shaw hoped to salvage the honor of his regiment in an assault planned against Fort Wagner, a Confederate stronghold on Morris Island, just outside Charleston's harbor. The plan was that if Wagner could be taken, Charleston would be wide open for invasion by land and sea.

To Shaw's regret, the role assigned the Fifty-Fourth was initially the modest one of simply serving as rear guard for the main attack force. But on July 16, several of its companies held off a Confederate attack long enough for a white regiment to retreat. The Fifty-Fourth had proved its mettle and, as a reward for bravery, was invited to be one of the leading regiments in the assault on Fort Wagner. Shaw eagerly accepted.

At twilight on July 18, the men of the Fifty-Fourth Massachusetts prepared to march on Fort Wagner. Both they and their young commander felt the weight of history on their shoulders. They knew that their conduct in the assault would affect how other recently mustered all-black units in the Union Army would be viewed. White skepticism about the black man's stomach for fighting, despite earlier displays of courage, still ran high in the North and was positively mocked in the South.

Although historians have discovered no corroboration for the claim, Harriet Tubman swore to her dying day that she was with the Fifty-Fourth as it began the assault on the high-packed sand walls of Fort Wagner. She claimed, in fact, that she prepared Colonel Shaw's last meal with her own hands. If she was telling the truth—and there's no good reason to doubt her—she would have accompanied the regiment on its rapid march to the Fort Wagner showdown.

Tubman also claimed to have witnessed the battle, even if only from afar. It didn't last long. As Shaw and his men double-timed toward the fort, wave after wave of them were slaughtered by savage volleys from Confederate cannon and musket. The Fifty-Fourth lost over 250 men, 40 percent of the regiment's total strength. Among the fallen was Shaw, who managed to reach the fort's parapet and dramatically brandish his sword before being mowed down. He was stripped and ignominiously tossed into a common grave with his slain men by the Confederate victors.

The nation was horrified by the Fifty-Fourth's loses but stirred by its remarkable courage. Its soldiers had shown once and for all that "colored" troops could fight just as well as white ones. Tubman, watching the slaughter from a distance, was too stunned by the sheer destruction of the assault to pay attention, at least right away, to the heroism. As she hauntingly remembered the horrible fighting,

> And then we saw the lightning, and that was the guns; and then we heard the thunder, and that was the big guns; and then we heard the rain falling, and that was drops of blood falling; and when we came to get in the crops, it was dead men that we reaped. (Conrad 1943, 181)

Wounded white soldiers were evacuated to Hilton Head, where Clara Barton and her team of nurses awaited them. Wounded black soldiers were shipped to Beaufort. Tubman traveled with them, doing her best to tend to their grievous injuries. Upon arrival, the men were carried in stretchers to an abandoned mansion that was designated General Hospital #10 for Colored Troops. Because fighting continued around Fort Wagner despite the failure of the initial assault, new convoys of wounded black soldiers arrived every day.

Conditions were primitive. Most of the men lay on the bare floor. A few of the luckier ones were on thin and filthy blankets. Wounds festered, fevers rose, and limbs were amputated without the benefit of anesthesia. Besides Tubman, there were only two physicians and one nurse to look after the more than five hundred patients.

The one bright spot in all this misery was that food was plentiful. Former slaves in the area who had been liberated by the Union Army gratefully supplied the wounded black soldiers with vegetables and fruit. For Tubman, tending the men was one long frustration. As she later described her experience,

> I'd go to the hospital early every morning. I'd get a big chunk of ice, and put it in a basin, and fill it with water; then I'd take a sponge and begin. First man I'd come to, I'd thrash away the flies and they'd rise, they would, like bees around a hive. Then I'd begin to bathe the wounds, and by the time I'd bathed off three or four, the fire and heat would have melted the ice and made the water warm, and it would be as red as clear blood. Then I'd go

and get some ice, and by the time I got to the next ones, the flies would be round the first ones black and thick as ever. (Bradford 1886, 51)

By the time that summer of suffering and sweltering drew to a close, Tubman was exhausted. She'd labored for the Union cause in the South a solid year-and-a-half. For the time being, she had nothing more to give. Sensing that her own health was in jeopardy, she realized she needed a rest. So she requested and received leave to return to her home in Auburn, both to recuperate her strength and to see her parents, whom she had missed dreadfully.

"THE COUNTRY OWES HER MUCH"

Tubman was gratified to discover that her parents were doing well. She stayed with them a few months, catching up with friends and family members, and then traveled in November to visit her brother Henry, who had settled in Ontario. By mid-November, she was back in the Department of the South. Its new commander, General Quincy Adams Gillmore, sent her to Folly Island, where she was put to work cooking and washing clothes at the commander's headquarters but also, and more importantly, interviewing refugee slaves to glean whatever military intelligence they might be able to provide. One visitor to the island reported that Tubman soon wanted to return home, but Gillmore thought her work with "contrabands escaping from the rebels too valuable to lose" (Larson 2003, 222). Apparently she supervised a number of scouts and spies while on Folly Island, because she was given $100 for "Secret Service" work. The money was used to recruit and pay informants (Grigg 2004, 97).

In early 1864, Tubman joined several regiments of white and black troops, including the Massachusetts Fifty-Fourth and Montgomery's Second South Carolina, intent on wreaking havoc in northeastern Florida. In all likelihood, her job was to cook and launder. As things turned out, her services as nurse were also needed. Upon arriving near the town of Olustee, Union forces encountered Confederate regiments, and one of the bloodiest battles of the war erupted. Before the Union forces retreated, one of the colored regiments was shattered, losing over half its troops. As the Confederates advanced, they killed many of the wounded black soldiers left on the ground. The rout created such an outcry in the North that any plans to retake Florida, a state that had little military value anyway, were shelved.

The wounded soldiers who made it off the battlefield were shipped to either Sanderson or Jacksonville, two Florida towns under federal control. Tubman probably nursed them there before returning with those fit to travel to Beaufort. Her duties as a military nurse continued throughout the entire spring of 1864, and she performed them with expertise and conscientiousness. One of the Department of the South's surgeons praised her medical skills and industry, "particularly her kindness to the sick and suffering of her own race" (Bradford 1886, 74).

Tubman requested another leave of absence in June 1864. She fully intended to return to South Carolina afterward, but as things turned out, she never did. After visiting with friends in New York City and Boston and spending some time with her family in Auburn, Tubman traveled to Camp William Penn, located near Philadelphia, to visit colored regiments in training. While there, she was persuaded by nurses from the U.S. Sanitary Commission that her expertise in treating sick and wounded soldiers and contrabands could be put to better use at Fortress Monroe in Hampton, Virginia, than in Beaufort. Tubman arrived there in March 1865.

U.S. SANITARY COMMISSION

The casualties in the Civil War were enormous—over six hundred thousand deaths, many more than in World War II. Two-thirds of those who perished succumbed to diseases such as dysentery, measles, tetanus, and fever; those who were wounded in battle but survived often required long periods of convalescence. It became immediately clear after the First Battle of Bull Run that the war effort would require enormous medical resources.

In the summer of 1861, Congress endorsed the creation of the U.S. Sanitary Commission, a private relief agency that offered medical supplies and care to wounded and sick Union soldiers. Inspired by the British Sanitary Commission's activities during the Crimean War—activities that brought Florence Nightingale to the world's attention—the U.S. Commission helped establish, supply, and operate dozens of hospitals and some thirty rest-and-recuperation homes during the war. Many of the era's notable women, including Louisa May Alcott, Dorothea Dix, and Clara Barton, served at one time or another as nurses for the commission.

Run by a board of directors operating out of New York City, the commission was enormously successful in fund-raising, receiving during the war years over $400 million in today's currency. It hosted huge sanitary fairs in major cities across the north to solicit contributions, and, in an especially creative fundraising tactic, auctioned off a single bag of flour, which was then promptly donated back to the commission so many times that it alone brought in a quarter of a million dollars.

The sheer volume of wounded and ill soldiers needing attention was sometimes more than the commission could adequately handle, as Tubman discovered during her time at Fortress Monroe in the final month of the war.

The commission continued its work on behalf of soldiers for a full year after the war's end, disbanding in May 1866.

She discovered disarray and inefficiency everywhere. Medical supplies, clothing, and bedding and even foodstuffs were in short supply, siphoned off to fighting units or "liberated" by dishonest quartermasters. After struggling for nearly three months to work with what she was given, a frustrated Tubman traveled to Washington, D.C., to lobby for assistance. Surgeon General Joseph Barnes gave her a sympathetic hearing and assured her that the badly needed supplies would be forthcoming. He even promised Tubman that he intended to appoint her head nurse of the black hospital at Fortress Monroe, an acknowledgment of the role she had played throughout the war as well as, finally, recognition that would bring her a regular salary. It didn't take long after she returned to Fortress Monroe in late July to realize that neither supplies nor title would arrive, so she turned toward Auburn. For Tubman, the war was over.

From May 1862 to July 1865, Tubman served as an unsalaried cook, laundress, servant, scout, spy, and nurse for the Union Army. She had reconnoitered and gathered intelligence useful for military missions, and she had accompanied both colored and white troops on at least three campaigns. She had risked her own health to nurse contrabands and whites who were suffering from the miasma of illnesses that enveloped the coastal regions of South Carolina and Florida, and she had labored tirelessly to help refugee slaves become self-sufficient economically. She received small sums of money from the authorities from time to time—the largest amount was the onetime grant of $200 to construct the Beaufort washhouse—but much of those funds went to pay informants. From first to last, throughout her entire military service, she was forced to work long hours above and beyond her official duties in order to feed and clothe herself and send money back home to Auburn. Few civilians gave more to the army and received less in return during the Civil War.

Everyone who witnessed Tubman's dedicated service during the war years recognized the injustice done to her by the government. Three years after its end, no less a person than General Rufus Saxton, military governor of the Department of the South during Tubman's time there, wrote a glowing recommendation in support of her application for a government pension. He praised her for "services rendered in the Union Army during the late war. I can bear witness to the value of her services in South Carolina and Florida. She was employed in the hospitals and as a spy. She made many a raid inside the enemy's lines, displaying remarkable courage, zeal, and fidelity." Saxton insisted that she was "as deserving of a pension from the Government for her services as any other of its faithful servants" (Bradford 1886, 76).

The pension would be years in coming, and even then given but reluctantly.

On her way back to Auburn in the summer of 1865, Tubman traveled by train, using a military pass. When the conductor walked down the aisles to check passengers' tickets, he refused to believe that Tubman's pass was legitimate. What would an illiterate black woman be doing with such a thing? He ordered her to leave her seat. Tubman refused, and four white male passengers physically manhandled her and locked her into the baggage car. She fought back and suffered for it with a broken arm and ribs that dogged her for months to come.

After four years of bloody civil war, slavery in the United States was a thing of the past. Racial prejudice wasn't.

9

Impoverished Legend

Such a servant of the country should be well paid by the country.

—Gerrit Smith (Bradford 1869, 67)

THE MORE THINGS CHANGE

In January 1865, the U.S. Congress passed the Thirteenth Amendment, thereby outlawing "slavery [and] involuntary servitude except as a punishment for crime whereof the party shall have been duly convicted." Eleven months later, it was ratified as part of the U.S. Constitution. After almost two hundred fifty years, legal slavery in North America was a thing of the past.

One year later, Congress overrode the veto of President Andrew Johnson to pass the Civil Rights Act, granting citizenship and all of its associated rights to ex-slaves. In quick succession, the Fourteenth and Fifteenth Amendments, both of which constitutionally guaranteed those civil rights, were passed and ratified. Before long, and for the first time in the nation's history, black citizens were elected to state and even federal legislatures.

Unfortunately, legal equality didn't eradicate the racism that was spawned by and, in turn, fueled slavery. Blacks in both the North and South were frequently discriminated against when it came to educational and economic opportunities. For the most part, whites and blacks lived in separate communities. Whatever crossover took place was typically the consequence of whites employing blacks as field hands, domestic servants,

THIRTEENTH, FOURTEENTH, AND FIFTEENTH AMENDMENTS

Three constitutional amendments emerged from the Civil War experience that fundamentally changed the legal status of black Americans—although, it might be argued, making less difference in their actual life circumstances.

The Thirteenth Amendment, ratified on December 6, 1865, abolished slavery once and for all in the United States. Congress outlawed slavery for the District of Columbia in 1862, and the Emancipation Proclamation of January 1863 did the same in the rebellious states of the Confederacy. But after the Civil War ended, there was no legal proscription in place to prevent southern states from reinstating human bondage. The Thirteenth Amendment ended that ominous possibility.

Still, it was met with some disapproval, even by Republicans who favored emancipation, because of their fear that it freed slaves without providing them opportunity for advancement. Future president James Garfield spoke for these critics when he asked, "What is freedom? Is it the bare privilege of not being chained? If this is all, then freedom is a bitter mockery, a cruel delusion" (Foner 1988, 66).

The Fourteenth Amendment, ratified on July 9, 1868, granted, among other things, citizenship to ex-slaves and guaranteed them equal protection under the law. The authors of the amendment deliberately used only the broadest language in writing the bill, obviously intending to encourage the widest possible application of its equal protection provision. The language also opened a wedge for ex-slave state legislatures to enact so-called black rules, or laws that curtailed legal rights for blacks under one pretext or another.

The Fifteenth Amendment, which forbade states from denying enfranchisement "on account of race, color, or previous condition of servitude," was ratified on February 3, 1870. Theoretically, the amendment granted blacks the right to vote in state and federal elections. It also left open the possibility that states could require certain threshold standards or tests for qualification to vote that were often specifically designed to exclude blacks. The amendment also neglected to give women the right to vote, which suffragettes Elizabeth Cady Stanton and Susan B. Anthony publicly condemned as yet "another humiliation" for women.

---

or physical laborers. In many southern states, including Tubman's own Maryland, flimsy legal ploys for keeping ex-slaves in virtual indentured servitude were successfully carried out.

Perhaps predictably, racial relations in the defeated southern states went from bad to worse. Emancipated blacks who dared to exercise their new liberties infuriated many already simmering whites and led to outbursts of violent reprisals. Acts of aggression against blacks perpetrated by individuals or mobs resentful of the federally enforced Reconstruction erupted again and again. One of its victims was John Tubman, the man Harriet married in 1844 and who took another wife after she fled to the North.

A little over two years after the war ended, John Tubman was gunned down in Dorchester County by a white man named Robert Vincent. According to a Baltimore newspaper, the two men squabbled the morning of Tubman's death about removing ashes from a house owned by Vincent. Tempers flared, and Vincent became so enraged that he went after Tubman with an ax, who managed to flee to safety. Later that day, the two men met by chance, and the quarrel between them erupted again. This time, Vincent shot Tubman pointblank in the forehead. Tubman's thirteen-year-old son witnessed the murder and later testified at Vincent's trial, contradicting the assailant's claim that he'd acted in self-defense. But the youngster's account was ignored, and the jury delivered a not-guilty verdict after deliberating for only ten minutes.

Given her years of witnessing white men and women abuse slaves and freedmen alike, Tubman was probably under no illusion that the end of the war and the enactment of constitutional protections meant that blacks would suddenly be treated with respect and fairness. Her vicious treatment in October 1865 when returning home to Auburn aboard a train was a particularly unpleasant reminder that the more things changed, the more they stayed the same. What especially bothered Tubman was the unsympathetic response to her mistreatment by the fellow passengers, immigrants all, who witnessed it. "Pitch the nigger out!" they shouted as she was manhandled (Bradford 1869, 46). Apparently even immigrants, whose own social status was considered lowly by white natives, felt superior to blacks.

Justifiably indignant at being treated in such a way after all she'd sacrificed for the war effort, Tubman not only physically resisted the assault on the train but afterward explored the possibility of legal action against the Camden & Amboy Railroad Company. One passenger who saw the abuse, a young white man, came up to her afterward, urged her to sue, and gave her his card, telling her he'd be glad to serve as a witness. With the help of some abolitionist friends she'd known for years, ads were placed in newspapers asking the young man to come forward. A report about her injuries was also solicited from the doctor who treated Tubman after the manhandling. Ultimately and rather inexplicably, however, the suit was never brought forward, and so the indignity she'd endured on the train went unanswered. In this regard, Tubman experienced the unhappy lot of most postwar black citizens.

HARD TIMES

Indignity wasn't the only wound Tubman suffered on that train. Because of her injuries—a broken arm and ribs—Tubman was unable to do much physical work during the fall and winter of 1865. Yet she had a household of relatives depending on her. By the time she arrived in Auburn, at least nine people, one of them a boarder, were living in the small frame house she'd purchased from Seward. If it hadn't been for her sister-in-law Catherine, who dwelt with her two children in the house, everyone would've gone hungry that winter. Things were so bad that they were forced to tear up the fence around the house as firewood for cooking and heating. It didn't help matters that Tubman's aged parents grumbled about the impoverishment—especially, in her mother's case, the scarcity of tobacco and tea, "more essential to her than food or clothing" (Bradford 1901, 145).

At one point, the household was completely without food. Tubman went off by herself for a while to pray. Then, grabbing a large pot and accompanied by Catherine, she set off to the town's outdoor market. The two women walked from stall to stall, and slowly but surely kind-hearted tradesmen gave them items—a bone, an onion, a few potatoes, and so on—from which Tubman was able to make a stew to feed her family.

Still, had it not been for the generosity of Tubman's admirers and friends like Wendell Phillips, Martha Wright, and the families of William Lloyd Garrison and Gerrit Smith, her first postwar winter back in Auburn would have been disastrous. They and others contributed much needed money, food, and clothing to her household. Gerrit Smith's wife, having heard that Rit was worried about not having any white laying-out clothes to be buried in when she died (an event nearly two decades away), actually sent her a set. Tubman was grateful for the charity but, in all likelihood, humiliated as well. Soliciting money and supplies for the rescue of slaves during her Underground Railroad days hadn't bothered her at all. As one observer noted, it pained Tubman to ask for handouts for herself. "She had a good deal of that honest pride [which] makes her unwilling to beg" (Larson 2003, 234).

Begging was one thing, demanding what she felt she was owed her quite another. Tubman wasn't at all inhibited about asking for what she considered her due from the U.S. government: back pay for her service during the war. As we saw in chapter 8, Tubman wasn't paid on a regular basis for her wartime activities. Instead, she was occasionally given small amounts of money, which, for the most part, she used to pay scouts and spies or to support slave refugees.

As early as July 1865, Tubman had personally petitioned Secretary of State William Seward, still recovering from his attempted assassination weeks earlier, for assistance in receiving what she believed the government justly owed her. Seward forwarded Tubman's request to General "Black Dave" Hunter who, while effusive in his praise of her services, was unable to make any headway with the government accountants. So she and her relatives suffered through the winter of 1865 to 1866 as best they could, without the federal support that was rightly hers.

When spring arrived and Harriet had recuperated from her injuries, she set about with her usual industry to earn money for her family. She took in boarders, which generated a bit of income but only added to the over-crowding of her small house; cared for local children; and hired herself out to do washing and housecleaning for Auburn's white families—chores that must have struck her admirers as sorrowfully incommensurate with what, given her Underground Railroad experience and war service, she was capable of. Additionally, she and other members of her household wove and sold baskets. She also cultivated a vegetable garden, fruit trees, and chickens for both household consumption and the market.

All this effort barely kept the wolf away from Tubman's door, and, in November 1867, anticipating another hard winter, Tubman visited Gerrit Smith at his home in Peterboro, New York, in the hope that he could pull strings with the government to get her the wartime back pay she deserved. She came laden with a packet of testimonials from army officers that lauded her skills as a nurse and scout. Sallie Holley, a prewar abolitionist and postwar suffragette, was at the Smith home when Tubman arrived, listened to her, and immediately dashed off a letter that appeared on November 30, 1867, in the *National Anti-Slavery Standard*, the weekly newspaper of the American Anti-Slavery Society. In it, Holley lauded Tubman's role during the war and solicited support for her. Tubman, wrote Holley, had more than demonstrated "a courage and self-devotion to the welfare of others." Why, then, was she so neglected by a nation which instead ought to be gratefully generous to her?

Once again, nothing came of Tubman's efforts. This was especially unfortunate because the winter of 1867 to 1868 proved to be just as bad as she had feared it would be. Things eventually became so desperate in her household that Tubman was compelled to go begging.

> The snow was very deep for months, and Harriet and the old people were completely snowed-in in their little home. The old man [Tubman's father] was laid up with rheumatism, and Harriet could not leave home for a long time to procure supplies of corn, if she could have made her way into the city. At length, stern necessity compelled her to plunge through the drifts to the city, and she appeared at the house of one of her firm and fast friends, and was directed to the room of one of the young ladies. She began to walk up and down, as she always does when in trouble. At length she said, "Miss Annie?" "What, Harriet?" A long pause; then again, "Miss Annie?" "Well, what is it, Harriet?" This was repeated four times, when the young lady, looking up, saw her eyes filled with tears. She then insisted on knowing what she wanted. And with a great effort, she said, "Miss Annie, could you lend me a quarter till Monday? I never asked it before." Kind friends immediately supplied all the wants of the family, but on Monday Harriet appeared with the quarter she had borrowed. (Bradford 1869, 111–112)

As news spread of Tubman's dire situation, even the *Auburn Daily Advertiser* came to her defense by publishing a letter on January 22, 1868, that expressed indignation at the government's neglect of her. "She hasn't yet succeeded in procuring any assistance from the Government for the acknowledged services," the author of the letter noted, "especially in securing the scouts in South Carolina who were so very successful in piloting our army about Port Royal, Hilton Head, and Beaufort."

Sallie Holley's description of Tubman in the *National Anti-Slavery Standard* as a woman devoted to the service of others continued to be accurate even during the hard personal times she endured. On two occasions at Christmastime, in 1867 and 1868, just when things were bleakest for her, she organized bazaars to raise money for ex-slaves in the southern states. She solicited donations ranging from clothing to baked goods from Auburn's citizens, and set the town's women, black and white alike, to sewing aprons, pincushions, rag dolls, and towels, all of which were to be sold at the fundraisers. (The dolls, especially popular despite their high cost of three dollars, quickly sold out on both occasions.) The proceeds from the bazaars raised hundreds of much appreciated dollars.

In addition to coordinating the fundraisers, Tubman continued to solicit private donations from her circle of wealthy white friends for the support of southern freedmen as well as other causes such as the work of the Salvation Army. At one point, after she had once again hit up William Seward, he exasperatedly told her, "You have worked for others long enough . . . If you ask for a donation for *yourself* I will give it to you, but I will not help you to rob yourself for others" (Bradford 1869, 112). There's no evidence, however, that his scolding dissuaded Tubman whatsoever in her campaign to help ex-slaves.

Despite his occasional frustration with her, Tubman and Seward remained close to the end of his life. His admiration for her was genuine, and if he sometimes urged her to be less concerned for others and more concerned for herself, it was only because he was so fond of her. For her part, Tubman's gratitude to Seward for his years of financial generosity to both her and her causes—not to mention the house and property he had sold to her at much less than he could have received for it on the open market—never wavered. When he died in 1872, never having fully recovered from the terrible wounds he received on the night of Lincoln's assassination and emotionally broken by the passing of his beloved wife and daughter just a few years earlier, Tubman appeared at his funeral.

> The great man lay in his coffin. Friends, children, and admirers were gathered there. Everything that love and wealth could do had been done; around him were floral emblems of every possible shape and design, that human ingenuity could suggest, or money could purchase. Just before the coffin was to be closed, a woman black as night stole quietly in, and laying a wreath of field flowers on his feet, as quietly glided out again.

The woman, of course, was Tubman. Her biographer Sarah Bradford, who recorded this event, concluded her description in a characteristically sentimental way: "This was the simple tribute of our sable friend, and her last token of love and gratitude to her kind benefactor. I think he would have said, 'This woman hath done more than ye all.'" A bit saccharine, as was Bradford's wont. But there's little doubt that Seward would have been touched by Tubman's tribute (Bradford 1886, 89–90).

A HAPPY INTERLUDE

The bazaars, or "Harriet Tubman's fairs" as they came to be called, were held at Auburn's Central Presbyterian Church, a predominantly white congregation, well attended by the town's abolitionist citizens. On March 18, 1869, an event took place there that gave Tubman some much needed joy: the Reverend Henry Fowler joined her in wedlock with Nelson Davis, a man who had boarded with Tubman since the winter of 1866 to 1867.

Davis was born into slavery near Elizabeth City, North Carolina. He escaped and made his way to Oneida, New York, where he lived for a while as Nelson Charles. (He took the surname of Fred Charles, the man who had owned him. This wasn't uncommon among ex-slaves. As we saw in earlier chapters, Tubman's brothers took the surname Stewart after the man for whom they had worked while they were slaves in Maryland.) In September 1863, shortly after the federal army began accepting black troops, Tubman's future husband traveled to Philadelphia and enlisted. Shipped to the Department of the South, he fought at the liberation of Jacksonville, Florida, and the fierce Battle of Olustee, both in February 1864. There's no hard evidence that he met Tubman while in Florida, although it's possible. Mustered out of the army at Brownsville, Texas, in November 1865, he moved with a fellow soldier to Auburn a year later, found lodgings at Tubman's house, and henceforth called himself Charles Nelson Davis. Around Auburn, everyone called him Nelson.

Only one photograph of Davis survives, taken in 1887. He's seated, a walking stick resting between his legs, and smoking a pipe. Despite being described as "a magnificent specimen in appearance," a "big, black, true African," Davis suffered from tuberculosis and would die, still a youngish man, a year after being photographed (Larson 2003, 253).

Despite his having taken another wife after she escaped bondage, Tubman considered herself married to John Tubman until she received news of his death in 1867. By then, Davis had been boarding with her for nearly a year. Over the next few months, their relationship deepened. It was a May-September romance: Davis was in his early twenties, and Harriet twice that. By all accounts, neither of them was bothered by the difference in their ages.

Their wedding was a big affair, announced and reported in Auburn newspapers and attended by many of the town's leading citizens, attesting to the esteem and affection the locals felt for Tubman. Both come through in one newspaper account of the event.

> The audience was large, consisting of the friends of the parties and a large number of first families in the city. Ladies and gentlemen who were interested in Harriet, and who for years had advised and assisted her, came to see her married. After the ceremony Rev. Mr. Fowler made some very touching and happy allusions to their past trials and apparently plain sailing the parties now had, when the ceremony ended amid the congratulations of the assembly, and the happy couple were duly embarked on the journey of life. (Clinton 2004, 199)

Not everyone was as convinced as Reverend Fowler that the marriage was so fortunate. Alice Brickler, Tubman's great-niece, was one of them. She wrote off Davis as a "colorless creature" whose tubercular condition she found distinctly unromantic. A friend, apparently forgetting that this was Tubman's second marriage, opined that Tubman's many fund-raising activities marked her as distinctively nondomestic and hence unsuited for marital bliss. Such reservations proved without merit. Tubman and Davis were married nearly twenty years, with no signs of unhappiness or incompatibility.

Still, their future wasn't exactly the plain sailing Reverend Fowler predicted. Davis did his best to help out with household finances. He worked in the family garden, hired himself out for odd jobs around town, and established a small brick-making business next to Tubman's home, apparently having been taught the trade as a slave. But water from the brickyard tended to flood out Tubman's garden, and, as Davis's physical condition grew worse over the years, he was less able to work and more expensive and time-consuming to nurse. The marriage brought Tubman emotional comfort, but it did little, if anything, to ease her financial worries.

SCENES FROM HER LIFE

Tubman's unsuccessful efforts in late 1867 to secure back pay from the federal government, as well as the suffering she and her family endured that winter, resolved several of her abolitionist friends in New York to do something to help her in more substantial ways than occasional handouts. Inspired by the freedmen fund-raiding bazaars she organized, they realized that a book about her life and adventures would sell well at such events. In the spring of 1868, they enlisted a woman from the town of

Geneva, located just a few miles west of Auburn, to write it. The intention was for all the proceeds to go directly to Tubman.

The woman chosen to author the book was Sarah Hopkins Bradford. Although not particularly active in the abolitionist movement herself, Bradford was certainly familiar with friends and relatives who had been. She was the sister of one of Central Presbyterian Church's pastors, Samuel Hopkins, a strong antislavery man, and her father, a New York congressman, was a close friend of William H. Seward, sworn enemy of the peculiar institution. Moreover, she knew firsthand the sacrifices that had been made to abolish slavery. She and her husband lost two sons in the Civil War.

Bradford had made a minor name for herself as an author of children's stories. In keeping with mid-nineteenth century literary conventions, there's a good deal of sentimental moralizing in them that strikes twenty-first-century sensibilities as tiresomely mawkish. That same tone comes through in Bradford's account of Tubman's life.

The book, entitled *Scenes in the Life of Harriet Tubman*, was a rushed affair. As Bradford herself admitted in it, she prepared it quickly, in the space of just a few weeks, because she wished to finish it up before a planned trip to Europe. To her credit, she approached the task in as conscientious a way as time and talent permitted.

To collect information, Bradford invited Tubman to spend a few days in her Geneva home so that she could hear the ex-slave's stories and record them as faithfully as possible. She determined not to include any claim of Tubman's that couldn't be corroborated by others. "Much has been left out which would have been highly interesting," she wrote, "because of the impossibility of substantiating by the testimony of others the truth of Harriet's statements. But whenever it has been possible to find those who were cognizant with the facts stated, they have been corroborated in every particular" (Bradford 1869, 4). She wanted, she wrote, to be as accurate as possible because "the story of Harriet Tubman needs not the drapery of fiction; the bare unadorned facts are enough to stir the hearts of the friends of humanity, the friends of liberty, the lovers of their country" (Bradford 1869, 3).

Additionally, Bradford felt it important to solicit testimonials and affidavits from political and military celebrities who could attest to Tubman's character and contributions. This wasn't an uncommon practice when it came to the memoirs of ex-slaves both before and after the war. Publishers felt the need to assure white readers' skepticism that black men and women were capable of the intelligence required for writing or even dictating a book.

There was another reason for Bradford's inclusion of testimonials. She frankly confessed in the very opening lines of her biography that the book's primary purpose was to raise funds for Tubman, so she believed it especially important to assure readers of her subject's worth. Consequently, a sizeable portion of the book was given over to epistolary praises of Tubman from the likes of Gerrit Smith, Wendell Phillips, Frederick Douglass, and General Saxton, military governor of the Department of the South during the war. Bradford also included the complete 1863 *Commonwealth* article on Tubman written by Franklin Sanborn, as well as newspaper accounts of her participation in the 1860 rescue of Charles Nalle in Troy, New York. Rounding out the volume was a rather lurid essay of uncertain authorship about the physical abuse or "whipping" of slave women, a punishment that Tubman herself had received as a child when hired out to an impatient mistress. The result was that less than half of the book was actually written by Bradford herself.

Scenes in the Life of Harriet Tubman was, in many respects, a confused hodge-podge of misleading information and incorrect chronologies, through which subsequent biographers have had to navigate carefully. One explanation for the book's poor quality is undoubtedly the haste in which it was written. It's also the case that Tubman herself may have been confused about the earliest details of her life, misremembering sequences of events, places, and names. One person familiar with the crafting of the book remarked that Bradford worked "as well as she can with Harriets [sic] disjointed materials," a reference, perhaps, to the jumble of documents Harriet presented to Bradford. The person also acknowledged that Bradford must have had a hard time understanding "Harriet's desultory talk," a probable reference to Tubman's episodes of narcolepsy (Larson 2003, 246). Finally, as one historian perceptively argues, Bradford was more interested in eliciting sympathy for Tubman's financial situation than presenting an accurate portrait of her life. Consequently, despite Bradford's insistence that she was offering unadorned facts, the book "begins and ends with sentimental depictions of Tubman as a kind of suffering saint" (Humez 2003, 85). In short, *Scenes* was more along the lines of the morality tales Bradford wrote for children than an objective and scrupulous-about-the-truth biography.

Even some of Bradford's friends and acquaintances noted the book's shortcomings. One Tubman well-wisher—the man who generously underwrote the cost of printing *Scenes*—strongly recommended that the book's errors be corrected in future editions. Another grumbled in a private letter about the book's inaccuracies. Dismissively referring to Bradford as "Mrs. Thingumbob," the writer complained that Bradford "is continually apologizing for haste, and going off to Europe. If she hadn't time to do the subject justice, why undertake it?" (Larson 2003, 246).

Still, Bradford's efforts shouldn't be totally dismissed. For all its inaccuracies, *Scenes* still provides information about Tubman's earliest years, or at least her recollections of them, that otherwise might have been lost.

Moreover, many of the epistolary testimonials to Tubman reproduced in the book were later lost to fire. Thanks to Bradford, transcripts of them were preserved.

What we don't know is Tubman's own evaluation of Bradford's biography. During the Civil War, she had remarked to a friend that she hoped one day to learn to read and write so that she could compose her memoirs (McGowan and Kashatus 2011, 123). She clearly thought the story of her life was worth sharing with others, and the fact that, a few years after *Scenes* appeared Tubman asked Bradford to put out a new edition, suggests that she was pleased with her efforts.

What, if any, reservations Tubman may have had about the book is unknown. But the financial rewards from its publication pleased her. Although its official publication date was 1869, copies were available to sell at the December 1868 freedmen charity bazaar she organized. The price, one dollar a copy, was considered by at least one of Tubman's acquaintances as too high. Nevertheless, upward of seventy were sold. The next month, on January 9, 1869, the *Boston Commonwealth* published an ad announcing: "Mrs. Sarah H. Bradford, of Geneva, New York, has made quite an interesting memoir of this devoted woman, which has been published in neat book-form and the proceeds of the sales of which go to her support, she being now very old and quite infirm."

Tubman was neither infirm nor old, so those alleged facts were most likely intended to pull at the heartstrings of prospective buyers. But the ad wonderfully succeeded and was further aided by a glowing review of the book written by Franklin Sanborn that encouraged readers to buy copies to support an Underground Railroad heroine who was "poor and partially disabled" (Larson 2003, 250). Bradford relinquished any right to royalties, so *Scenes* eventually brought in over $1,200 to Tubman. It was more than enough to pay off the mortgage on her house, although the funds do not seem to have been used for that because the home wasn't fully hers until 1873. Most likely the royalties were used to pay interest on the mortgage, cover any other debts Tubman may have incurred, and fund everyday living expenses. There's even some evidence that the royalties were held in trust for Tubman and doled out to her as she needed them. If that's the case, it indicates a paternalistic concern on the part of her white friends that she wasn't a responsible minder of her own finances. Because of her generosity, they may have worried, with some justification, that a sizeable percentage of her royalties would be given to charity were they handed over to her in a lump sum.

Around the time that *Scenes* appeared, an Auburn banker named Charles Wood launched a campaign to urge the government to reward Tubman for her war service. He drafted a document that described her activities in the Department of the South and estimated that she was owed nearly $1,000 for her scouting alone. Wood based his calculation on the standard $60 to $75 per month pay rate for military scouts, but cut it in half because Tubman was never officially commissioned. He also pointed out that Tubman had encouraged scores of slave refugees from the Combahee River raid to join the federal army. The bounty for enlisting troops during the war ranged all the way up to $300, but Tubman hadn't been given a cent.

The conclusion urged on Congress by Wood was that "Harriet is entitled to several thousands of dollars pay—there can be no doubt" (Clinton 2004, 197). Once submitted, his petition got buried. It would be years more

---

CIVIL WAR PENSIONS

Tubman's difficulty in securing a federal pension for her war service was partly the product of racism. It's also the case that the allocation of federal pensions to Union Civil War veterans and their widows and orphans was a bureaucratic mare's nest as well as, eventually, a substantial drain on the national budget. (Pensions for Confederate veterans were left up to their individual states.)

The federal pension system went through several different stages, beginning in 1862 with a congressional allocation of funds for slain and disabled veterans and their families. The actual dollar amount depended on a soldier's rank and injury. A private listed as totally disabled, for example, was entitled to a monthly pension of $8, eventually rising to $30 by the beginning of the twentieth century. Civil War widows' benefits ceased if they remarried, a regulation that wasn't suspended until 1901.

In 1879, largely in response to thousands of veterans' petitions, Congress passed the Arrears Act, which awarded lump payments to soldiers to cover the time period between when they became eligible for pensions and when they actually applied for them. Disability pensions were awarded only for wartime mishaps, not for injuries or illnesses after military service. This changed eleven years later with the Dependent Pension Act, which granted annuities to all disabled veterans, regardless of whether or not their infirmities stemmed from their war service. The act swelled the numbers of veterans who applied for pensions, soon accounting for a full 40 percent of the federal budget. Desperate to raise revenue for the pensions, President William McKinley levied an astounding 49 percent tariff on selected importations, satisfying veterans but enraging consumers. In 1907, pension benefits were extended yet again to cover old age. By 1910, 90 percent of surviving Civil War veterans were receiving monthly federal checks. The last one of them died in 1956.

Although field nurses weren't officially considered veterans, who were defined as being in the employment of the United States Army for at least ninety days during the Civil War, they too finally begin receiving pensions, $12 monthly, in 1892.

before Tubman received any federal benefits. In the meantime, she had to make do with what she could earn, royalties from *Scenes,* and charity.

THE GOLD SCAM

Ben Ross died in 1871. Although Tubman mourned her father, who had been crippled by rheumatism for years and unable to work, his passing meant that she had one less mouth to feed. Two years later, she was finally able to pay off the mortgage on her house after William Seward's son Henry forgave part of the debt following his own father's death. This left Tubman without any savings or cash reserves to fall back on, which may explain why she fell victim to a couple of con artists in the late summer of 1873.

In the years following the Civil War, rumors that gold had been squirreled away by diehard Confederate loyalists in the final weeks of the conflict and subsequently discovered by treasure seekers were everywhere. Nearly all of them were false, fueled by wild imagination and appropriated by criminals for the purposes of scamming unwitting victims. These flim-flam artists claimed that they had uncovered a cache of gold and were willing to sell it below its actual value for ready and hard cash. When they found someone gullible enough to believe them, they arranged to take the cash with the promise that the gold was forthcoming. Of course, it never was.

In mid-September 1873, a couple of mulatto grifters named Stevenson and Thomas tried to pull off a Confederate gold scam in Seneca Falls, New York. Meeting with no success, they moved on to Auburn, where they made contact with Tubman's brother, John Stewart. They assured him that they knew how to get their hands on "a large sum of gold," currently held by an ex-slave in South Carolina named Harris who was afraid to cash any of it in lest he be accused of thievery. The cache, they assured Stewart, was worth a cool $5,000, but they were willing to let him have it for $2,000 in greenbacks, explaining that what their South Carolina acquaintance needed more than gold was cash currency.

When Stewart told his sister about the offer, Tubman was immediately interested, especially because she'd actually seen a trunk load of discovered Confederate gold and silver in Beaufort during the war. She invited Stevenson and Thomas to stay with her for a few days while she scurried to come up with the $2,000 they wanted. Auburn's bankers, sensing something fishy about the whole affair, turned her down when she asked for a loan, insisting that they'd have to actually see the gold first. Several wealthy men to whom she turned next likewise wanted nothing to do with the whole affair and even warned her not to get involved with what they immediately suspected was a swindle.

But Tubman was convinced that Stevenson and Thomas were legitimate, and she persevered looking for an underwriter, until she managed to convince a local entrepreneur named Anthony Shimer to front the money. She was acquainted with him through the Central Presbyterian Church and knew him to be one of Auburn's more adventurous entrepreneurs, a daring that made him one of the city's richest men by the time he died at the century's end. His willingness to take a chance on a dodgy venture met with the disapproval of his bankers, who tried to dissuade him from withdrawing the money Tubman required.

Arrangements were made for Shimer, his reluctant banker, and Tubman to deliver the cash to the man posing as Harris, the South Carolina freedman who was offering the gold for sale. When Harris failed to show up at the rendezvous point, Stevenson convinced them that he was frightened of white people. The new plan was for Stevenson to take Tubman and the cash to the freedman, who was supposedly hiding in a nearby wood with the gold, while her white companions waited in a nearby tavern.

This alone should have sounded alarm bells, but the prospect of an easy profit was too tempting for Tubman to pull back from the deal. What happened next was a comedy of errors. Tubman and Stevenson found Harris sitting next to a box that he said held the gold. When Tubman went to open it, he fumbled in his pockets and told her that he'd forgotten to bring the key. He and Stevenson left, supposedly to retrieve the key, leaving Tubman alone with the box. Although dusk was settling in and her eyesight wasn't as sharp as it once was, she realized, on inspecting the box, that it had no keyhole. Nervously suspecting (finally!) that she'd been tricked, she tried to grope her way out of the woods in the dark, but she was frightened by white shapes that she later said she thought were ghosts. Suddenly, out of the gloom, Harris and Stevenson appeared at her side, at which point she lost consciousness, probably because the two men covered her mouth and nose with an ether-soaked cloth. Then they robbed her of the $2,000 in cash, tied and gagged her, and took off, never to be heard from again.

When Tubman came to, she dragged herself, still bound, to the tavern. Along the way, she had to lift herself by her chin over fences because her hands were behind her back. The next morning, constables located the "gold" box and found it to be filled with stones. A furious Shimer demanded his money back and, when he realized it was gone, claimed that Tubman had agreed to put up her house as collateral on the loan. No one believed him, and he was forced to swallow the loss. Tubman, for her part, was so physically and emotionally shaken by her ordeal that she needed a few days to recover her equilibrium.

It is a measure of the respect and affection Auburnians felt for Tubman that no one suspected she or her brother had been accomplices in swindling Shimer out of his money. Even he had no suspicion along those lines.

At worst, they believed Tubman had shown particularly bad judgment in getting mixed up in the whole affair in the first place. The fact that she had done so underscored for them the continuous financial worries that beset her, and a wave of public sympathy for her jumpstarted the stalled petition on her behalf that Charles Wood had filed in 1869. One of New York's congressmen pushed the issue to the point of actually getting a bill onto the floor of the House of Representatives. H.R. 3786 described Tubman as having worked in "various capacities of nurse, scout and spy" during the war, of contributing "great service and value to the Government," and of being utterly uncompensated for her pains. The bill requested a modest appropriation of $2,000 for Tubman. It made it through the House but died in the Senate.

On the face of things, it does seem strange that Tubman, a woman who in prewar years had successfully evaded slave catchers by navigating in the dark through woods and swamps, should have become so discombobulated on the night of her misadventure. Even more surprising, given her reputation for fearlessness, is her report that she was frightened by what at the time she took to be ghosts. (The apparitions turned out to be white cows.) Two contemporary historians, Kate Clifford Larson and Jean M. Humez, argue that Tubman's testimony of what happened that night actually might have been a clever smoke screen to protect herself against suspicions of collusion with the three flimflam artists who took off with Shimer's money. "She may have had a very particular self-protective strategy in mind," writes Humez. "She may have been playing the fool, in order to divert suspicion and avoid danger" (Humez 2003, 89, 90). Larson even suggests that Tubman may have played into "existing racialized expectations of the superstitious black woman, thereby providing herself with ample protection from voices [like Shimer's] that may have been searching for a clearer explanation of the mysterious sequence of events" (Larson 2003, 259).

MOSES OF HER PEOPLE

The next few years of Tubman's life were relatively uneventful, but there were a few high and low watermarks that we know about.

One year after the gold scam, Tubman and Davis adopted an infant girl to whom they gave the name Gertie Davis. We know next to nothing about her except that she married in 1900. Judging by the affection in which she was held by her nieces and nephews, Tubman's relationship with Gertie was, in all likelihood, warmly affectionate and playful. Tubman always held family in high regard, and, despite being childless herself, she had a wonderful way with children, as evidenced by a story that one of her grandnieces was fond of telling.

[Tubman] and mother were talking as they say in the yard. Tiring of their conversation, I wandered off in the tall grasses to pick the wild flowers. Suddenly I became aware of something moving toward me in the grass. So smoothly did it glide and with so little noise, I was frightened! Then reason conquered fear and I knew it was Aunt Harriet, flat on her stomach and with only the use of her arms and serpentine movements of her body, gliding smoothly along. Mother helped her back to her chair and they laughed. (McGowan and Kashatus 2011, 126)

Tubman and her husband continued earning money for their household of relatives, friends, and borders in the ways they always had. They grew produce for their table and to sell or barter, and Nelson continued working, as best he could, in the brickyard. But his tuberculosis continued its progress, and his ability to contribute to the household's upkeep was proportionately diminished. He finally died of the disease in 1888, still a relatively young man.

We also know that, for a time, Harriet and Nelson raised hogs to sell because one of the city newspapers reported in the summer of 1884 that her entire herd was sickening, and that many swine had already perished. The origin of their ailment was never discovered. Tubman suspected that some household arsenic, used for killing vermin, had made its way into the kitchen garbage collected from Auburn's houses on which she fed her hogs. It's unknown if Tubman collected Auburnians' garbage as a private citizen or if she had contracted with the city. Given her spirit of entrepreneurship, the second seems distinctly possible.

The loss of her hogs came on the heels of an equally costly tragedy that had struck less than two years earlier. Sometime in 1882, the wooden frame house she had purchased from Seward and lived in since returning from the war caught fire and burned to the ground. Especially painful was the loss of all the documentation she'd collected over the years testifying to her wartime services. Tubman, Davis, and Gertie stayed at her brother John's house while a new brick home was built on the foundation of the old wooden one. Her mother Rit, who had died in 1880 at close to one hundred years of age, was spared the dislocation.

By the mid-1880s, Davis's illness, as well as her own declining health—the headaches and narcoleptic episodes were increasing, as was rheumatism that she apparently inherited from her father—prompted Tubman to make yet another effort to secure a government pension. When this one failed as well, she contacted Sarah Bradford about reissuing *Scenes in the Life of Harriet Tubman*, which had brought Tubman much needed funds seventeen years earlier. Bradford was happy to accommodate but decided it would be better to rewrite and update her biography instead of simply reissuing *Scenes*. She titled the new version *Harriet, Moses of Her People*, and justified its appearance in her preface by confessing that *Scenes* had been written too hastily. She also made it clear that this biography, like the first one, was intended primarily as a fund raiser for Tubman, who "labored without any remuneration" for the government during the Civil War (Bradford 1886, 6).

A good deal of the first biography made its way into *Moses,* however, along with some of the misinformation that bedeviled the first book. Bradford also carried over, with a few additions, the documentary testimonials to Tubman's character and service with which she padded *Scenes.* She also included Sanborn's *Commonwealth* article about Tubman, as well as the newspaper account of the rescue of Charles Nalle.

In the new biography, perhaps to lend what she considered the ring of literary authenticity, Bradford made much heavier use of slave dialect than she had in *Scenes,* sometimes to the point of inadvertent caricature. The sparse narrative of the original biography was considerably fleshed out—often in the sentimental style that was Bradford's signature—and episodic descriptions of Tubman's life in Auburn were added. It still needs to be read with the same critical eye that's appropriate to *Scenes.*

When the book was published in 1886, Bradford once again graciously foreswore royalties so that all the profits could go to Tubman. The book brought in some badly needed income, especially after Sanborn invited Tubman to Boston and hosted a book launch to publicize it. But it wasn't enough to fund a project that Tubman had dreamed about for some time: building a hospital and rest home for black folks. As in her Underground Railroad days, however, the absence of funds was a problem that she refused to let get in her way.

10

Mother Tubman

Her own sands are nearly run, but she hopes, 'ere she goes home, to see this work, a hospital, well under way. Her last breath and her last efforts will be spent in the cause of those for whom she has already risked so much.

—Sarah Bradford (1886, 7)

"ARE YOU SAVED?"

When Nelson Davis finally died of tuberculosis in October 1888, his funeral was held at the Thompson Memorial AME Zion Church in Auburn. After returning from the war, Tubman had worshipped at Central Presbyterian, the church favored by many of the city's leading abolitionists. But when Nelson was elected a trustee of Zion shortly after he and Tubman wed, she began attending services there with him. She remained a loyal member of the church for the rest of her life, even pledging $500 in 1891 when the congregation relocated to a new building. (It's not at all clear, by the way, how or even whether or not Tubman honored the pledge.)

Tubman's faith had always been central in her life. As with most slaves and ex-slaves, the Exodus story of Moses leading the Hebrews out of Egyptian bondage was an especially significant story for her, both before her escape and afterward, when she conducted slaves to freedom. The Bible promised liberation for all people who found themselves oppressed or in bondage, and even though she couldn't read, Tubman knew a good deal of it by heart from hearing it read by others. As we'll see, her reported final words were a quotation from the Bible.

Unsurprisingly, given the depth of her faith, Tubman was a person of deep and constant prayer. Quaker and Underground Railroad stationmaster Thomas Garrett once said of her, "I never met with any person of any color who had more confidence in the voice of God, as spoken direct to her soul" (Whyman 1896, 112). Tubman also frequently sang hymns and religious spirituals she'd learned as a child. Quite often, when appearing to audiences in later life, she spontaneously punctuated her spoken remarks with snatches of song. According to those who heard her, she had a remarkably pleasing voice, even as an elderly woman.

Somewhat unusual for a member of the AME tradition, Tubman fasted on Fridays her entire adult life. She learned the discipline, she said, from her father, who told her that if "he denies himself for the sufferings of his Lord and Master, Jesus will sustain him" (Bradford 1869, 109). What wasn't at all unusual for an African Methodist Episcopalian was Tubman's willingness to throw herself into church-sponsored charity work, whether it meant collecting clothes for orphaned black children or visiting the homes of sick parishioners. Service to others, sustained by her faith, was an essential part of who she was.

Nor was it only the dispossessed and enslaved that stirred Tubman's compassion. Sarah Bradford records that Tubman strove to view slaveholders and even leaders of the Confederacy as misguided men and women who acted as they did more from cultural conditioning than inherent wickedness.

> Harriet's charity for all the human race is unbounded. It embraces even the slaveholder—it sympathizes even with Jeff Davis, and rejoices at his departure to other lands, with some prospect of peace for the future. She says, "I think there's many a slaveholder'll get to Heaven. They don't know no better. They acts up to the light they have. You take that sweet little child (pointing to a lonely baby)—'pears more like an angel than anything else—take her down there, let her never know nothing 'bout niggers but they was made to be whipped, and she'll grow up to use the whip on 'em just like the rest. No, Missus, it's because they don't know no better." (Bradford 1869, 112–113)

The AME Zion milieu, which unabashedly encouraged its members to praise God with voice and body during worship, was certainly a better fit for her than the more staid Central Presbyterian congregation. Typically sitting at the front of the church, perhaps because her hearing was failing, it wasn't unusual for Tubman to bound up from her pew during the service, filled with religious fervor. One such spontaneous episode was witnessed by Reverend James Mason, who met her after she'd been a member of Zion for about ten years. He remembers that "she arose and commenced to speak in a hesitating voice." But in just seconds, "in a shrill voice, she commenced to give testimony to God's goodness and long suffering. Soon she was shouting, and so were others" (Larson 2003, 262). Mason, impressed by her zeal, asked someone who she was and was startled and delighted to learn that she was "the Underground Railroad Moses." Introducing himself to her after the service, she immediately asked if he was saved. When he responded affirmatively, "she remarked: 'Glory to God,' and shouted again" (Humez 2003, 334).

Within the confines of AME Zion, Tubman's religious fervor was seen as a sign of her deep faith. In other contexts, however, it caused uneasiness and invited derision. In 1884, for example, the *Auburn Daily Advertiser* reported a disturbance she caused in the street on which the city jail was located. While visiting and praying with a nephew who had been arrested for theft, she fell into one of her religious ecstasies. When she exited the jail, according to the newspaper report, "she was seized with what is familiarly known as the 'power,' and began shouting and singing." Tubman raised such a ruckus that a deputy sheriff had to lead her back inside the jail and call a nearby physician who "succeeded in quieting her, after a time" (Humez 2003, 93).

The "power," visions that came to Tubman all her life but especially after the horrible head wound she suffered as a young girl, were often but not always religious in nature. Sometimes the experiences were visual, as when before her escape from bondage she saw white women in flowing gowns beckoning to her. She often saw herself flying and looking down upon the landscape below her. At other times they were auditory, reminding her of flowing water or screams. Often they were music that sounded so sweet to her that she concluded it had a heavenly origin.

Once when she was a girl, she was returning home, accompanied by a couple other children, after a hard day's work of carting manure. Suddenly she experienced a flood of music filling the air, and then saw a vision "which she described in language which sounded like the old prophets in its grand flow." Her two companions report that the "Master" was called in and tried several times to rouse Tubman, presuming that she had fallen into a strange kind of sleep. But Tubman protested each time that she wasn't sleeping (Humez 2003, 181).

On other occasions, Tubman's visions took on frighteningly apocalyptic tones that seemed to foresee disaster. In at least two instances, witnesses reported that she became agitated with a vision of people drowning just prior to a ship disaster off Martha's Vineyard, and again just before an earthquake struck in South America. During that second episode, she ran into a neighbor's house, crying that a "dreadful thing was happening somewhere, the ground was opening, and the houses were falling in, and the people being killed faster than they was [sic] in the war" (Bradford 1901, 147–148).

Tubman's fellow AMEers had no difficulty taking her visions as genuine revelations from God or portents of the future. Her white friends, however, were ambivalent. In her *Scenes in the Life of Harriet Tubman*, Bradford deliberately shies away from describing too many of Tubman's "dreams and visions" lest they "might bring discredit upon [her] story." But she can't resist offering a broad description of what she calls Tubman's "somnolency"—what the Auburn newspaper later referred to as the "power"—which hints at her skepticism.

> When these turns of somnolency come upon Harriet, she imagines that her "spirit" leaves her body, and visits other scenes and places, not only in this world, but in the world of spirits. And her ideas of these scenes show, to say the least of it, a vividness of imagination seldom equaled in the soarings of the most cultivated minds.
>
> Not long since, the writer, on going into Harriet's room in the morning, sat down by her and began to read that wonderful and glorious description of the heavenly Jerusalem in the two last chapters of Revelations. When the reading was finished, Harriet burst into a rhapsody which perfectly amazed her hearer—telling of what she had seen in one of these visions, sights which no one could doubt had been real to her, and which no human imagination could have conceived, it would seem, unless in dream or vision. There was a wild poetry in these descriptions which seemed to border almost on inspiration, but by many they might be characterized as the ravings of insanity. All that can be said is, however, if this woman is insane, there has been a wonderful "method in her madness." (Bradford 1869, 55–56)

In 1896, *The Woman's Era*, a newspaper for black women, ran a feature on Tubman, complete with a Civil War-era image of her holding a rifle, which referred to her as a "Black Joan of Arc." It's likely that Tubman had never heard of the fifteenth-century French peasant girl who became both a military hero and a saint. It's also true that the feature author laid things on a bit thick in praising "this great leader [who] in days and actions . . . caused strong men to quail" (*Woman's Era* 1896). But the comparison between Tubman and Joan of Arc is apposite. Both believed that God personally called them to great and dangerous deeds, both had visions that sustained their spiritual strength, and both saw the world through essentially religious lenses. Tubman's great motivation, like Joan's, was freedom from oppression, and it was a motive sustained from first to last by her faith.

JOHN BROWN HALL

Despite her chronic poverty, exacerbated in large part by the government's refusal to offer her remuneration or pension for her wartime services, Tubman continued to open her doors to both relatives and strangers who needed a place to live, a meal, or a small handout. Given her reputation for generosity, people occasionally took advantage of her, especially when she aged, but such instances did nothing to slacken her willingness to help everyone who asked.

In the 1880s, her house was especially crowded with people who relied on her. "At no one time," wrote someone who knew her, "can I recall the little home to have sheltered less than six or eight wrecks of humanity entirely dependent upon Harriet for their all" (Telford in Larson 2003, 203). Two of her aging brothers lived with her, as did a nephew and his infant daughter. There were others as well. As one of her contemporaries recalled, Tubman's roof sheltered "a great number of young and old, black and white, all poorer than she." She also took in children, both those accompanied by their mothers and those who were orphans. One particularly tragic case was a blind woman who showed up on her doorstep with four little children after the husband and father had driven them away. The poorest of the poor made their way to her house: "the aged . . . the babe deserted, the demented, the epileptic, the blind, the paralyzed, the consumptive." Nor were her guests always black. She also took in "an incorrigible white woman" shunned by whites after she experienced numerous run-ins with the law and had an illegitimate child (Larson 2003, 276–277).

Tubman's husband Nelson Davis had been a helpmate to her in feeding the people for whom she had taken responsibility. But in the last few years of his life his energy waned; by the time he finally died, his income-earning ability had dwindled to nearly nothing. Tubman kept the household in food and fuel by selling chickens and eggs, produce from her garden, child-minding, and performing cleaning chores around town. As usual, the generosity of her white friends kept her and her wards afloat. Without them, she would have been left in genuine distress. As it was, her household's members typically lived day to day.

So it was surprising—shocking, actually—when Tubman showed up at a public auction to bid on a twenty-five-and-a-half acre lot adjacent to her own seven-acre holding on the outskirts of Auburn. The property, which had once belonged to William Seward's wife's family, had two frame houses, two barns, and a long, narrow brick building. Her description of what happened at the auction is colorful. It sheds light on not only her courage and determination, but also on the dismissively patronizing way she was treated by at least some of the local whites.

They [the other bidders] was all white folks. There I was like a blackberry in a pail of milk, but I was hid down in a corner, and no one knowed who was bidding. The man began pretty low, and I kept going up by fifties. He got to twelve hundred, thirteen hundred, fourteen hundred, and still that voice in the corner kept going up by fifties. At last it got up to fourteen hundred and fifty, and then others stopped bidding, and the man said, "All done! Who is the buyer?" "Harriet Tubman," I shouted. "What! That old nigger?" they said. "Old woman, how are you ever going to pay for that lot of land?" "I'm going home to tell the Lord Jesus all about it," I said. (Bradford 1901, 149–150)

Tubman did a bit more than that. She went straight to AME Zion and persuaded its elders to cosign a $1,000 bank mortgage. Church leaders also began soliciting funds from generous donors to pay down the debt of the purchase, eventually raising over $200. With this money in hand, as well as the few dollars she took with her to the auction, the sale was finalized. It came to be called Tubman's "large parcel."

Why did she make the astoundingly reckless decision to place herself in such debt, even as she was struggling to put food on her table and fuel in her fireplace?

The answer is that Tubman wanted the land and buildings to found a residence and hospital for indigent, aged, and invalid blacks. She planned to call it the John Brown Hall, after her fiery abolitionist friend and mentor who had led the ill-fated raid on Harpers Ferry in 1859. At the time, the hospices and care facilities that existed in the state of New York—and most everywhere else in the nation, for that matter—refused to admit black men and women. Tubman's plan was to do something to rectify the situation by turning the long brick building on the large parcel into a residence for homeless blacks, whether they were born free or were ex-slaves. As she said, she wished to offer "an asylum for aged colored people" (Larson 2003, 280). Her intention was to do on a larger scale what she'd been doing in her home for years: rescuing those most in need of help.

For the next few years, however, she was unable to launch her project. Encumbered by the debt she took on in purchasing the large parcel, she had no money to convert the brick building on it into a livable refuge. So for the time being, she rented the land and outbuildings to anyone who could use them, and continued to take those who needed help into her own home.

Partly as a means of defraying her mortgage expenses, Tubman asked Sarah Bradford to put out a new edition of the *Moses* biography. Bradford agreed to do so, as long as funds could be found to cover the printing costs. Tubman contacted her usual circle of patrons for help in raising half of the needed $100, claiming that she could front $50 herself. The new edition appeared in 1886, but sales weren't sufficient to pay off the mortgage debt on the new property. Tubman continued to be plagued by financial worries.

Throughout the 1890s, her prospects improved, although still not enough to free her from debt. In June 1890, Congress passed the Dependent Pension Act granting pensions to disabled war veterans or their dependents and widows. Tubman applied almost immediately after the act became law, but the process took another five years before she was finally granted a tiny monthly pension of $8 as well as a lump sum of $500 to cover back benefits, dating from when she first applied for the pension. For the first time in her life, Tubman had a steady income, even if it was miserably inadequate.

In part, the delay was because her late husband had used one name, Nelson Charles, when he joined the Eighth United States Colored Troop and another, Nelson Davis, after he was mustered out. Tubman understandably filled out the pension application form using the name he used when the two were married, and it took over a year and a half for the War Department to sort out the ensuing confusion. Having certified that Davis had indeed served honorably during the war, Tubman's petition was then handed over to the Pension Bureau, which took another three and a half years to collect and accept affidavits from Tubman and others attesting to the fact that Davis, as well as her first husband, was, indeed, dead.

Things improved a bit more one year later when *The Chautauquan* published an article about Tubman that chastised the government for its miserly treatment of her. "It seems strange that one who has done so much for her country and been in the thick of the battles with shots failing all about her, should never have had recognition from the Government in a substantial way" (Holt 1896, 461). This prompted Tubman's white supporters to once again launch a campaign to persuade the government to pay her properly for her wartime services. This time, the charge was led by her New York congressman, Sereno Payne.

Payne argued that Tubman was owed a soldier's pension of $25 per month because of her services on the Combahee River raid and other military excursions. The problem was that neither the War Department nor State Department had any documentation that showed that Tubman had acted in an official soldierly capacity during the war. There were affidavits that testified to her usefulness as a spy and scout, but for some of the members of the board examining her case, they didn't justify a full soldier's pension. The opposition was especially led by a South Carolina congressman, who clearly disliked the idea of a black woman being recognized as a bona fide soldier. As a way out of the impasse, other members of the board suggested that Tubman be awarded a nurse's pension, which was just a few dollars more than a widow's pension. Finally, in 1899, thirty-five years after her wartime service ended, the House of Representatives approved a pension for Tubman of $25 per month, which the Senate then reduced to $20.

By then, beginning in 1895, Harriet had converted the brick building on the large parcel into a residence that could accommodate six or seven elderly blacks at a time. Her dream of opening John Brown Hall was finally realized, but the going remained rough, even after the larger pension kicked in. Simply paying the taxes on the two properties was an enormous strain on her resources, leading her, at one point, to sell off her cattle and at another to remortgage her own home.

In 1896, apparently at the instigation of her white Auburn supporters, who realized that the administration of John Brown Hall was becoming an increasingly vexing and bewildering burden for Tubman, it was incorporated and a board of directors appointed to oversee its finances.

It was around this same time that Tubman finally faced the fact that she would never be able to raise on her own the funds needed to open and operate the asylum she envisioned. She began looking around for an organization that was stable and wealthy enough to take the project on. She first turned to the recently formed National Association of Colored Women, a logical enough choice, but the organization's directors declined her invitation; the large mortgage that was still held on the property dissuaded them. Three years later, in 1902, she succeeded in persuading AME Zion to accept the property, under the conditions that the AME would fund the day-to-day operation of John Brown Hall.

The transfer of the deed proved more complicated than expected. Because of some legal technicality, city officials determined in early 1903 that the document needed to be rewritten and resubmitted. AME Zion was ready to do so, but it seems that Tubman balked because some of her white friends, worried about her lack of means to support herself, had persuaded her that she should've sold the property instead of handing it over lock, stock, and barrel to the church. Actually, the deal was even worse than that. Under the agreement, the church assumed the mortgage debt, but Tubman remained responsible for paying the property's taxes and insurance. She eventually even had to agree to foot the bill for repairs and maintenance on the buildings. In return, she was allowed to remain on the property for the rest of her life. Finally, in early summer of 1903, realizing that she really had no other viable option, Tubman agreed. The deed transfer was rewritten, and the deal was struck. AME Zion began an aggressive fund-raising campaign for what was now called the Harriet Tubman Home for Aged and Infirm Negroes. Apparently naming the project after John Brown, as Tubman originally had, was deemed needlessly controversial.

There were two other changes from Tubman's original plans. In the first place, AME overseers decided that the Home, described by a journalist as a "home . . . for worthy indigent, aged colored people of the state of New York, and elsewhere," would charge residents a $100 entrance fee. (By the time the home actually opened five years later, the fee had been raised to $150.) The dissonance of requiring such an enormous sum either escaped the overseers or, if noticed, was deemed an unfortunate necessity for the upkeep of the project. Tubman, however, resisted it mightily. "They make a rule that nobody should come in without having a hundred dollars," she said. "I wanted to make a rule that no body should come in unless they didn't have no money at all" (*New York Sun* 1909). But her protest notwithstanding, the fee policy was maintained. To add insult to injury, when Tubman became an increasingly infirm resident at the Home during her final two years, she was charged a $10 per week nursing fee.

The other change from Tubman's original vision for the home was the expansion of its mission. Although she definitely disapproved of the first change, it's unclear what her response was to this one. The AME Zion overseers heartily endorsed Tubman's plans to turn the large portion property into a refuge for "aged and infirm colored people who are constantly seeking shelter." They also decided that "when the trustees see their way clear to do so, they shall establish on the ground beside the home, a school of domestic science where girls may be taught the various branches of industrial education" (McGowan and Kashatus 2011, 139). The object of the school was to "train and fit colored girls as to be able to do everything belonging to household service" (Humez 2003, 104).

Part of the justification for the school was its perceived income-generating possibilities. As the AME Zion overseers recognized, the project of training domestic servants was "particularly popular with the white people in this western part of the state of New York," who were always looking for qualified maids and cooks (McGowan and Kashatus 2011, 139). The hope was that that they would donate to the upkeep of the school out of sheer self-interest.

There was another motive as well, and it fed into a larger debate among leaders of the nation's black community as well as their white well-wishers about how blacks ought best to be educated. One school of thought, led by former slave Booker T. Washington, argued that blacks were best served by being taught skills that would enable them to earn a decent wage, raise their economic status, and eventually move them into middle class respectability. More traditional learning that offered instruction in the liberal arts, he argued, was of little benefit to blacks at this stage of their existence in the United States. What was important, first and foremost, was establishing them on a solid economic footing, and that was achieved by learning trades. Washington's Tuskegee Institute in Alabama served as the center of gravity for the "industrial education" approach he championed.

The other school, represented by the Harvard-trained sociologist W.E.B. Du Bois, insisted that Washington's approach to educating blacks was essentially accommodationist, feeding the white presumption that blacks were intellectually inferior. Regardless of its intentions, industrial education kept blacks at a lower social, and hence economic, level than whites. What was needed to even out the imbalance was an academic education every bit as rigorous and enlightening as the one white children received.

Economic success for the nation's blacks, Du Bois insisted, was dependent upon training the mind as well as the hands.

Still, for all AME Zion's efforts, the Harriet Tubman Home, much less the planned school for girls, simply didn't have the funds to open its doors until five years before Tubman's death. Beginning in 1907, a high-powered fund-raising campaign was launched to finally get the project off the ground. Among other strategies, notices were placed in newspapers and sent to churches asking every black person in the state of New York to contribute $1 to the effort. Moreover, the AME Zion regional conference voted to sustain the project with a much-needed annual subsidy of $200.

The Home was at last dedicated and officially opened on June 23, 1908, offering space for five residents. Auburn threw a parade in Tubman's honor, with black Civil War veterans, the Ithaca colored band, and several dozen local "young colored people" leading an entourage of carriages, in one of which rode Tubman.

When the parade arrived at its destination, Tubman, showing every one of her eighty-six years, draped a U.S. flag around her shoulders and stood to speak.

> When called upon by the chairman for a few words of welcome the aged woman stated that she had but started the work for the rising generation to take up. "I did not take up this work for my own benefit," said she, "but for those of my race who need help. The work is now well started and I know God will raise up others to take care of the future. All I ask is united effort, for united we stand, divided we fall." (Humez 2003, 106)

"I SUFFERED ENOUGH TO BELIEVE IT"

For the first few years after her return to Auburn from the war, Tubman devoted herself to supporting relatives and acquaintances who were dependent upon her and on collecting material and money to aid freedmen in the South. By the mid-1880s, she felt able to extend her activities a bit further and became involved, although only tangentially, in the women's suffrage movement. Always an engaging public speaker, Tubman was invited to address several women's associations in Auburn, New York City, Boston, and Washington, D.C., throughout the 1880s and 1890s.

Tubman had worked with many of the women who became suffrage leaders back in her Underground Railroad days because many of them had been just as ardently in favor of abolitionism as of women's rights. It was, in fact, the refusal of male-dominated abolitionist circles to welcome women into leadership positions that had served as one of the motivations to agitate for suffrage. Woman such as Lucretia Mott, Mary Cady Stanton, and Sarah and Angelina Grimké clearly saw a parallel between the enslavement of blacks and the suppression of women.

The famous 1848 Seneca Falls Convention, which passed a Declaration of Sentiments calling for legal equity when it came to property and divorce, stopped short of demanding voting rights for women. Then, in the years immediately following the Civil War and largely through the efforts of Frederick Douglass, more attention was paid to enfranchising black men than women. "Negro suffrage," wrote Douglass in the July 1, 1858, issue of the *Anti-Slavery Reporter,* was a cause of which there was none "more sacred" or "urgent." Women who agitated for the right to vote, thereby drawing attention and energy away from the campaign to win voting rights for blacks, were acting in a manner that "does not seem generous." In the years following the 1870 ratification of the Fifteenth Amendment, focus on the enfranchisement of women returned.

In 1888, for example, Tubman was invited to speak at Auburn's cumbersomely named Non-Partisan Society for Political Education for Women. Specifically asked to share stories of her exploits on the Underground Railroad, she made it clear that she believed women were as capable as men of performing any number of tasks traditionally reserved for the "stronger" sex. Women, the *Auburn Morning Dispatch* (March 15, 1888) reported her as saying, had performed "brave and fearless deeds" and even "sacrificed all for their country," courageously venturing "where bullets mowed down men" to "administer to the injured, to bind up their wounds and [afterward] to tend them through weary months of suffering in the army hospitals." Then she posed a pointedly defiant question that must have thrilled her listeners. "If those deeds do not place woman as man's equal," she asked, "what do?"

A few years later, in 1896, Tubman was the keynoter at the second annual Washington-based meeting of the National League of Colored Women (NLCW). The NLCW had been founded the preceding year as an alternative to the National American Woman Suffrage Association (NAWSA), an organization that contained some decidedly racist elements which, despite rhetoric about sisterhood, tended to sideline the concerns and interests of black women. She was hailed by delegates as a genuine hero, and encomiums of "this noble mother of Israel," "black Joan of Arc," and "Mother Tubman" were given her.

Later that year, no less a suffrage champion than Susan B. Anthony introduced Tubman to a cheering assembly at a convention in Rochester, New York. One observer was struck by the contrast between her cheap clothes, frayed straw bonnet, and worn face and the eloquence of her remarks. It was at this meeting that Tubman uttered the words for which she's perhaps most remembered: "I was the conductor on the Underground Railroad for eight years, and I can say what most conductors can't say— I never ran my train off the track and I never lost a passenger" (Bradford 1901, 142).

SUFFRAGE AND ABOLITIONISM

Tubman's postwar participation in the women's suffrage movement was a natural outgrowth of her prewar abolitionism, because it was the antislavery movement that especially mobilized women to protest their own lack of enfranchisement in U.S. culture. As Quaker abolitionist Abby Kelly said, "In striving to cut [the slave's] irons off, we found most surely that we were manacled *ourselves*" (Barney 2011, 350).

Many women became active abolitionists in the antebellum years. These included luminaries such as Angelina and Sarah Grimké, Lucretia Mott, Elizabeth Margaret Chandler, Lydia Marie Child, Elizabeth Cady Stanton, and Abby Kelly. Their public speaking scandalized many men, including abolitionists, and eventually led to a rupture in the American Anti-Slavery Society, with *Liberator* editor William Lloyd Garrison siding with the women against critics such as Arthur and Lewis Tappan, wealthy businessmen who underwrote the abolitionist movement. Moreover, the World Anti-Slavery Convention that met in London in 1840 refused to seat two women delegates from the United States.

So women abolitionists began to agitate not only for emancipation but for their own rights as well, holding a national convention in 1848 in Seneca Falls, New York, in which they produced a Declaration of Sentiments, patterned after the Declaration of Independence, outlining their demands. Written primarily by Elizabeth Cady Stanton, the declaration called for voting and property rights for women, reform of divorce laws, and equal opportunities for women in business and religion.

The final three points in the declaration were especially stirring. They charged that male-dominated culture had "created a false public sentiment by giving to the world a different code of morals for men and women, by which moral delinquencies which exclude women from society, are not only tolerated but deemed of little account in man; usurped the prerogative of Jehovah himself, claiming it as [a man's right] right to assign for her a sphere of action, when that belongs to her conscience and her God; [and] endeavored, in every way that [it] could to destroy her confidence in her own powers, to lessen her self-respect, and to make her willing to lead a dependent and abject life."

After emancipation, suffragettes, as they came to be called, continued to lobby for equal protection and opportunities under the law. On August 26, 1920, the Nineteenth Amendment, giving women the right to vote, was finally ratified. It came a full half century after the abolitionist movement, which women did so much to promote, culminated in the Fifteenth Amendment's enfranchisement of black men.

As late as 1905, when Tubman was over eighty years old, she traveled to Rochester to attend a suffrage meeting, selling a cow to pay the train fare. When she and her traveling companion, a white woman named Emily Howland, reached the station, they went their separate ways for the night, Howland to a comfortable lodging room and Tubman to a hard bench in the train station's waiting room because she knew that no public house would offer lodgings to a black woman. She probably couldn't have afforded a room anyway. When Howland discovered how Tubman had spent the night, she was horrified enough to scold the conference planners about not providing accommodations for black attendees.

There's no doubt that Tubman was in favor of voting rights for women. When queried once about whether she believed her gender should be allowed to vote, she simply replied, "I suffered enough to believe it" (Sterling 1984, 411). Few women of her generation had done more to demonstrate that tenacity, courage, ingenuity, and dedication were not male-specific virtues.

Nonetheless, Tubman's role in the suffrage movement ought not to be exaggerated. While it's certainly true that she was more than willing to speak to suffrage gatherings, available records of her remarks indicate that she nearly always focused on her experiences on the Underground Railroad and her service during the war. Her primary function at these events was to inspire attendees with her life story. Moreover, she never missed an opportunity to solicit financial aid for her home for indigent blacks. It's likely that she accepted as many speaking invitations as she did primarily for the purpose of fund-raising. First and foremost, her focus was on her vision of an Auburn asylum.

The claim that Tubman was an important voice in the U.S. suffrage movement was first explored by Earl Conrad, who published a groundbreaking biography, *Harriet Tubman: Negro Soldier and Abolitionist*, in 1942. One of his primary assumptions going into his research on Tubman is that she was just as important a black participant in U.S. suffrage as Sojourner Truth. But in researching his book, he was surprised to encounter resistance from Carrie Chapman Catt (1859–1947), who succeeded Susan B. Anthony as the leader of the NAWSA, the premier women's rights organization in the late nineteenth and early twentieth centuries. Conrad expected that when he contacted Catt, she would confirm his assumption that Tubman had played a significant role in the suffrage struggle. Instead, Catt insisted (somewhat doubtfully) that she had never heard of Tubman and that, therefore, she couldn't have "had much, if anything, to do with the woman suffrage movement." After hearing a bit about Tubman's connections with abolitionists turned suffragists, the most that Catt would concede was that Tubman "undoubtedly agreed with the proposition of the women to gain the vote, but her idea was far away from that as an aim. She did not assist the suffragists or the woman suffrage movement at any time. It was they who were attempting to assist her" (Sernett 2007, 154, 155).

In light of Catt's testimony, Conrad eventually described Tubman as a fellow traveler rather than a central figure in the U.S. suffrage movement, and this seems to be an accurate appraisal. Nevertheless, as one contemporary scholar puts it, "Feminists and women's groups of varied political orientations continue to employ Tubman as emblematic of their own struggles for equity and justice, and as long as America falls short of these goals, the symbolic use of Harriet Tubman remains important" (Sernett 2007, 163).

SUNSET ON A BRIGHT CLEAR DAY

As the nineteenth century drew to a close, Tubman, who had sunk into relative obscurity in the years immediately following the Civil War, once again caught the public's imagination. Newspaper and magazine articles about her appeared, especially in retrospectives about abolitionism that regularly appeared whenever one of the movement's aging luminaries died. Publicity about her efforts to found an asylum for blacks who were too old and infirm to care for themselves, as well as her speaking engagements at suffrage gatherings, also improved her visibility. Nor was her fame limited to the North American side of the Atlantic. Queen Victoria, who read and was impressed by Bradford's 1886 biography of her, sent Tubman a medal commemorating the queen's 1897 Diamond Jubilee and a white shawl.

Victoria also invited Tubman to visit her at Buckingham Palace. Even if she'd had the funds to finance the journey, Tubman's health wouldn't have allowed her to go. In her late seventies by the century's end, she was growing increasingly feeble, with a number of ailments, not the least of which was the rheumatism that had crippled her father, Ben.

At around the time of Victoria's invitation, Tubman endured surgery on her skull in the hope that it would do something to relieve the headaches that had afflicted her ever since she'd been struck in the head with an iron weight as a girl. She underwent the procedure without the benefit of anesthesia, instead "mumbling prayers through teeth clenched on [a] bullet," something she'd seen wounded soldiers under the surgeon's knife do many times during the war. Her description of what happened, told to someone who asked why her head was shaved, is harrowing.

> "When I was in Boston I walked out one day," recalled Tubman, "I saw a great big building, I asked a man what it was, and he said it was a hospital. So I went right in, and I saw a young man there, and I said, 'Sir, are you a doctor?' And he said he was; then I said 'Sir, do you think you could cut my head open?'" The doctor must have been taken aback by Tubman's abrupt request, because she quickly went on to describe for him the "aching and buzzing" in her head that prevented her from sleeping. So he agreed to do what he could for her.

> And he said, "Lay right down on this here table," and I lay down.
> "Didn't he give you anything to deaden the pain, Harriet?"

> No sir; I just lay down like a lamb before the slaughter, and he sawed open my skull, and raised it up, and now it feels more comfortable.

"Did you suffer much?"

"Yes, sir, it hurt, of course; but I got up and put on my bonnet and started to walk home, but my legs kind of give out under me, and they sent for a [sic] ambulance and sent me home." (Bradford 1901, 152–153)

Tubman's description of her skull surgery was recorded in the 1901 edition of Bradford's *Moses*, which included additional and up-to-date material. Bradford decided to reissue the book because, on a visit to Tubman's home, she was dismayed both by Tubman's physical condition and the general squalor of her living conditions. Apparently, Tubman was no longer able to do as much physical labor as she once had. Bradford determined that she wouldn't allow Tubman to sink into abject poverty, and publishing a new edition of the book, the proceeds of which she intended to supervise, was one way to prevent that. Soliciting financial aid from Tubman's well-wishers was another.

It wasn't simply the threat of poverty to the aging Tubman that alarmed Bradford and others. They were also concerned, as they had been for years, about con artists taking advantage of either her generous nature or her desperate poverty, as had happened two decades earlier in the gold scam fiasco. Her high public profile made her an easily locatable mark.

On at least two occasions in her final years, the fears of her friends proved well-founded. In 1905, a man came to her home seeking shelter. After she invited him in, Tubman discovered that he was carrying a revolver. She was so frightened that she stayed awake all night, and finally got rid of the man in the morning by giving him $5, which she borrowed from an acquaintance. The stranger, apparently unsatisfied with such a small sum, then made his way to the home of Emily Howland, the woman who accompanied Tubman that same year to a suffrage conference in Rochester. Once there, he told Howland that he was a friend of Tubman's who'd barely escaped a lynching in the South and, with this sob story, swindled her out of over $500.

Although not as hair-raising, Tubman was robbed again two years later by a visitor who discovered that she had $34 in the house. The loss of so much money was barely short of a disaster for her household. Even more painfully, the stolen money was a Christmas gift to Tubman.

By 1910, an increasingly feeble Tubman, nearing her nineties, was largely confined to a wheelchair. One year later, after a lengthy illness, she bowed to the inevitable by moving out of her own house to become one of the tenants of the Harriet Tubman Home. The only income she had was the $20 monthly federal pension, and the cost of caring for her was $10 a week. Friends and admirers from around the country sent in donations to make sure that she received the attention she needed.

One year after moving into the asylum, realizing that her time was running out, she made a will. Her three legatees were all women. Two were nieces, and the third, a member of AME Zion, charged with overseeing the Harriet Tubman Home, was a friend.

Even though an increasingly frail ward of the asylum she founded, Tubman retained her independent spirit. She intensely disliked being coddled and was particularly annoyed when visitors, noticing her rheumatic hands, offered to cut her food for her. She did, however, remain as mentally sharp as ever and, right up until the year of her death, entertained fellow residents and visitors with stories of her adventures.

The final winter of her life was hard on her, confining her to bed. She was described as "very thin and weak so emaciated that her nurse can lift her about very easily" (Humez 2003, 117). She died on March 10, 1913, aged ninety-one, from what one local newspaper rather improbably described as a pneumonia that had lasted for eighteen months. Friends gathered around her bed to share her last few hours. Although the account may be embellished to some extent, the description left to us of her departure has the ring of truth. Clergy conducted a service in Tubman's room, in which she participated as best she could, receiving the sacrament and singing as much as her coughing and uneasy breathing allowed. "To the clergymen she said, 'Give my love to all the churches' and after a severe coughing spell she blurted out in a thick voice a farewell passage which she had learned from the gospel of Matthew: 'I go away to prepare a place for you, and where I am ye may be also'" (Humez 2003, 118).

Alice Brickler, the granddaughter of one of her brothers, later recounted what she had been told about the day of her great aunt's death.

> For sometime before her death, Aunt Harriet had lost the use of her legs. She spent her time in a wheel chair and then finally was confined to her bed. It is said that on the day of her death, her strength returned to her. She arose from her bed with little assistance, ate heartily, walked about the rooms of the Old Ladies' Home which she liked so much and then went back to bed and her final rest. Whether this is true or not, it is typical of her. She believed in mind [over] matter. Regardless of how impossible a task might seem, if it were her task she tackled it with a determination to win. I've always enjoyed believing this story as a fitting finish chapter to her life. It was right that her sun should go down on a bright day out of a clear sky. (Humez 2003, 118)

Tubman's funeral was held three days later, commencing with a service at the Tubman Home, and then proceeding to her church. Several hundred locals and visitors came to say their farewells and follow her flag-draped coffin to the Fort Hill cemetery, where she was laid to rest beside her brother William Henry and his son. She was wearing the medal sent her by Queen Victoria.

Auburnians clearly weren't ready to let her go. They launched a fund-raising campaign to purchase a commemorative bronze plaque in

---

Queen Victoria's Gift

Queen Victoria officially celebrated her Diamond Jubilee in June 22, 1897, although events commemorating the anniversary were observed throughout the entire year. To honor her sixty-year reign, commemorative medals were struck and awarded to different groups of people.

Three versions of the medals were made and distributed. The first was struck in gold and given to members of the royal family, the second in silver for people lower in rank, and the third in bronze for people of still lower rank. Additional ones were awarded to mayors and police.

Victoria had read Sarah Bradford's 1886 *Moses* biography and was impressed enough to include Tubman in the list of medal honorees. We don't have a description of the medal she sent Tubman, but it was probably a bronze one. She also sent a letter of invitation for Tubman to travel to London for the Jubilee celebration and a fine white silk, lace, and linen shawl.

Tubman was immensely proud of the gifts. She later told an acquaintance that she'd handled the letter so often that it "was worn to a shadow" and eventually lost (Larson 2003, 385). The medal was buried with her, and the shawl, beautiful even today, is currently on exhibit in the Collection of the Smithsonian National Museum of African American History and Culture.

---

her honor and invited Booker T. Washington to speak at its June 1914 unveiling ceremony. Mounted on the wall of the country courthouse, the plaque carried a likeness of Tubman and the following inscription:

> In Memory of Harriet Tubman.
> Born a slave in Maryland about 1821.
> Died in Auburn, N.Y. March 10th, 1913.
> Called the "Moses" of her people during the Civil War,
> with rare courage, she led over
> three hundred Negroes up from slavery to freedom,
> and rendered invaluable service as a nurse and spy.
> With implicit trust in God, she braved every danger and
> overcame every obstacle; withal she possessed extraordinary
> foresight and judgment so that she truthfully said—
> *"On my Underground Railroad I never run my train off*
> *the track and I never lost a passenger."*
> (Larson 2003, 290)

Except for the exaggerated number of rescued slaves, the plaque commemorating Tubman's life and character got it exactly right.

Why Harriet Tubman Matters

I am confident that . . . she has a rare discernment,
and a deep and sublime philanthropy.

—Gerritt Smith (Bradford 1869, 5)

In my opinion there are few captains, perhaps few colonels,
who have done more for the loyal cause since the war began,
and few men who did before that time more for the colored race,
than our fearless and most sagacious friend, Harriet.

—Wendell Phillips (Bradford 1869, 6)

When Harriet Tubman died in 1913, rich in years and accomplishments, she hoped that the home for indigent blacks that she founded in Auburn, New York, would be her enduring legacy. It was the culmination of a dream that she'd cherished for years. She wanted to name the institution, which opened its doors in 1908, in honor of her old abolitionist fellow warrior John Brown, but church elders and town officials insisted on naming it after her instead of Brown. This was a disappointment to Tubman. Still, newspaper reports of the home's official opening reported that Tubman, close to ninety years of age, was otherwise delighted. She wore a stars-and-stripes banner draped shawl-like across her shoulders and gave a short but rousing speech.

Scarcely ten years later, with funds nearly dried up, and the last of its residents dead, the Harriet Tubman Home closed its doors. The AME Zion Church, which had taken over the ownership and management of it, didn't want to pump any more resources into what struck church elders as a money trap. The house and a few other buildings on the property sat empty and decaying for two decades until finally put up for auction by town officials, eager to recoup back taxes. The prospect of erasing a visible link to a woman who, in her day, had been praised as "the Moses of her people" alarmed and awakened church officials, and they raised money to retain ownership of the site, even though the buildings were falling apart.

Just as the home she founded slid into ruin, so the memory of Harriet Tubman nearly vanished in those years, at least among white Americans. This was remarkable, because in the 1850s, she had been one of the nation's most admired—and, south of the Mason-Dixon line, reviled—opponents of slavery. Her daring rescues of slaves on the Underground Railroad as well as her exploits during the Civil War made her famous. No less a figure than Frederick Douglass was effusive and utterly sincere in his praise of her. When Tubman asked for a testimonial from him after the war, his reply was both unequivocal and hauntingly beautiful.

> You ask for what you do not need when you call upon me for a word of commendation. I need such words from you far more than you can need them from me, especially where your superior labors and devotion to the cause of the lately enslaved of our land are known as I know them. The difference between us is very marked. Most that I have done and suffered in the service of our cause has been in public, and I have received much encouragement at every step of the way. You on the other hand have labored in a private way. I have wrought in the day—you in the night. I have had the applause of the crowd and the satisfaction that comes of being approved by the multitude, while the most that you have done has been witnessed by a few trembling, scarred, and foot-sore bondmen and women, whom you have led out of the house of bondage, and whose heartfelt "God bless you" has been your only reward. The midnight sky and the silent stars have been the witnesses of your devotion to freedom and of your heroism. Excepting John Brown—of sacred memory—I know of no one who has willingly encountered more perils and hardships to serve our enslaved people than you have. (Bradford 1869, 7–8)

Yet just a few short years after Tubman's death, she slipped from the national consciousness into near-obscurity.

* * *

That changed in the 1930s, when Earl Conrad, a white union organizer and leftist, began researching her life and interviewing the few remaining people who had personally known her. Although he had a hard time finding a publisher—another indication of just how far Tubman had sunk into obscurity—his 1943 biography of her that brought her back to the public eye. Her life story was soon a standard staple of children's and juvenile literature. Beginning in the 1950s, books for young readers about her abounded, and the stream has only increased as she became an iconic black heroine. There are now, in fact, more books about her for youngsters than about Frederick Douglass or Sojourner Truth, and the Tubman juvenilia far outnumber books about her written for adults (Sernett 2007, 22). Her name is so well known to youngsters, especially ones of color, that one Georgia teacher reported that her students answer "Harriet Tubman" for every question she asks them because that's the only name they recognize. The teacher's immediate point was that her kids needed a better grasp of black history. Her story also underscores just how well known Tubman now is (Sernett 2007, 12).

Nor is it just kids who admire her. The year after Conrad's book was released, the United States government named a Liberty ship after her—she was the first black woman so honored—and to coincide with the ship's launching, the National Council of Negro Women urged Americans to buy "Harriet Tubman War Bonds for Freedom." Three decades later, the U.S. Post Office issued two commemorative postage stamps bearing her features. Tubman has been inducted into the National Women's Hall of Fame and the Maryland Women's Hall of Fame. She has been honored as one of the one hundred most important African Americans and has even had an asteroid named after her.

President Barack Obama announced plans in his second term to put Tubman's face on the $20 bill. The Trump administration, however, distanced itself from that commitment, announcing in early 2019 that Andrew Jackson would remain on the bill for the foreseeable future. It's unclear what the reasons for this decision are. They may be similar to Lynne Cheney's complaint twenty-five years earlier, when she served as Chair of the National Endowment for the Humanities, that interest in Tubman was unduly inflated by political correctness (Cheney 1994).

The spat over whose face belongs on the $20 bill is just the latest skirmish between people who have either co-opted Tubman as an ally or demonized her as the over-admired darling of politically correct advocates. Booker T. Washington, for example, whose primary concern was helping black people achieve upward mobility into middle-class respectability, presented her as a sterling role model. In a speech he gave at a dedication ceremony honoring her a year after her death, he said that Tubman "made it possible for the white race to know the black race, to place a different estimate on it. In too many sections of our country, the white man knows the criminal Negro, but he knows little about the law-abiding Negro" (Humez 2003, 122). Washington's conclusion was that Tubman was an exemplary law-abider, an encomium which flew in the face of the fact that she regularly violated civil and state laws, first by "stealing" herself from the man who owned her, and then "stealing" dozens of others from their masters.

At the time of her rediscovery in the mid-1940s, leftists tried to co-opt her as a revolutionary icon in their political and unionization campaigns. Before publishing his full-length biography of her, Conrad wrote a short pamphlet for the American Communist Party, characterizing Tubman as a "Negro soldier" who fought for a new world order. But this is an anachronistic reading. The key Marxist category of class warfare, much less classical Marxism's reduction of racism to economic inequality, were quite foreign to Tubman.

More recently, a statue of Tubman in Battle Creek, Michigan, that depicts her holding a rifle, as well as a proposed painting of her in Maryland likewise portraying her with a weapon in her hand, have stirred up controversy among gun-rights opponents and those who wish to adopt Tubman as a proponent of pacifistic civil disobedience. It can hardly be denied that Tubman endorsed violence, if that's what it took, to end slavery in the United States. John Brown's willingness to resort to armed revolt was, in fact, one of the reasons she admired and supported him. It's telling that in her first book-length biography, published in 1869, the frontispiece is a sketch of Tubman holding a rifle.

Many of the books for juvenile readers written about her distort, unwittingly or otherwise, what we know of her life, in order to cater to their young audience's taste for adventure and derring-do. Moreover, the fact that special interest groups have sometimes tried to refashion her in their image in order to claim her as an ally has contributed to the distortion. The mystification surrounding her life is compounded by the fact that the primary sources nearly always relied upon by the juvenilia authors are two books written by Tubman's contemporary, Sarah Bradford, the first in 1869 and the second in 1886 (rereleased with additional material in a 1901 edition).

Both of these biographies, but especially the first, are hodgepodges of different accounts of Tubman's life, some of them relayed by Tubman herself and others by people who knew her. Bradford tended to exaggerate, much like the later children's books authors, in order to make her heroine seem more exciting. For example, she claimed that Tubman had made nineteen trips to the South to rescue some three hundred slaves, and that irate slave owners had put out a $40,000 bounty on her head, both of which are egregious exaggerations. Bradford also tended to praise her subject in purple prose, which is certainly an honest expression of her admiration but does little to further our understanding of Tubman. She writes, for example, that Tubman's "name (we say it advisedly and without exaggeration) deserves to be handed down to posterity side by side with the [name] of Joan of Arc" (Bradford 1869, 1).

The distortions can't, however, be laid completely to Bradford's hero-worship of her subject. Tubman frequently embellished her recollections with each retelling, depending on the audience with whom she was sharing it. Moreover, like all of us, her memory of past events was filtered through any number of subsequent prisms, again resulting in different versions of the same story depending on when she repeated it in middle or old age.

As a consequence, serious biographers have found it a daunting task to separate the historical Tubman from the legendary or mythical one. Black historian Benjamin Quarles goes so far as to describe her life narrative as a "tissue of improbabilities verging on the impossible" (Quarles 1988, 57). All historical figures are beclouded, to one extent or another, in mystery. But after her return to public view in the 1940s, Tubman virtually disappeared again behind a screen of myth-making. Interestingly, she seems to have sensed as early as her service in the Civil War that this was a danger. She remarked at least once that she wanted to learn to read and write so that she could compose the story of her life instead of leaving it to others.

In a way, however, she did write her own story. As already mentioned, Sarah Bradford's two biographies of her are at least, in part, based on Tubman's own recollections. Earl Conrad's biography started the process of distinguishing fact from fiction in Bradford's work, and, in the 1990s, African American historian James McGowan edited an online resource, *The Harriet Tubman Journal,* which offered scholars opportunities for even more rigorous investigation. In her 2003 *Harriet Tubman: The Life and the Life Stories,* Jean Humez collected dozens of documents, drawn from people who knew Tubman, as well as contemporaneous newspaper accounts of her, that shed valuable light on the historical woman behind the legend. Finally, a recent spate of biographies written by Catherine Clinton, Kate Clifford Larson, and Milton Sernett have each done a masterful job of delving beneath the Tubman myth. Larson's book is especially helpful.

*   *   *

In thinking about why Tubman matters, therefore, it's important to keep in mind that she plays both historical and mythical roles in U.S. culture and that it's often difficult to completely distinguish between them, especially when it comes to her work on the Underground Railroad, activity that was necessarily shrouded in secrecy for the sake of safety. Nevertheless, it's possible to discern several objective Tubman legacies that show us why she matters.

One of her life's legacies, although certainly not one she intended, is a warning about how easy it is for an historical figure, particularly a dynamic one like Tubman who stirs imagination and arouses emotions, to gradually disappear behind hagiography. This disappearance is especially disconcerting when it occurs to a black person who was born in circumstances that would have kept her anonymous had she not escaped from bondage, and who subsequently vanished from public memory for an entire generation after her death. The renaissance of interest in her and scholarship regarding her life and times are reminders of how important it is to resist the imperialism of myth-making, especially with men and women in the U.S. experience who, because of their ethnicity, may be marginalized in the first place.

A second and much more concrete legacy, although one that's curiously overlooked by many commentators, is the sheer number of descendants, certainly numbering in the thousands, of the slaves she rescued from bondage. Many of them gather each Memorial Day in Auburn, New York, where Tubman made her home in the second half of her life, to commemorate her. There's disagreement about just how many rescue trips southward, especially to the Eastern Shore where she was born, Tubman actually made, but the most likely number is twelve or thirteen, during which she freed between seventy and ninety people. The number of her rescues swelled during the Civil War, the most dramatic instance of which was the Combahee River raid in South Carolina's Low Country, when nearly one thousand slaves who labored on rice and cotton plantations were liberated from bondage. Tubman served as a scout on that military expedition.

Her rescues, as well as her war service, remind us of another legacy Tubman has left: her remarkable example of courage and determination in the face of adversity. In every aspect of her long life, she drew upon a self-discipline and resolve that inspired both her contemporaries and those of us today who hear her story.

Courage is a complex virtue. There's physical courage, in which we risk danger to our material well-being, and moral courage, in which for the sake of conscience, we defy public opinion or received wisdom. There is also courage as fearlessness in the face of immediate danger, and courage as fortitude or endurance in the face of long-term adversity. Tubman displayed courage in all of these ways.

What immediately elicits the applause of most of her admirers is the high drama of her physical courage: her daring escape from slavery, her twelve to thirteen returns to Maryland to rescue other slaves from bondage, her participation in the furious and bloody 1860 rescue of Charles Nalle, a fugitive slave, from rendition back to bondage in Virginia, and her valor as a scout and spy in the Civil War.

It was an excruciating ordeal to escape from slavery, even in Upper South states in which there were at least some Underground Railroad stations willing to help fugitives. Slaves rarely traveled more than a few miles from their owner's property (unless, of course, they were sold) and, consequently, had only a vague sense of how to get to the north and freedom. The North Star served as just about their only guide. Moreover, they likewise had little idea how far they would have to travel to get to a free state. Slave owners frequently exaggerated the distance, telling their slaves it was thousands and thousands of miles, to deter escape attempts. Finally, fugitive slaves suffered from snow, heat, rain, and hunger and had to be on a constant watch for roving bands of slave catchers, either those commissioned by law or unofficial bounty hunters. It took a good deal of physical courage to even contemplate a run for freedom and, once undertaken, even more to see it through to the end.

When Harriet Tubman made her break for freedom in 1849—and that a woman slave would make a run for freedom on her own was nearly unheard of—she left behind a husband, parents, and siblings. But she resolved to return to Maryland, regardless of the risk to herself, to rescue them all. She was nearly successful in her goal; as it turned out, her husband refused to accompany her, and one of her sisters died before Tubman could get her to freedom.

Returning to the South probably required more courage than her initial flight. Once free, ex-slaves were horrified by the thought of being returned to bondage, and, in the 1850s, when it became clear that they weren't safe from rendition even in free states, many of them migrated to slave-free Canada. Consequently, few considered the possibility of putting themselves in danger's way by actually returning to the locations where they had been enslaved in order to lead others to freedom. There's no evidence that Tubman hesitated for a moment in returning for her family members. When the war that had been brewing for years finally erupted in 1861, Tubman once more showed no hesitation in joining Union forces in South Carolina as a scout and spy, participating in at least one military expedition and possibly two more.

Physical courage is one thing, moral courage another. Very often it's easier to stand up to physical threats than to buck conventional morality. Although her journeys southward demanded a certain amount of secrecy and anonymity, in the late 1850s, she began to speak out publicly, thereby risking unwelcome attention to her status as a fugitive, against the institution of slavery at abolitionist meetings in New York, Massachusetts, and Pennsylvania. The abolitionist movement, which called for immediate, uncompensated emancipation as well as racial equality under the law, represented a minority opinion in antebellum United Sates, and persons who publicly defended it were frequently accused, strange as it seems today, of being immoral, unpatriotic, and un-Christian. It took a good deal of moral courage on the part of a white person to withstand such opprobrium, and even more for a black one like Tubman, who additionally had to face racially inspired fury.

The bigotry that Tubman defied wasn't simply from proslavery supporters and antiabolitionists. Along with other blacks of her generation, she faced it even from well-wishers. Despite their good intentions, many whites involved in abolitionism and the Underground Railroad typically addressed Tubman in patronizing tones or referred to her in condescending ways. In recording conversations with her, they tried to capture her dialect in an argot that made her seem not simply unlettered but simple-minded. At least some of the reason she became such a celebrity abolitionist is that white audiences found it incredible that a black woman could actually have accomplished what she had. She was a curious novelty to them. After her wartime service, she was physically beaten and thrown off a train by rowdies who objected to her riding in the same car as whites and became enraged at her stalwart insistence that she had as much right to be on the train as anyone else. She doggedly petitioned Congress for years, until her war service was finally recognized with a pitifully small pension, even though her applications were dismissed time and again as unworthy. Her white benefactors, including Sarah Bradford, condescendingly doled out funds that were rightfully hers on the pretext that she was irresponsibly generous with money. Moral courage in the face of such racism, even if most of it was unintentional, was a quality that Tubman certainly displayed.

Her opposition to slavery wasn't Tubman's only public display of moral courage. After the war and the legal end of slavery, she spoke occasionally in support of the suffrage movement, another wildly unpopular position to take at the time. Her participation in the movement remained relatively marginal, but that's attributable to the fact that during the postwar years, she was scrambling to support a growing number of people dependent on her.

It's especially during those postwar years that Tubman exemplified courage as fortitude, the self-discipline to endure hardship. In rescuing her family members from slavery, she became the single person to whom they constantly looked for material, as well as emotional, support. Her parents, her siblings, her nieces and nephews, and eventually her second husband and a score of unrelated acquaintances, depended upon her for their upkeep. At times, they seemed nearly helpless when it came to making the simplest decisions or accomplishing the easiest of tasks unless she was there to guide them. Moreover, some of them, especially her mother, could sometimes be quite ungrateful to her by complaining that life as a free person was harder than life as a slave, the cutting insinuation being that Tubman had done her relatives a disservice by rescuing them from slavery. Their neediness placed an enormous burden upon her, but it was one she willingly shouldered out of love and loyalty to family. And when all of her family members had been seen to, she converted her property, as we saw earlier, into a haven for indigent strangers.

The selflessly dedicated way in which she served as materfamilias for relatives and friends indicates another powerful legacy of Tubman's: she broke conventional gender roles of the mid-nineteenth century. In her circle, she was the breadwinner and the problem-solver, and everyone in her family acknowledged as much, even if sometimes only implicitly and sometimes begrudgingly. They may have balked at a woman being the head of the family, but they were too reliant on Tubman's ingenuity, generosity, and wise leadership to really want it any other way.

Mention has already been made of the rarity of female slaves running on their own to freedom. Slave fugitives were most often single men, and, when women escaped, they were almost accompanied and protected by male relatives. But Tubman took out on her own—and this after a prior attempt that she aborted only because the two brothers who accompanied her got cold feet and returned home. She, ever the responsible family member, felt obliged to return with them.

Moreover, the courage and canniness she displayed on her many trips to the Eastern Shore to rescue others were qualities that her contemporaries tended to associate exclusively with men. When leading slaves to freedom, Tubman insisted on their absolute obedience to her instructions. She carried a pistol with her and let it be known to the people she guided that she was more than willing to use it against slave catchers or against any fugitive who jeopardized the safety of others. She reconnoitered terrain; slept on the ground in foul weather; stole corn and grain from fields; and, in general, played the part of a scout behind enemy lines as she guided slaves to liberty.

She also broke conventional gender standards in her willingness to resort to violence in the struggle against slavery. It wasn't just that she carried a pistol when she conducted fugitives on the Underground Railroad. She was also willing to take part in actual fighting.

Tubman was sympathetic to John Brown's idealistic but ultimately ill-planned vision of fomenting a slave revolution, and there's some reason to believe that she would have joined him on the infamous Harpers Ferry raid had she not been ill at the time. Brown was so impressed with her martial spirit that he called her "General Tubman," and even referred to her with masculine pronouns. So did many other persons, even if not so directly, when they called her the "Moses of her people." No doubt doing so was, by today's standards, a rather offensive denial that women were capable of actions and virtues normally reserved for men. But ascribing to her what were considered to be masculine qualities nevertheless attested both to the admiration felt for Tubman by her contemporaries, as well as the extent to which her extraordinary life didn't fit easily into conventional gender categories.

Her status as a person of action more than willing to fight for an end to slavery was further attested by her Civil War service. There's no evidence that Tubman was ever actually involved in combat during those years, but she did recruit and train scouts from Low Country ex-slaves, and she traveled with the Union military expedition up the Combahee River, facing submerged torpedoes as well as Confederate troops on land, as well as, probably, campaigns in Florida and at the bloody debacle of Fort Wagner. After the war, when she repeatedly applied for a veteran's pension, one of the obstacles she encountered was the inability of bureaucrats to believe that a woman, especially a black one, could have actually participated in the war as anything more than a behind-the-lines cook; servant; or, at most, nurse.

Both the courage of her personal life and her willingness to take "unladylike" action in the struggle against slavery suggest yet another reason why Tubman matters: she gave the lie to the general belief at the time that black persons were largely incapable of self-determination. As a consequence, she inspired other African Americans during her lifetime, both in the struggle against slavery and in the postwar years when, although legal bondage was ended, black codes, Jim Crow laws, economic inequality, and racial discrimination were normative.

As noted in chapters 1 and 4, a common defense of slavery in the antebellum years was that it was actually a beneficial institution. Blacks, so this line of thinking went, were essentially childlike, unable to care for themselves without white supervision. Slave owners provided them with food, shelter, and direction in life, and cared for them in their sicknesses and old age. This essentially racist attitude that black people needed white guidance wasn't only used as a justification for slavery. It was also widely believed throughout the entire nation, and resulted in the misconception, widely held for years, that slavery was eventually eliminated almost exclusively by white abolitionists, white politicians, and white soldiers.

Tubman, and others like her, demonstrated the absolute falsity of this stereotype. Slaves frequently asserted self-determination, ranging from acts of everyday resistance to their owners' instructions, to escape, to overt revolt. Tubman in particular displayed a streak of independence from an early age, and while still a slave, became something of an entrepreneur by saving enough money to buy a team of oxen, which she then rented out. Moreover, many ex-slaves and freedmen were active collaborators in the abolitionist movement. They served as conductors and stationmasters on the Underground Railroad, gave lectures to antislavery gatherings, wrote books and edited newspapers, served on vigilance committees that offered relief to fugitives and kept watch for slavecatchers, and eventually served in the Civil War as troops.

Tubman, although not unique, was enough of a rarity and exceptional personality to attract special attention and thereby challenging the myth of black passivity. Along with Sojourner Truth, she was the only black woman who was widely known for her escape from slavery. Even before Sarah Bradford's 1869 biography of her appeared, Tubman had gained notoriety as word of her rescue trips to the south spread. She was also a dynamic speaker, able to transfix audiences with tales of her rescues, acting out scenes and playing different parts. Abraham Lincoln is reported to have said when he met Harriet Beecher Stowe that she was the woman who wrote the big book that started the Civil War. A similar commendation can be made of Tubman: she was the black woman whose courage and daring both inspired and empowered her own people and demonstrated to whites just how actively involved in their own liberation blacks were.

As explored more fully in chapter 10, Tubman's activism was also an inspiration after the war to many women in the suffrage movement, women who frequently had labored shoulder-to-shoulder with her for the abolition of slavery. Tubman was often invited to speak to their gatherings and conventions, and even though she usually confined herself to repeating stories about her Underground Railroad and Civil War service years on such occasions, the example of a woman who was largely self-sufficient in a man's world was eagerly noted and embraced. It's little wonder that in our own time, Tubman has become an icon for both African Americans and women.

*   *   *

It seems fitting that Rosa Parks, who became an icon for the Civil Rights Movement of the 1950s and 1960s, was born just a month before Tubman died in March 1913. It's as if Tubman passed on the baton she carried so admirably her whole life to Parks. Like Tubman, Parks was a black woman who displayed a courageous willingness to step outside of conventional norms about appropriate gender and ethnic behavior to assert both her own dignity as a human being and the right of blacks to enjoy the same rights and privileges as whites. It's unsurprising that, in a 2008 survey of two thousand high school students, Tubman and Parks were voted two of the top three most admired Americans (Wineberg and Monte-Sano 2008).

The third was Martin Luther King Jr.

Timeline

1822
Harriet Tubman is born in February or March on Anthony Thompson's plantation in the Peters Neck district of Dorchester County, Eastern Shore, Maryland. Her birth name is Araminta, and she's called "Minty." At least three of her grandparents were probably born in Africa. Her parents are Ben Ross and Harriet "Rit" Green. Along with her mother, Harriet is owned by Edward Brodess, a minor, whose property is held in trust by Thompson.

1828–1836
Araminta is hired out to local whites for a variety of jobs but is unsuited for many them. Toward the end of this period, she suffers a head wound that nearly kills her and leads to recurring headaches and blackouts that plague her for the rest of her life. Although always religious, she becomes intensely so after the head wound, and frequently experiences visions.

1831–1833
William Lloyd Garrison publishes the inaugural issue of the abolitionist newspaper the *Liberator* on January 1. That same year, the term "Underground Railroad" is coined to describe secret escape routes for fugitive slaves. Two years later, the American Anti-Slavery Society is founded. In August, Nat Turner leads a slave revolt in Southampton County, Virginia, killing nearly sixty whites. In response, already restrictive slave laws throughout the South are tightened even more by frightened legislators.

1836–1844
Araminta works for John Stewart, cutting and hauling timber, a job for which she's well suited. Her father, Ben, who also works for Stewart, is freed in 1840. Araminta marries a free black, John Tubman, in 1844 and begins using "Harriet" as her first name. It's unclear why.

1849

Tubman's owner, Edward Brodess, dies in March. In September, fearing that she'll be sold by his debt-ridden widow, Tubman makes a run for freedom with two of her brothers, Ben and Henry. The brothers grow discouraged and persuade Tubman to return with them. Undaunted, she runs again a few weeks later, this time on her own. With the help of safe houses on the Underground Railroad, she makes it to Philadelphia and freedom.

1850

As part of a brokered congressional deal to ease tensions between free and slave states, Senator John C. Calhoun proposes the Fugitive Slave Act. Replacing a less draconian 1793 law, the act requires magistrates and even private citizens in free states, under threat of penalty, to cooperate in the capture and return of runaway slaves. Several northern states vow to disobey the law. The abolitionist movement grows steadily.

1850–1857

Between working a number of domestic jobs in Philadelphia and Cape May, New Jersey, Tubman launches the first of her thirteen rescue trips, collaborating with Underground Railroad stationmasters such as William Still and Thomas Garrett. In 1850, she brings her niece and her niece's children to freedom. By 1857, she's rescued her brothers and parents as well as nonrelated slaves, for a total of some seventy people. She is gravely disappointed, however, when her husband, John, who has remarried in her absence, refuses to go north with her in fall 1851. She is also unable to rescue one of her sisters and her sister's children. Because of the Fugitive Slave Act, Tubman begins guiding her refugees to Canada. She and her family make St. Catharines, Ontario, their home base for a while.

1858–1859

Tubman meets with abolitionist John Brown. She approves of his plans for an armed uprising of slaves, and he admiringly refers to her as "General Tubman." Brown's raid on the arsenal at Harpers Ferry in October 1859 ends in disaster, and he's hanged in December. A few months earlier, Tubman buys a house and plot of land in Auburn, New York, from William Seward. Auburn will be her home for the rest of her life. She begins lecturing in New York, Boston, and elsewhere about her adventures on the Underground Railroad and acquires notoriety as the "Moses of her people."

1860–1861

Tubman participates in the April 1860 rescue of Charles Nalle, a runaway captured in Troy, New York, under the Fugitive Slave Act. In November, Republican Abraham Lincoln is elected to the presidency. In protest, South Carolina secedes from the Union in December, eventually followed by ten other slave states. The Civil War begins in April 1861 with the assault on Fort Sumter, in South Carolina's Charleston Harbor.

1862–1865
Tubman volunteers her services in the war effort and is stationed at Hilton Head, South Carolina. While there, she cooks, nurses, scouts, and recruits and supervises a network of local spies. In June 1863, she and Colonel James Montgomery lead a raid up the Combahee River, destroying crops and buildings and rescuing some seven hundred slaves. In 1865, she relocates briefly to Virginia's Fortress Monroe as a nurse. On a train home after her war service, she's attacked by white men, who object to her presence in the passenger car, and is severely injured.

1865–1885
The Thirteenth Amendment abolishes slavery in the United States in December 1865. Tubman struggles to make ends meet in Auburn, where she now lives with her aging parents and assorted acquaintances and siblings. She grows and sells food, does domestic labor, and minds children. She also becomes active in raising relief funds for freed slaves in the South. In 1867, she receives word that her husband, John, has been murdered in Maryland. The Fourteenth Amendment grants citizenship to all black persons in 1868; two years later, the Fifteenth Amendment prohibits denying voting rights to anyone because of race. In an effort to raise much-needed funds for Tubman, Sarah Bradford publishes *Scenes in the Life of Harriet Tubman* in 1869. That same year, Tubman marries Nelson Davis, a younger man who fought in the Civil War. Davis begins a small brick-making business but is in poor health, suffering from consumption. In 1873, Tubman falls victim to the "gold swindle." Her parents die—Ben in 1871, and Rit in 1880.

1886–1903
Bradford publishes *Harriet: The Moses of Her People*, an updated biography, in 1886. It runs through two more editions during Tubman's life. Nelson Davis dies two years later, and Tubman becomes peripherally involved in the suffrage movement, lecturing from time to time at meetings. In 1896, she borrows money to buy a plot of land, on which she hopes to found a home and hospital for indigent blacks. Even with private donations, however, she's unable to raise enough funds to see the project through. Age is also beginning to slow her down. In 1903, bowing to necessity, she transfers ownership of the project to the AME Zion Church.

1908–1913
The Harriet Tubman Home finally opens in 1908. Tubman, progressively disabled by rheumatism and pulmonary difficulties, becomes one of its residents. She dies on March 10, 1913, in her early nineties.

1914

Auburn citizens dedicate a memorial plaque to Tubman. Booker T. Washington speaks at its unveiling and dedication.

1920

The Harriet Tubman Home closes its doors.

PRIMARY DOCUMENTS

Harriet Tubman's Escape from Slavery (1849)

In Scenes in the Life of Harriet Tubman, *Sarah Bradford's first biography of her, Tubman related the story of her 1849 run for freedom. She tells Bradford of her constant fear as a slave that she would be sold down South to a rice or cotton planter, a fate that all Upper South slaves dreaded, as well as the unhappy fact that her husband, John, a free black man, refused to take her anxiety seriously.*

After receiving word that two of her sisters had been impressed into a chain gang headed southward (this isn't quite accurate; either Tubman misremembered or Bradford distorted what Tubman told her), she resolved to flee with three (actually, two) of her brothers. After setting out, probably in September, they lost their nerve and eventually persuaded her to return with them to bondage. Tubman was determined to try again, however, and a month later, she did so. Taking out on her own, with some help from a Quaker family named Leverton, who managed a station on the Underground Railroad, Tubman was successful this time.

Tubman's account of her escape captures the heartbreak of leaving loved ones—especially, in Tubman's case, her mother and her husband, John—that fugitive slaves endured, as well as the joy they experienced upon reaching a free soil state, such as Pennsylvania. As Tubman confesses here, leaving behind one's old life, even a life of bondage, could be a frightening and lonely business.

The slaves were told that their master's will provided that none of them should be sold out of the State. This satisfied most of them, and they were very happy. But Harriet was not satisfied; she never closed her eyes that she did not imagine she saw the horsemen coming, and heard the screams of women and children, as they were being dragged away to a far worse slavery than that they were enduring there. Harriet was married at this time to a free negro, who not only did not trouble himself about her fears, but did his best to betray her, and bring her back after she escaped. She would start up at night with the cry, "Oh, dey're comin', dey're comin', I mus' go!"

Her husband called her a fool, and said she was like old Cudjo, who when a joke went round, never laughed till half an hour after everybody else got through, and so just as all danger was past she began to be frightened. But still Harriet in fancy saw the horsemen coming, and heard the screams of terrified women and children. "And all that time, in my dreams and visions," she said, "I seemed to see a line, and on the other side of that line were green fields, and lovely flowers, and beautiful white ladies, who stretched out their arms to me over the line, but I couldn't reach them nohow. I always fell before I got to the line."

One Saturday it was whispered in the quarters that two of Harriet's sisters had been sent off with the chain-gang. That morning she started, having persuaded three of her brothers to accompany her, but they had not gone far when the brothers, appalled by the dangers before and behind them, determined to go back, and in spite of her remonstrances dragged her with them. In fear and terror, she remained over Sunday, and on Monday night a negro from another part of the plantation came privately to tell Harriet that herself and brothers were to be carried off that night. The poor old mother, who belonged to the same mistress, was just going to milk. Harriet wanted to get away without letting her know, because she knew that she would raise an uproar and prevent her going, or insist upon going with her, and the time for this was not yet. But she must give some intimation to those she was going to leave of her intention, and send such a farewell as she might to the friends and relations on the plantation. Those communications were generally made by singing. They sang as they walked along the country roads, and the chorus was taken up by others, and the uninitiated knew not the hidden meaning of the words—

> When dat ar ole chariot comes,
> I'm gwine to lebe you;
> I'm boun' for de promised land,
> I'm gwine to lebe you.

These words meant something more than a journey to the Heavenly Canaan. Harriet said, "Here, mother, go 'long; I'll do the milkin' to-night and bring it in." The old woman went to her cabin. Harriet took down her sun-bonnet, and went on to the "big house," where some of her relatives lived as house servants. She thought she could trust Mary, but there were others in the kitchen, and she could say nothing. Mary began to frolic with her. She threw her across the kitchen, and ran out, knowing that Mary would follow her. But just as they turned the corner of the house, the master to whom Harriet was now hired, came riding up on his horse. Mary darted back, and Harriet thought there was no way now but to sing. But "the Doctor" [Dr. Anthony C. Thompson] as the master was called, was regarded with special awe by his slaves; if they were singing or talking together in the field, or on the road, and "the Doctor" appeared, all was hushed till he passed. But Harriet had no time for ceremony; her friends must have a warning; and whether the Doctor thought her "imperent" or not, she must sing him farewell. So on she went to meet him, singing:

> I'm sorry I'm gwine to lebe you,
> Farewell, oh farewell;
> But I'll meet you in the mornin',
> Farewell, oh farewell.

The Doctor passed, and she bowed as she went on, still singing:

I'll meet you in the mornin',
I'm boun' for de promised land,
On the oder side of Jordan,
Boun' for de promised land.

She reached the gate and looked round; the Doctor had stopped his horse, and had turned around in the saddle, and was looking at her as if there might be more in this than "met the ear." Harriet closed the gate, went on a little way, came back, the Doctor still gazing at her. She lifted up the gate as if she had not latched it properly, waved her hand to him, and burst out again:

I'll meet you in the mornin',
Safe in de promised land,
On the oder side of Jordan,
Boun' for de promised land.

And she started on her journey, "not knowing whither she went," except that she was going to follow the north star, till it led her to liberty. Cautiously and by night she traveled, cunningly feeling her way, and finding out who were friends; till after a long and painful journey she found, in answer to careful inquiries, that she had at last crossed that magic "line" which then separated the land of bondage from the land of freedom; for this was before we were commanded by law to take part in the iniquity of slavery, and aid in taking and sending back those poor hunted fugitives who had manhood and intelligence enough to enable them to make their way thus far towards freedom.

"When I found I had crossed dat line," she said, "I looked at my hands to see if I was de same pusson. There was such a glory ober ebery ting; de sun came like gold through the trees, and ober the fields, and I felt like I was in Heaben."

But then came the bitter drop in the cup of joy. She said she felt like a man who was put in State Prison for twenty-five years. All these twenty-five years he was thinking of his home, and longing for the time when he would see it again. At last the day comes—he leaves the prison gates—he makes his way to his old home, but his old home is not there. The house has been pulled down, and a new one has been put up in its place; his family and friends are gone nobody knows where; there is no one to take him by the hand, no one to welcome him.

"So it was with me," she said. "I had crossed the line. I was free; but there was no one to welcome me to the land of freedom. I was a stranger in a strange land; and my home, after all, was down in Maryland; because my father, my mother, my brothers, and sisters, and friends were there. But I was free, and they should be free. I would make a home in the North and bring them there, God helping me. Oh, how I prayed then," she said; "I said to de Lord, 'I'm gwine to hole stiddy on to you, an' I know you'll see me through.'"

Source: Sarah Bradford. *Scenes in the Life of Harriet Tubman.* Auburn, NY: W. J. Moses, Printer, 1869, 15–20.

Statement Made by Martin I. Townsend, Counsel for the Fugitive Slave Charles Nalle (1860)

The Fugitive Slave Act of 1850 led to a crackdown on refugee slaves living in free states. Local magistrates and private citizens were required, under threat of legal penalty, to assist in the capture and return of fugitives. Many northern state officials chose to ignore the law; some towns and regions became known as sanctuaries or safe havens for runaways. Nonetheless, the decade leading up to the Civil War was a period in which ex-slaves living in free states were in constant danger of being snatched by legal authorities or private slave catchers and returned to bondage.

Charles Nalle was one of them. Born a slave in Virginia around 1821, he escaped to the North in 1858, and eventually made his way to Troy, New York, where he worked as a laborer. While there, the illiterate Nalle asked a journalist, Horace Avril (misspelled Averill in this document), to write letters to family members still in servitude in Virginia. Instead, Avril turned him in to officials, who had no choice but to arrest him on April 27, 1860.

Nalle had been boarding with a member of the Troy vigilance committee, and as soon as word of his arrest spread, abolitionists sprang into action. Attorney Martin Townsend, author of this eyewitness account, immediately applied for a writ of habeas corpus while a large crowd of angry protesters gathered outside the building where Nalle was being held.

Tubman happened to be on a visit to Troy when Nalle was captured, and she played a leading and dramatic role in his rescue from officers of the law. Townsend's recollection of her actions, corroborated by other firsthand accounts, is a testament to Tubman's willingness to put herself in danger's way to help slaves and ex-slaves. At the time, she was in her late thirties, about the same age as Nalle, and was still physically strong and capable of enduring a good deal of pain. Townsend is clearly impressed by her courage and stamina during the rescue. He's equally impressed, as he indicates at the end of his account, by her ongoing efforts to help indigent blacks in both the South and the North.

The verse with which Townsend ends his recollection is a reworking of the third stanza of the hymn "I Love Thy Kingdom, Lord." In the original, "her" refers to the Church.

For her my tears shall fall,
For her my prayers ascend;
To her my cares and toils be given
Till toils and cares shall end.

Nalle is an octoroon; his wife has the same infusion of Caucasian blood. She was the daughter of her master, and had, with her sister, been bred by him in his family, as his own child. When the father died, both of these daughters were married and had large families of children. Under the highly Christian national laws of "Old Virginny," these children were the slaves of their grandfather. The old man died, leaving a will, whereby he manumitted his daughters and their children, and provided for the purchase of the freedom of their husbands. The manumission of the children and grandchildren took effect; but the estate was insufficient to purchase the husbands of his daughters, and the father of his grandchildren. The manumitted, by another Christian, "conservative," and "national" provision of law, were forced to leave the State, while the slave husbands remained in slavery. Nalle and his brother-in-law were allowed for a while to visit their families outside Virginia about once a year, but were at length ordered to provide themselves with new wives, as they would be allowed to visit their former ones no more. It was after this that Nalle and his brother-in-law started for the land of freedom, guided by the steady light of the north star. Thank God, neither family now need fear any earthly master or the bay of the blood-hound dogging their fugitive steps.

Nalle returned to Troy with his family about July, 1860, and resided with them there for more than seven years. They are all now residents of the city of Washington, D.C. Nalle and his family are persons of refined manners, and of the highest respectability. Several of his children are red-haired, and a stranger would discover no trace of African blood in their complexions or features. It was the head of this family whom H. F. Averill proposed to doom to returnless exile and lifelong slavery.

When Nalle was brought from Commissioner [Miles] Beach's office into the street, Harriet Tubman, who had been standing with the excited crowd, rushed amongst the foremost to Nalle, and running one of her arms around his manacled arm, held on to him without ever loosening her hold through the more than half-hour's struggle to Judge [George] Gould's office, and from Judge Gould's office to the dock, where Nalle's liberation was accomplished. In the melee, she was repeatedly beaten over the head with policemen's clubs, but she never for a moment released her hold, but cheered Nalle and his friends with her voice, and struggled with the officers until they were literally worn out with their exertions, and Nalle was separated from them.

True, she had strong and earnest helpers in her struggle, some of whom had white faces as well as human hearts, and are now in Heaven. But she exposed herself to the fury of the sympathizers with slavery, without fear, and suffered their blows without flinching. Harriet crossed the river with the crowd, in the ferry-boat, and when the men who led the assault upon the door of Judge Stewart's office, were stricken down, Harriet and a number of other colored women rushed over their bodies, brought Nalle out, and putting him in the first wagon passing, started him for the West.

A livery team, driven by a colored man, was immediately sent on to relieve the other, and Nalle was seen about Troy no more until he returned a free man by purchase from his master. Harriet also disappeared, and the crowd dispersed. How she came to be in Troy that day, is entirely unknown to our citizens; and where she hid herself after the rescue, is equally a mystery. But her struggle was in the sight of a thousand, perhaps of five thousand spectators.

This woman of whom you have been reading is poor, and partially disabled from her injuries; yet she supports cheerfully and uncomplainingly herself and her old parents, and always has several poor children in her house, who are dependent entirely upon her exertions. At present she has three of these children for whom she is providing, while their parents are working to pay back money borrowed to bring them on. She also maintains by her exertions among the good people of Auburn, two schools of freedmen at the South, providing them teachers and sending them clothes and books. She never asks for anything for herself, but she does ask the charity of the public for "her people."

> For them her tears will fall, For them her prayers ascend;
> To them her toils and cares be given,
> Till toils and cares will end.

If any persons are disposed to aid her in her benevolent efforts, they may send donations to Rev. S. M. Hopkins, Professor in the Auburn Theological Seminary, who will make such disposition of the funds sent as may be designated by the donors.

Source: Sarah Bradford. *Scenes in the Life of Harriet Tubman.* Auburn, NY: W. J. Moses, Printer, 1869, 100–104.

Two Accounts of the Combahee River Raid Victory (1863)

Determined to play a part in the Civil War, Tubman volunteered for service and was sent to Beaufort, South Carolina, where the headquarters of General David Hunter, governor of the Department of the South, was located. Unlike many Union officers, Hunter was a strong opponent of slavery, who pushed for enlisting black troops in the Union cause. While governor of the department, he issued a declaration of emancipation for all slaves in his military district, an order subsequently rescinded by Abraham Lincoln.

In Beaufort, Tubman served as a laundress, cook, and nurse. Craving more direct participation in the war effort, she also recruited and supervised spies, refugee slaves familiar with the Lowcountry tidal area, to describe the lay of the land for the Union Army. Thanks to the reconnaissance intelligence she gathered, an expeditionary force, commanded by Colonel James Montgomery, a past associate of John Brown's during the Bloody Kansas years, went up the Combahee River on June 2, 1863. Tubman accompanied the force, guiding the troop transports around Confederate torpedoes hidden in the river's water. The expedition was a complete success, routing rebel forces stationed along the river, burning several plantations, securing stockpiles of supplies, and freeing some seven hundred slaves.

In the first selection, Bradford recounts Tubman's recollection of the raid. Especially noteworthy is her account of the ecstatic jubilation displayed by the rescued slaves, and the extemporaneous song she crooned to calm the excited refugees so that they could board the transports in an orderly way. Two lines of the song especially stand out:

> *Come along! Come along! Don't be alarmed,*
> *Uncle Sam is rich enough to give you all a farm.*

The second selection, an excited and slightly repetitious journalistic account of a rally celebrating the Combahee River Raid's success, praises Tubman, the "Moses of her people," for both her oratorical skill as well as her martial courage—despite, the author remarks, her being a black woman. It's not completely clear whether this comment is intended ironically or reveals the time's prejudicial views of women and black persons. The journalist does go on to say that Tubman's performance outstrips that of many whites, who fancied themselves superior simply by virtue of "the cuticle in which their Creator condescended to envelop them."

One phrasing in this selection especially reveals the excitement its author felt over the raid's success. In referring to the rescue of the slaves, he calls them "recreated black humanity," transformed by their passage from "chattels" to free men and women.

When our armies and gun-boats first appeared in any part of the South, many of the poor negroes were as much afraid of "de Yankee Buckra" as of their own masters. It was almost impossible to win their confidence, or to get information from them. But to Harriet they would tell anything; and so it became quite important that she should accompany expeditions going up the rivers, or into unexplored parts of the country, to control and get information from those whom they took with them as guides.

General Hunter asked her at one time if she would go with several gun-boats up the Combahee River, the object of the expedition being to take up the torpedoes placed by the rebels in the river, to destroy railroads and bridges, and to cut off supplies from the rebel troops. She said she would go if Colonel Montgomery was to be appointed commander of the expedition. Colonel Montgomery was one of John Brown's men, and was well known to Harriet. Accordingly, Colonel Montgomery was appointed to the command, and Harriet, with several men under her, the principal of whom was J. Plowden, whose pass I have, accompanied the expedition. Harriet describes in the most graphic manner the appearance of the plantations as they passed up the river; the frightened negroes leaving their work and taking to the woods, at sight of the gun-boats; then coming to peer out like startled deer, and scudding away like the wind at the sound of the steam-whistle. "Well," said one old negro, "Mas'r said de Yankees had horns and tails, but I nebber beliebed it till now." But the word was passed along by the mysterious telegraphic communication existing among these simple people, that these were "Lincoln's gun-boats come to set them free." In vain, then, the drivers used their whips in their efforts to hurry the poor creatures back to their quarters; they all turned and ran for the gun-boats. They came down every road, across every field, just as they had left their work and their cabins; women with children clinging around their necks, hanging to their dresses, running behind, all making at full speed for "Lincoln's gun-boats." Eight hundred poor wretches at one time crowded the banks, with their hands extended toward their deliverers, and they were all taken off upon the gun-boats, and carried down to Beaufort.

"I nebber see such a sight," said Harriet; "we laughed, an' laughed, an' laughed. Here you'd see a woman wid a pail on her head, rice a smokin' in it jus' as she'd taken it from de fire, young one hangin' on behind, one han' roun' her forehead to hold on, 'tother han' diggin' into de rice-pot, eatin' wid all its might; hold of her dress two or three more; down her back a bag wid a pig in it. One woman brought two pigs, a white one an' a black one; we took 'em all on board; named de white pig Beauregard, and de black pig Jeff Davis. Sometimes de women would come wid twins hangin' roun' der necks; 'pears like I nebber see so many twins in my life; bags on der shoulders, baskets on der heads, and young ones taggin' behin', all loaded; pigs squealin', chickens screamin', young ones squallin'." And so they came pouring down to the gun-boats. When they stood on the shore, and the small boats put out to take them off, they all wanted to get in at once. After the boats were crowded, they would hold on to them so that they could not leave the shore. The oarsmen would beat them on their hands, but they would not let go; they were afraid the gun-boats would go off and leave them, and all wanted to make sure of one of these arks of refuge. At length Colonel Montgomery shouted from the upper deck, above the clamor of appealing tones, "Moses, you'll have to give em a song." Then Harriet lifted up her voice, and sang:

Of all the whole creation in the East or in the West,
The glorious Yankee nation is the greatest and the best.
Come along! Come along! don't be alarmed,
Uncle Sam is rich enough to give you all a farm.

At the end of every verse, the negroes in their enthusiasm would throw up their hands and shout "Glory," and the row-boats would take that opportunity to push off; and so at last they were all brought on board. The masters fled; houses and barns and railroad bridges were burned, tracks torn up, torpedoes destroyed, and the object of the expedition was fully accomplished.

This fearless woman was often sent into the rebel lines as a spy, and brought back valuable information as to the position of armies and batteries; she has been in battle when the shot was falling like hail, and the bodies of dead and wounded men were dropping around her like leaves in autumn; but the thought of fear never seems to have had place for a moment in her mind. She had her duty to perform, and she expected to be taken care of till it was done.

Source: Sarah Bradford. *Harriet: The Moses of Her People*. New York: George R. Lockwood & Son, 1886, 98–102.

Celebration Following the Combahee River Raid

June 6, 1863

At Beaufort a few days since, I had the satisfaction of witnessing the return of the gallant Col. Montgomery from a successful raid into the enemy's country, having with him the trophies of war in the shape of 780 black chattels, now recreated and made freemen, and thousands of dollars worth of rice and other property.

As I witnessed the moving mass of recreated black humanity on its way from the boat to the church in Beaufort, where they were quartered for the moment, with the filth and tatters of slavery still hanging to their degraded persons, my heart went up in gratitude to God for the change which had been wrought on South Carolina soil. The emblem of liberty and a nation's glory, as it floated over these poor, defenseless children of oppression, never looked to me so glorious, and never thrilled any heart with a more honest pride.

I doubt whether this church was ever before filled with such a crowd of devout worshippers—whether it was ever before appropriated to so good a purpose—whether so true a gospel had ever before been preached within its walls. I certainly never felt such swelling emotions of gratitude to the Great Ruler at this moment.

Col. Montgomery and his gallant band of 300 black soldiers, under the guidance of a black woman, dashed into the enemies' [sic] country, struck a bold and effective blow, destroying millions of dollars worth of commissary stores, cotton and lordly dwellings, and striking terror to the heart of rebellion, brought off near 800 slaves and thousands of dollars worth of property, without losing a man or receiving a scratch. It was a glorious consummation.

After they were all fairly disposed of in the church, they were addressed in strains of thrilling eloquence by their gallant deliverer; to which they responded in a song—

There is a white robe for thee.

A song so appropriate and so heartfelt and cordial as to bring unbidden tears.

The Colonel was followed by a speech from the black woman who led the raid, and under whose inspiration it was originated and conducted. For sound sense and real native eloquence, her address would do honor to any man, and it created a great sensation.

And now a word of this woman—this black heroine—this fugitive slave. She is now called "Moses," having inherited the name, for the many daring feats she has accomplished in behalf of the bondmen and the many slaves she has set free. She was formerly a slave in Virginia—she determined upon "freedom or death" and escaped to Canada. She there planned the deliverance of all her kindred, and made nine successful trips to different slave states, effecting the escape of over 180 slaves and their successful establishment in Canada. Since the rebellion she has devoted herself to her great work of delivering the bondmen, with an energy and sagacity that cannot be exceeded. Many and many times she has penetrated the enemy's lines and discovered their situation and condition, and escaped without injury, but not without extreme hazard. True, she is but a woman, and a "nigger" at that, but in patriotism, sagacity, energy, ability and all that elevates human character, she is head and shoulders above all the copperheads in the land, and above many who vaunt their patriotism and boast their philanthropy, swaggering of their superiority because of the cuticle in which their Creator condescended to envelop them.

Source: "From Florida: Colonel Montgomery's Raid." *Wisconsin State Journal,* June 20, 1863.

Thomas Garrett's Reminiscence of Tubman as Underground Railroad Conductor (1868)

Thomas Garrett's home in Wilmington, Delaware, was one of the most important Underground Railroad stations in the East. In this testimonial, solicited by Tubman biographer Sarah Bradford, he recalls two of her rescues. The first took place in November 1856, when Tubman led Joe and Ben Bailey, Peter Pennington, and Eliza Manokey to freedom. The trek northward, which went all the way to Canada, was an especially grueling one for Tubman. She caught a chill that turned into pneumonia, and she remained ill throughout the winter. The second rescue Garrett describes took place six months later, when Tubman led her parents, Ben and Rit, to the North.

Garrett also remarks on Tubman's absolute certainty that God had commissioned her to lead slaves to freedom. She believed this gave her license to make tenacious requests of him for the funds necessary to finance her rescue missions. Although Garrett's account humorously suggests that Tubman's demands for money were sometimes disconcerting, he was astounded that the cash she needed somehow always became available.

Garrett was convinced that Tubman and her work on the Underground Railroad were genuinely inspired by God. "In truth," he marveled, "I never met with any person, of any color, who had more confidence in the voice of God, as spoken direct to her soul." Coming from a Quaker who was himself intensely devout, this was high praise indeed.

WILMINGTON, 6th Mo., 1868.

MY FRIEND: Thy favor of the 12th reached me yesterday, requesting such reminiscences as I could give respecting the remarkable labors of Harriet Tubman, in aiding her colored friends from bondage. I may begin by saying, living as I have in a slave State, and the laws being very severe where any proof could be made of any one aiding slaves on their way to freedom, I have not felt at liberty to keep any written word of Harriet's or my own labors, except in numbering those whom I have aided. For that reason I cannot furnish so interesting an account of Harriet's labors as I otherwise could, and now would be glad to do; for in truth I never met with any person, of any color, who had more confidence in the voice of God, as spoken direct to her soul. She has frequently told me that she talked with God, and he talked with her every day of her life, and she has declared to me that she felt no more fear of being arrested by her former master, or any other person, when in his immediate neighborhood, than she did in the State of New York, or Canada, for she said she never ventured only where God sent her, and her faith in the Supreme Power truly was great.

I have now been confined to my room with indisposition more than four weeks, and cannot sit to write much; but I feel so much interested in

Harriet, that I will try to give some of the most remarkable incidents that now present themselves to my mind. The date of the commencement of her labors, I cannot certainly give; but I think it must have been about 1845; from that time till 1860, I think she must have brought from the neighborhood where she had been held as a slave, from 60 to 80 persons, from Maryland, some 80 miles from here. No slave who placed himself under her care, was ever arrested that I have heard of; she mostly had her regular stopping places on her route; but in one instance, when she had several stout men with her, some 30 miles below here, she said that God told her to stop, which she did; and then asked him what she must do. He told her to leave the road, and turn to the left; she obeyed, and soon came to a small stream of tide water; there was no boat, no bridge; she again inquired of her Guide what she was to do. She was told to go through. It was cold, in the month of March; but having confidence in her Guide, she went in; the water came up to her armpits; the men refused to follow till they saw her safe on the opposite shore. They then followed, and, if I mistake not, she had soon to wade a second stream; soon after which she came to a cabin of colored people, who took them all in, put them to bed, and dried their clothes, ready to proceed next night on their journey. Harriet had run out of money, and gave them some of her underclothing to pay for their kindness. When she called on me two days after, she was so hoarse she could hardly speak, and was also suffering with violent toothache. The strange part of the story we found to be, that the masters of these men had put up the previous day, at the railroad station near where she left, an advertisement for them, offering a large reward for their apprehension; but they made a safe exit. She at one time brought as many as seven or eight, several of whom were women and children. She was well known here in Chester County and Philadelphia, and respected by all true abolitionists. I had been in the habit of furnishing her and those who accompanied her, as she returned from her acts of mercy, with new shoes; and on one occasion when I had not seen her for three months, she came into my store. I said, "Harriet, I am glad to see thee! I suppose thee wants a pair of new shoes." Her reply was, "I want more than that." I, in jest, said, "I have always been liberal with thee, and wish to be; but I am not rich, and cannot afford to give much." Her reply was: "God tells me you have money for me." I asked her "if God never deceived her?" She said, "No!" "Well! How much does thee want?" After studying a moment, she said: "About twenty-three dollars." I then gave her twenty-four dollars and some odd cents, the net proceeds of five pounds sterling, received through Eliza Wigham, of Scotland, for her. I had given some accounts of Harriet's labor to the Anti-Slavery Society of Edinburgh, of which Eliza Wigham was Secretary. On the reading of my letter, a gentleman present said he would send Harriet four pounds if he knew of any way to get it to her. Eliza Wigham offered to forward it to me for her, and that was the first money ever received by me for her. Some twelve months after, she called on me again, and said that God told her I had some money for her, but not so much as before. I had, a few days previous, received the net proceeds of one pound ten shillings from Europe for her. To say the least there was something remarkable in these facts, whether clairvoyance, or the divine impression on her mind from the source of all power, I cannot tell; but certain it was she had a guide within herself other than the written word, for she never had any education. She brought away her aged parents in a singular manner. They started with an old horse, fitted out in primitive style with a straw collar, a pair of old chaise wheels, with a board on the axle to sit on, another board swung with ropes, fastened to the axle, to rest their feet on. She got her parents, who were both slaves belonging to different masters, on this rude vehicle to the railroad, put them in the cars, turned Jehu herself, and drove to town in a style that no human being ever did before or since; but she was happy at having arrived safe. Next day, I furnished her with money to take them all to Canada. I afterward sold their horse, and sent them the balance of the proceeds. I believe that Harriet succeeded in freeing all her relatives but one sister and her three children.

Thy friend,

THOS. GARRETT.

Source: Sarah Bradford. *Harriet: The Moses of Her People.* New York: George R. Lockwood & Son, 1886, 83–88.

"Moses" (1874)

William Wells Brown (1814–1884) was an ex-slave who, along with Frederick Douglass, became the preeminent black author of his generation. Born in Kentucky, he escaped to Ohio and freedom when he was twenty years old. Settling in Boston, he became a leading abolitionist and published articles and reviews that quickly earned him a reputation. In 1847, he published his memoir of life as a slave, and in 1853 published Clotel, *often credited as the first novel written by a U.S. black. It's based on the alleged affair between Thomas Jefferson and his slave Sally Hemmings.*

In 1874, Wells published The Rising Sun, *a personal account of the abolitionist movement in the United States. In the book, he profiled many of the leading abolitionists, and one of them was Harriet Tubman, the "Moses of her people."*

For eight or ten years previous to the breaking out of the Rebellion [the Civil War], all who frequented anti-slavery conventions, lectures, picnics, and fairs, could not fail to have seen a black woman of medium size, upper front teeth gone, smiling countenance, attired in coarse, but neat apparel, with an old-fashioned reticule or bag, suspended by her side, and who, on taking her seat, would at once drop off into a sound sleep. This woman was Harriet Tubman, better known as "Moses."

She first came to Boston in 1854, and was soon a welcome visitor to the homes of the leading Abolitionists, who were always attentive listeners to her strange and eventful stories. Her plantation life, where she was born a slave at the South, was cruelly interesting. Her back and shoulders, marked with the biting lash, told how inhuman was the institution from which she had fled. A blow upon the head had caused partial deafness, and inflicted an injury which made her fall asleep the moment she was seated. Moses had no education, yet the most refined person would listen for hours while she related the intensely interesting incidents of her life, told in the simplest manner, but always seasoned with good sense.

During her sojourn in Boston, Moses made several visits to the South, and it was these that gave her the cognomen of "Moses." Men from Canada, who had made their escape years before, and whose families were still in the prison-house of slavery, would seek out Moses, and get her to go and bring their dear ones away. How strange! This woman—one of the most ordinary looking of her race; unlettered; no idea of geography; asleep half of the time—would penetrate the interior slave states, hide in the woods during the day, feed on the bondsman's homely fare at night, bring off whole families of slaves, and pilot them to Canada, after running the gauntlet of the most difficult parts of the southern country. No fugitive was ever captured who had Moses for a leader.

Source: William Wells Brown. *The Rising Son; or, the Antecedents and Advancement of the Colored Race.* Boston: A. G. Brown & Co., 1882, 537–538.

Dedication of the Harriet Tubman Home for Black Indigents (1908)

In 1896, Tubman purchased a twenty-five-acre parcel of land adjacent to her property, with the intention of establishing on it a self-sufficient community for indigent and ailing blacks. She acquired the land at a public auction, even though she had nearly no money of her own, and paid for it with the help of a bank loan, a new mortgage on her own home, and the generous contributions of friends and supporters.

Tubman was in her seventies at the time of the purchase and beginning to feel the weight of her years. Eventually admitting that she hadn't the energy or resources to achieve her dream on her own, she transferred ownership of the parcel to the AME Zion Church, in which she was a member, in 1903. Five years later, thanks to the promise of an annual subsidy from the church as well as a one-time fee for residents—a policy Tubman vigorously disapproved—the Harriet Tubman Home finally became a reality. Toward the end of her life, infirm and unable to care for herself, she became one of its residents.

In this newspaper account of the home's 1908 dedication, Auburn's affection for Tubman is obvious. Equally clear is that even at an advanced age, she was still able to hold an audience spellbound with stories about her Underground Railroad days.

Unfortunately, the home didn't long survive her. After her death, it limped along for a while before closing its doors in 1920.

With the stars and stripes wound around her shoulders, a band playing national airs and a concourse of members of her race gathered about her to pay tribute to her lifetime struggle in behalf of the colored people of America, aged Harriet Tubman Davis, the Moses of her race, yesterday experienced one of the happiest moments of her life, a period to which she has looked forward for a score or more of years, the dedication of a home for aged and friendless colored people. The delays in the consummation of her efforts have been many and tedious, but the Harriet Tubman Home is today an accomplished fact, and her 95 years have at last been crowned with success.

Now the A.M.E. Zion Church of America has taken upon itself the work of establishing the Home on a successful basis and yesterday marked the opening of the home for the reception of those who wish to take advantage of it. At the present time the sum of $150 gives the applicant life privileges. Mr. and Mrs. Asa Lewis have recently been placed in charge of the Home as overseers and managers with their residence upon the property. The property will gradually be improved and the land cultivated as funds will permit. There are an abundance of fruit trees and the entire property is tillable. At the lately adjourned [A.M.E.] conference of western New York held at Binghamton, it was voted to take an annual collection for the maintenance fund of the Home, and it is estimated that this sum will not be less than $200 per year.

The Home has been tidily fitted up with comfortable furniture, plenty of clean, white linen, enameled beds, etc. . . .

One of the most active persons on the grounds was Harriet herself and everywhere she went groups of people gathered about her to listen to her stories of her work.

When called upon by the chairman for a few words of welcome the aged woman stated that she had but started the work for the rising generation to take up. "I did not take up this work for my own benefit," said she, "but for those of my race who need help. The work is now well started and I know God will raise up others to take care of the future. All I ask is united effort, for 'united we stand: divided we fall.'"

Harriet stated that the first payment she made on the present property was a York shilling. As she ceased speaking Perry Williams unfurled the flag behind her and the band played The Star Spangled Banner amid the applause of the throng.

Source: "Tubman Home Open," *Auburn (NY) Citizen*, June 24, 1908.

Tubman's Obituary (1913)

Newspapers across the land ran long and generally admiring obituaries of Tubman when she died on March 10, 1913. Their descriptions of her varied in accuracy. The most common errors were exaggerations of the number of slaves she rescued from bondage, indicating the mythic status that her years with the Underground Railroad had achieved in the popular imagination.

In this death notice from an Auburn newspaper, details of Tubman's death, including her final words, are reported. The bulk of the article (not excerpted in this selection) offered a fulsome and relatively accurate biography of her. The medal sent to her by Queen Victoria that is mentioned in the obituary was buried with Tubman when she was laid to rest on March 13 in Auburn's Fort Hill Cemetery.

HARRIET TUBMAN IS DEAD

"I GO TO PREPARE A PLACE FOR YOU"

THE LAST WORDS SHE UTTERED.

BORN IN SLAVERY NEARLY 100 YEARS AGO

Harriet Tubman Davis, Aunt Harriet, died last night of pneumonia at the home she founded on South Street Road near here. Born lowly, she lived a life of exalted self-sacrifice and her end closes a career that has taken its place in American history. Her true services to the black race were never known but her true worth could never have been rewarded by human agency.

Harriet's death was indeed the passing of a brave woman. There was no regret but on the contrary she rejoiced in her final hours. Conscious within a few hours of her final passing she joined with those who came to pray for her and the final scene in the long drama of her life was quite as thrilling as the many that had gone before.

Yesterday afternoon when the trained nurse, Mrs. Martha Ridgeway of Elmira, and Dr. G. B. Mack had decided that her death was but the question of a few hours, Harriet asked for her friends, Rev. Charles A. Smith and Rev. E. U. A. Brooks, clergyman of the Zion A. M. E. Church. They with Eliza E. Peterson, national superintendent for temperance work among colored people of the W.C.T.U., who came here from Texarkana, Tex., to see Harriet, and others, joined in a final service which Harriet directed. She joined in the singing when her cough did not prevent, and after receiving the sacrament she sank back in bed ready to die.

LOVE TO ALL THE CHURCHES

To the clergyman she said "Give my love to all the churches" and after a severe coughing spell she blurted out in a thick voice this farewell passage which she had learned from Matthew: "I go away to prepare a place for you, and where I am ye may be also." She soon afterward lapsed into a comatose condition and death came at 8:30 o'clock last evening. Those present when she died included Rev. and Mrs. Smith and Miss Ridgeway, the colored nurse.

Two grandnieces of Harriet, Miss Alida Stewart and Miss Eva Stewart, were in Washington attending the inaugural [of Woodrow Wilson] and had not returned to Auburn. Harriet's nephew, William H. Stewart and his son, Charles Stewart, were in attendance during the final hours.

Harriet's age was unknown. Born a slave of slave parents her lowly origin did not become a matter of sufficient moment to demand chronicling until it was too late to obtain other than a vague story of her childhood.

Today, more-than half a century after John Brown said "I bring you one of the bravest and best persons on this continent" when he presented Harriet to Wendell Phillips, a glance over her remarkable career shows that the hero of Harper's Ferry might well be quoted in selecting Harriet Tubman's epitaph . . .

EXACT AGE NOT ESTABLISHED

Her age has never been established, but it is known that she was over 90 years and possibly was even more than 95 years. To a reporter, who met her some time before she was finally compelled to remain at the Home, she replied to the questions of her age: "Indeed I don't know, Sir. I am somewhere's about 90 to 95. I don't know when I was born, but I am pretty near

95." She was in the office of the Superintendent of Charities F. J. Lattimore at the time, and her mind was unusually clear.

MEDAL FROM QUEEN VICTORIA

It is no exaggeration to say that Harriet Tubman, as she is best known, furnishes a career of self sacrifice that, in her services to the Negro race, does not fall far short of the brilliancy of Joan of Arc, Grace Darling or Florence Nightingale. She has been honored by thousands and exalted personages have been equally eager to pay homage with humble folk that she labored for. She was a friend of William Lloyd Garrison, Wendell Phillips, John Brown, Gerrit Smith, Seward, Lincoln and others connected with the Anti-Slavery period. One of the treasured possessions that she leaves behind is a small medal given her by Queen Victoria. . .

Harriet leaves very little property, and so far as known her possessions include the seven acres, little brick house and, barns on the place out on South Street road where she lived so many years.

The arrangements for the funeral were incomplete at a late hour this afternoon. Rev. Charles A. Smith and Rev. E. U. A. Brooks are in charge of the matter and expect to complete the arrangements late today.

Source: *Auburn (NY) Citizen*, March 11, 1913.

Bibliography

Adams, Nehemiah. *A South-Side View of Slavery; or, Three Months at the South in 1854.* Boston, MA: T. R. Marvin & B. B. Mussey, 1854.

American Anti-Slavery Society. *The Anti-Slavery History of the John-Brown Year; Being the Twenty-Seventh Annual Report of the American Anti-Slavery Society.* New York: Anti-Slavery Society, 1861.

Barney, William L. *The Oxford Encyclopedia of the Civil War.* New York: Oxford University Press, 2011.

Blassingame, John H. (ed.). *The Frederick Douglass Papers.* New Haven, CT: Yale University Press, 1982.

Blassingame, John H. *The Slave Community: Plantation Life in the Antebellum South.* New York: Oxford University Press, 1979.

Blassingame, John H. (ed.). *Slave Testimony: Two Centuries of Letters, Speeches, Interviews, and Autobiographies.* Baton Rouge, LA: Louisiana State University, 1977.

Bordewich, Fergus M. *America's Great Debate: Henry Clay, Stephen A. Douglas, and the Compromise That Preserved the Union.* New York: Simon & Schuster, 2012.

Bradford, Sarah. *Harriet, Moses of Her People.* New York: George R. Lockwood and Son, 1886.

Bradford, Sarah. *Harriet, Moses of Her People.* New York: J. H. Little, 1901.

Bradford, Sarah. *Scenes in the Life of Harriet Tubman.* Auburn, NY: W. J. Moses, 1869.

Brown, William Wells. *The Rising Son; or, the Antecedents and Advancement of the Colored Race.* Boston, MA: A. G. Brown, 1874.

Calhoun, John C. "Remarks of Mr. Calhoun, of South Carolina, on the Reception of Abolition Petitions Delivered to the Senate of the United States, February 1837." In *The Senate, 1789–1989: Classic Speeches* Vol. 3, edited by Wendy Wolf, 175–178. Washington, DC: Government Printing Office, 1994.

Cartwright, Samuel. "Diseases and Peculiarities of the Negro Race." *De Bow's Southern and Western Review* XI (September 1851).

Cheney, Lynne. "The End of History." *Wall Street Journal* (October 20, 1994).

Clinton, Catherine. *Harriet Tubman: The Road to Freedom.* New York: Little, Brown, 2004.

Cobb, Thomas R. R. *An Inquiry into the Law of Negro Slavery in the United States of America.* Philadelphia, PA: T & J. W. Johnson, 1858.

Congressional Globe, 33rd Congress, 1st Session.

Conrad, Earl. *Harriet Tubman.* Washington, DC: The Associated Publishers, 1943.

Donald, David Herbert. *Charles Sumner and the Coming of the Civil War.* New York: Alfred A. Knopf, 1960.

Douglass, Frederick. *Life and Times of Frederick Douglass.* Boston, MA: De Wolfe & Fiske Co., 1882.

Douglass, Frederick. *My Bondage and My Freedom.* Edited by John Stauffer. New York: Modern Library, 2003.

Douglass, Frederick. *Narrative of the Life of Frederick Douglass, an American Slave, Written by Himself.* (1845). Edited by John R. McKivigan IV, Peter P. Hinks, and Heather L. Kaufman. New Haven, CT: Yale University Press, 2016.

Drayton, Daniel. *Personal Memoir of Daniel Drayton, for Four Years and Four Months a Prisoner (for Charity's Sake) in Washington Jail.* Boston, MA: Bela Marsh, 1855.

Drew, Benjamin. *The Refugee: A North-Side View of Slavery.* (1856). Toronto: Dundurn Press, 2008.

Duncan, Russell. *Blue Eyed Child of Fortune: The Civil War Letters of Colonel Robert Gould Shaw.* Athens, GA: University of Georgia Press, 1999.

Faust, Drew Gilpin. *The Ideology of Slavery: Proslavery Thought in the Antebellum South, 1830–1860.* Baton Rouge, LA: Louisiana State University Press, 1981.

Ferrell, Claudine L. *The Abolitionist Movement.* Westport, CT: Greenwood Press, 2006.

Fitzhugh, George. *Sociology for the South; or, the Failure of Free Society.* Richmond, VA: A. Morris, 1854.

Foner, Eric. *Nat Turner.* Trenton, NJ: Prentice Hall, 1972.

Foner, Eric. *Reconstruction: America's Unfinished Revolution, 1863–1877.* New York: Harper & Row, 1988.

Franklin, John Hope, and Loren Schweninger. *Runaway Slaves: Rebels on the Plantation.* New York: Oxford University Press, 1999.

Gara, Larry. *The Liberty Line: The Legend of the Underground Railroad.* Lexington, KY: University Press of Kentucky, 1996.

Gienapp, William E. *The Civil War and Reconstruction: A Documentary Collection*. New York: W. W. Norton, 2001)

Greenberg, Kenneth S. *The Confessions of Nat Turner, and Related Documents*. Boston, MA: Bedford/St. Martin's, 1996.

Grigg, Jeff W. *Combahee River Raid: Harriet Tubman and Lowcountry Liberation*. Charleston, SC: The History Press, 2004.

Hamilton, Holman. *Prologue to Conflict: The Crisis and Compromise of 1850*. Lexington, KY: University Press of Kentucky, 2005.

Hammond, James H. *Selections from the Letters and Speeches*. New York: John F. Trow & Co., 1866.

Harris, Norman D. *The History of Negro Servitude in Illinois, and the Slavery Agitation in the State, 1719–1864*. Chicago, IL: A.C. McGlurg, 1904.

Hendricks, Gerret, Derick op de Graeff, Francis Daniell Pastorius, and Abraham op den Graef. "Resolution of Germantown Mennonites." In *American Antislavery Writings*, edited by James G. Basker. New York: The Library of America, 2012.

Higginson, Thomas Wentworth. *Army Life in a Black Regiment*. (1869). New York: W. W. Norton, 1984.

Holt, Rosa Belle. "A Heroine in Ebony." *The Chautauquan* 23 (July 1896): 459–462.

Horton, James Oliver, and Lois E. Horton. *Slavery and the Making of America*. New York: Oxford University Press, 2005.

Humez, Jean M. *Harriet Tubman: The Life and the Stories*. Madison, WI: University of Wisconsin Press, 2003.

Jefferson, Thomas. *Life and Selected Writings*. Edited by Adrienne Koch and William Peden. New York: Modern Library Classics, 1944.

Larson, Kate Clifford. *Bound for the Promised Land: Harriet Tubman, Portrait of an American Hero*. New York: Ballantine, 2003.

Lincoln, Abraham. *The Collected Works of Abraham Lincoln*. Edited by Roy P. Basler. New Brunswick, NJ: Rutgers University Press, 1953.

Looby, Christopher (ed.). *The Complete Civil War Journal and Selected Letters of Thomas Wentworth Higginson*. Chicago, IL: University of Chicago Press, 2000.

Lowry, Beverly. *Harriet Tubman: Imagining a Life*. New York: Anchor, 2008.

May, Samuel J. *Some Recollections of Our Antislavery Conflict*. (1869). Stoughton, WI: Books on Demand, 2013.

McGowan, James A., and William C. Kashatus. *Harriet Tubman: A Biography*. Santa Barbara, CA: Greenwood, 2011.

Miller, Edward A., Jr. *Lincoln's Abolitionist General: The Biography of David Hunter*. Columbia, SC: University of South Carolina Press, 1977.

Nevins, Allan. *Ordeal of the Union: A House Dividing, 1852–1857.* New York: Charles Scribner's Sons, 1947.

New York Sun, The. "The Moses of Her People; Proposed Memorial to Harriet Tubman, a Negress." (May 2, 1909).

Northup, Solomon. *Twelve Years a Slave.* (1853). Mineola, NY: Dover, 2014.

Oakes, James. *Slavery and Freedom: An Interpretation of the Old South.* New York: Alfred A. Knopf, 1990.

Oakes, James. *To Purge This Land with Blood.* New York: Harper & Row, 1970.

Parker, John. *His Promised Land: The Autobiography of John P. Parker.* Edited by Stuart Seely Sprague. New York: W. W. Norton, 1996.

Parker, William. "The Freedman's Story." *The Atlantic Monthly* XVII (February and March 1866): 152–166, 276–295.

Pearson, Elizabeth Ware. *Letters from Port Royal.* Boston, MA: W. B. Clarke, 1906.

Quarles, Benjamin. "Harriet Tubman's Unlikely Leadership." In *Black Leaders of the Nineteenth Century.* Edited by Leon Litwack and August Meier, 43–57. Urbana, IL: University of Illinois Press, 1988.

Richardson, James Daniel (ed.). *A Compilation of the Messages and Papers of the Presidents.* Washington, DC: Bureau of National Literature and Art, 2007.

Rodriguez, Junius P. (ed.). *Slavery in the United States: A Social, Political, and Historical Encyclopedia.* Santa Barbara, CA: ABC-CLIO, 2007.

Sanborn, Franklin B. "Harriet Tubman." *Commonwealth* (Boston), August 12, 1863. Contained as an appendix in Bradford, 1886.

Schott, Thomas E. *Alexander H. Stephens of Georgia: A Biography.* Baton Rouge, LA: Louisiana State University Press, 1988.

Sernett, Milton C. *Harriet Tubman: Myth, Memory, and History.* Durham, NC: Duke University Press, 2007.

Siebert, Wilbur H. *The Underground Railroad from Slavery to Freedom.* Mineola, NY: Dover, 2006.

Stauffer, John. *Giants: The Parallel Lives of Frederick Douglass and Abraham Lincoln.* New York: Twelve, 2008.

Steckel, Richard H. "Women, Health, and Work under Plantation Slavery in the United States." In *More Than Chattel: Black Women and Slavery in the Americas.* Edited by David Barry Gaspar and Darlene Clark Hine, 43–60. Bloomington, IN: Indiana University Press, 1996.

Sterling, Dorothy. *We Are Your Sisters: Black Women in the Nineteenth Century.* New York: W. W. Norton, 1984.

Still, William. *The Underground Railroad.* (1872). Mineola, NY: Dover, 2007.

Telford, Emma P. "Harriet: The Modern Moses of Heroism and Visions." Auburn, NY: Cayuga County Museum, c. 1905, typescript. Quoted in Humez 2003 and Larson 2003.

Thoreau, Henry David. "A Plea for Captain John Brown." In *Henry David Thoreau: Collected Essays and Poems*. Edited by Elizabeth Hall Witherell. New York: Library of America, 2001.

Tragle, Henry Irving. *The Southampton Slave Revolt of 1831: A Compilation of Source Material*. New York: Vintage, 1973.

Walker, David. *Appeal to the Colored Citizens of the World*. (1829). Edited by Peter P. Hinks. University Park, PA: Pennsylvania State University Press, 2006.

Walters, Kerry. *American Slave Revolts and Conspiracies*. Santa Barbara, CA: ABC-CLIO, 2015.

Walters, Kerry. *The Underground Railroad*. Santa Barbara, CA: ABC-CLIO, 2012.

Walters, Ronald G. *American Reformers, 1815–1860*. New York: Hill and Wang, 1978.

Ward, Samuel Ringgold. *Autobiography of a Fugitive Slave*. (1855). Scotts Valley, CA: CreateSpace, 2010.

Whittier, John Greenleaf. "The Branded Hand." In *Poems*. Boston, MA: Sanborn, Carter, & Bazin, 1856.

Whyman, Lillie B. Chase. "Harriet Tubman." *New England Magazine* 14.1 (March 1896).

Wineberg, Sam, and Chauncey Monte-Sano. "Who Is a Famous American? Charting Historical Memory across the Curriculum." *Phil Delta Kappa* 98/9 (May 2008): 643–648.

Winks, Robin W. *The Blacks in Canada: A History*. 2nd edition. Montreal and Kingston: McGill-Queen's University Press, 2008.

Woman's Era, The. "Eminent Women." Volume 3.1 (1896).

Index

Abolitionism, 62–69; antislavery petitions, 67; attitudes to Underground Railroad, 69; disagreement between Garrison, William Lloyd and Douglass, Frederick, 68; early figures, 63; gradual or immediate emancipation, 63; newspapers, 78; role of women, 68–69; societies, 63; splintering, 67–68; and suffrage movement, 176 (*see also* Tubman, Harriet: and suffrage movement)

Adams, Charles Francis, 80

Alcott, Louisa May, 121, 143

American Colonization Society, 23, 24, 63

American Methodist Episcopal (AME) Church, 24, 72; history of, 73

Andrew, John, 123, 140

Anthony, Susan B., 175

Appeal to the Colored Citizens of the World (David Walker), 13

Atchison, David Rice, 53

Barnes, Joseph, 144

Barton, Clara, 141

Beecher, Lyman, 64

Benezet, Anthony, 22, 62

Birney, James G., 68

Black laws. *See* Slavery and laws

Bleeding Kansas. *See* Kansas Civil War

Bradford, Sarah Hopkins. *See Harriet, Moses of Her People*; *Scenes in the Life of Harriet Tubman*

Brickler, Alice (HT's grandniece), 154, 180

Brodess, Edward, 20, 27

Brodess, Eliza Ann, 27, 44, 50, 74

Brodess, Joseph, 26, 27, 43–44

Brodess, Mary, 26

Brown, Henry "Box", 58, 62

Brown, John, 111–118; constitutional convention, 115; Harpers Ferry raid, 117–118; involvement in Kansas Civil War, 111–115; meets HT, 114; trial and execution, 117

Brown, William Wells, 131

Butler, Benjamin, 123

Calhoun, John, 3

Canadian fugitive settlements, 81, 106–107

Cartwright, Samuel, 53

Catt, Carrie Chapman, 171, 177

Chandler, Margaret, 176

Chapman, Maria, 69

Chase, Salmon, 89

Chestnut, Mary Boykin, 14, 17

Child, Marie W., 68, 176

Civil Rights Act (1866), 147

Civil War pensions, 158. *See also* Tubman, Harriet: struggle for wartime pension
Clay, Henry, 23, 78, 79–80, 89
Cobb, Thomas R., 4, 6
Coded spirituals, 49
College of William and Mary, 4
Combahee River raid, 135–138, 204–208. *See also* Montgomery, James; Tubman, Harriet
Conrad, Earl, 177, 184
Considerations on the Keeping of Negroes (John Woolman), 22
Cooley, Chloe, 101
Cotton gin, 2, 3, 62
Cuffee, Paul, 24

Davis, Nelson (HT's second husband), 153–154, 165
Dix, Dorothea, 143
Douglas, Stephen, 80
Douglass, Frederick, 11, 25, 58, 60, 81, 175; shelters fugitives, 77
Dover Eight, 102–103
Drapetomania, 53–54
Drayton, Daniel, 61
Dred Scott v. Sandford, 7, 11
Drew, Tomas, 4
Du Bois, W.E.B., 173–174

Eastern Shore, 20–25; crops, 21; earliest settlers, 21; freedmen, 22–25; Quakers, 21–22
An Exhortation & Caution to Friends Concerning Buying or Keeping of Negroes (George Keith), 62

Fifteenth Amendment, 147, 148
Fillmore, Millard, 80
Flournoy, John Jacobus, 17
Fort Wagner, 140–141
Fourteenth Amendment, 147, 148
Franklin, Benjamin, 72

Garner, Margaret, 65
Garrett, Thomas, 51, 75, 81, 96–97, 166, 176

Garrison, William Lloyd, 24, 80, 150; immediate emancipation, 66; pacifism, 66–67
Gaston, William, 6–7
Gideon's Army. *See* New England Freedmen's Aid Society
Green, Harriet or Rit (HT's mother), 26
Green, Modesty (HT's maternal grandmother), 26
Green, Samuel, 8; arrest and imprisonment, 103
Grimké, Angelina, 68, 176
Grimké, Sarah, 68, 176
Gullah, 129, 130

Hammond, James Henry, 3
Harpers Ferry raid. *See* Brown, John
Harriet (HT's niece), 45
Harriet, Moses of Her People (Sarah Hopkins Bradford), 162–163, 170, 186–187
Harriet Tubman: Negro Soldier and Abolitionist (Earl Conrad), 177
Head, Francis Bond, 101
Heney, Lynne, 185
Higginson, Thomas Wentworth, 69, 116, 120; dislikes Montgomery, James, 139; as Union officer, 132
Howland, Emily, 176
Hunter, David, 128; emancipates Low Country slaves, 128–129, 150

Jayhawkers, 139
Jefferson, Thomas, 10, 23
Jesus of Lubeck, 2
Johnson, Herschel, 80

Kansas Civil War, 90–91, 113–115; Osawatomie massacre, 114; Pottawatomie massacre, 113–114. *See also* Brown, John; Jayhawkers
Kansas-Nebraska Act, 89–90
Kelly, Abby, 176
Kessiah (HT's niece), 45, 74
A Key to Uncle Tom's Cabin (Harriet Beecher Stowe), 91

King, Martin Luther, Jr., 193
King, Roswell, 17

Lay, Benjamin, 22
Letters on Slavery (John Rankin), 64
Leverton, Hannah, 50
Liberty party, 68
Lincoln, Abraham, 8, 68, 129
Logue, Sarah, 16
Loguen, Jermain Wesley, 114
Lovejoy, Elijah, 112, 113
Lucas, Alice (HT's possible
    grandniece), 111
Lundy, Benjamin, 64–65

Madison, James, 23
Mason, James, 167
Mills, John, 45
Monroe, James, 23
Montgomery, James, 133–134; his
    methods questioned, 138–139; as
    Jayhawker, 133; as Union officer,
    134–138
Morrison, Toni, 65
Mott, Lucretia, 68, 81

Nalle, Charles, 57; rescue of, 118–119,
    120–121, 201–204
New England Colored Citizens'
    Convention, 116
New England Freedmen's Aid Society,
    123, 124
Nineteenth Amendment, 176
North Carolina v. Mann, 5
North Carolina v. Will, 6, 7
A North-Side View of Slavery
    (Benjamin Drew), 88
Notes on the State of Virginia
    (Thomas Jefferson), 10

Obama, Barack, 185

Parker, John, 11
Parks, Rosa, 193
Pattison, Atthow, 26, 28, 43
Payne, Sereno, 171
Peculiar institution (slavery), 3

Philadelphia: as haven for fugitive
    slaves, 72; racial tension in, 73
Phillips, Wendell, 150
Pierce, Franklin, 90
Popular sovereignty, 90, 112, 113
Port Royal Experiment, 128
Post-war racial discrimination,
    147–148
Predeaux, Henry. *See* Dover Eight
Prigg v. Pennsylvania, 77

Quakers and slavery, 21–22, 62, 72
Quarles, Benjamin, 187
Quitman, John, 16

Rankin, John, 63
Robinson, John Bell, 122
Ross, Ben (HT's brother), 28, 40, 46
Ross, Ben (HT's father), 26, 40, 159
Ross, Henry (HT's brother), 40, 46
Ross, John (HT's brother), 40, 159
Ross, Linah (HT's sister), 41
Ross, Mariah or Rhody (HT's sister),
    20, 41
Ross, Robert (HT's brother), 82
Ross, Soph (HT's sister), 28, 41
Ruffin, Thomas, 5–7
Ruggles, David, 57

Sanborn, Franklin, 115, 163; authors
    first public account of HT, 138
Saxton, Rufus, 132, 144
Scenes in the Life of Harriet Tubman
    (Sarah Hopkins Bradford), 155–157,
    186–187
Secret Six, 114, 117
Seneca Falls Convention, 175
Seward, William, 90, 123, 150, 152;
    generosity to HT, 108–109; "Higher
    Law" speech, 107, 108; "Irresistible
    Conflict" speech, 108; presidential
    aspirations, 108
Shaw, Robert, 138, 139, 140–141
Sherman, William Tecumseh, 139
Simcoe, John Graves, 101
Slave rescues: Burns, Anthony, 120;
    Christiana, 119; Drayton, Daniel, 61;

Slave rescues (*cont.*)
    Henry, William, 119–120; Walker,
    Jonathan, 61. *See also* Nalle, Charles
Slavery and Canada, 101
Slavery and laws, 3–8, 23; 1793
    Fugitive Slave Act, 77; 1850 Fugitive
    Slave Act, 57, 58, 80; Articles of
    Confederation, 4; Compromise of
    1850, 78–81, 89 (*see also* Kansas-
    Nebraska Act); Louisiana Slave
    Code, 5; Missouri Compromise, 7,
    89; Northwest Ordinance, 5; U.S.
    Constitution, 4
Slaves: as perpetual outsiders, 8–11; as
    resistors, 12–16; as self-stealing,
    55–56, 192; as soldiers, 129
Smith, Gerrit, 112, 118, 150
Sociology for the South (George
    Fitzhugh), 88
Southside View of Slavery (Nehemiah
    Adams), 88
Stanton, Edwin, 129
Stanton, Elizabeth Cady, 176
Stephens, Alexander, 90
Stewart, John, 38
Stewart's canal, 38–39
Still, William, 56, 57, 58, 59, 75, 81
Stowe, Harriet Beecher, 68. *See also*
    Uncle Tom's Cabin
Sumner, Charles, 90

Taney, Roger, 7
Tappan, Arthur, 67, 176
Tappan, Lewis, 67, 176
Taylor, Zachary, 79
Thirteenth Amendment, 58, 147, 148
Thompson, Absalom, 37
Thompson, Anthony, 26, 27
Thompson, Anthony C., 37, 40, 48, 200
Trump (Donald) Administration, 185
Truth, Sojourner, 109, 193
Tubman, Harriet: adopts Gertie Davis,
    161–162; attempts to rescue John
    Tubman, 76–77; birth, 26; breaks
    gender roles, 191; Brodess tries to
    sell her, 35, 36, 47; buys Auburn
    home, 107; buys property for John

Brown Hall, 169–170;
commemorative plaque, 181;
cooptation of, 186; courage of,
188–191; death and funeral,
180–181, 214–216; death of Nelson
Davis, 162, 165; discipline as
Underground Railroad conductor,
83–84; early childhood, 29–33;
establishes John Brown Hall,
171–172; fails to rescue sister Rachel,
95, 98, 102, 104, 111; falls into
obscurity, 178, 184, 187; financial
struggles, 109, 122, 150–153; first
flight to freedom, 46–47; generosity,
109, 152, 157, 179; and gold scam,
159–161; Harriet Tubman Home
(formerly John Brown Hall), 172,
174, 183–184, 212–214; head injury,
34–35; health, 31, 33–35, 43, 95,
123, 150, 162, 178–179; hired by
James Cook, 30–34; house burns,
162; investigates Atthow Pattison's
will, 43; jobs as a fugitive slave, 74,
109; and John Brown, 111, 116, 117;
legacy, 184–186, 187–192; marriage
to John Tubman, 41–42; marriage to
Nelson Davis, 153–154; as
materfamilias, 110, 149–150, 162,
169; narcolepsy, 35, 162; physical
strength, 39; physically assaulted,
145; public speaking, abolitionism,
105, 109, 115, 116, 211–212;
relationship with Seward family,
107, 108, 109, 152–153; religion, 35,
94, 165–168; rescues Bailey brothers,
98–101; rescues Ben, Henry, and
Robert, 82–85; rescues Charles
Nalle, 120–121, 201–204; rescues
Henry Hooper, 95; rescues Jacob
Jackson, 82; rescues Kessiah, 74–75;
rescues Moses, 75; rescues parents,
104; rescues Tilly, 97; skull surgery,
178–179; struggle for wartime
pension, 144, 150, 151, 157–159, 161,
170–171; successful flight to
freedom, 47–51, 199–201; and
suffrage movement, 174–178, 193;

tactics as Underground Railroad conductor, 92–94, 209–211; Victoria's gifts to, 178; visions, on violence, 15–16, 33, 167–168, 191–192; war service as nurse and factotum, 130–131, 141–142; war service as scout, 135–138; war service at Department of the South, 123–143; war service at Department of the South as advocate for contraband, 131; war service at Fort Wagner, 140–142; war service at Fortress Monroe, 123, 143; war service in Florida campaigns, 142–143; war service on Combahee River raid, 135–138, 204–208

Tubman, John (HT's first husband), 39, 41–42; murder of, 148–149

Tubman, Margaret (HT's possible niece), 110–111

Turner, Nat, 14–15, 42

Uncle Tom's Cabin (Harriet Beecher Stowe), 8, 64, 88, 91

Underground Railroad, 50, 54–55; breakdown of, 122; dangers of, 56; eastern and western routes, 59–60; origin of name, 54; secrecy, 55, 58, 75; terminology, 55; water routes, 60–62

United States Sanitary Commission, 143

Victoria, 178, 180, 181

Vigilance committees, 56–57

Vrooman, William, 101

Walker, Jonathan, 61

Ward, Samuel Ringgold, 120

Washington, Booker T., 173, 181, 185

Whitney, Eli, 2, 62; and cotton gin, 2, 3, 62

Whittier, John Greenleaf, 61

Wood, Charles, 157

Woolman, John, 62

World Anti-Slavery Convention, 176

About the Author

Kerry Walters is professor emeritus of philosophy and peace and justice studies at Gettysburg College, Pennsylvania, where he taught for thirty years. He is the author or editor of forty-five books, many of which have won awards and been translated. His works include *The Underground Railroad* (ABC-CLIO); *Lincoln, the Rise of the Republicans, and the Coming of the Civil War* (ABC-CLIO); and *American Slave Revolts and Conspiracies* (ABC-CLIO). He has also written a number of biographies about figures such as Oscar Romero, Theresa of Calcutta, and Benjamin Franklin.